CONTEMPORARY
JAPANESE
ARCHITECTS

JAPAN LIBRARY

CONTEMPORARY

JAPANESE

ARCHITECTS

Profiles in Design

Igarashi Taro
TRANSLATED BY David Noble

Japan Publishing Industry Foundation for Culture

Note on Romanization
This book follows the Hepburn system of romanization. Except for place names found on international maps, long vowels are indicated by macrons. The tradition of placing the family name first has been followed for Japanese, Chinese, and Korean names.

Contemporary Japanese Architects: Profiles in Design
by Igarashi Taro. Translated by David Noble.

Published by
Japan Publishing Industry Foundation for Culture (JPIC)
3-12-3 Kanda-Jinbocho, Chiyoda-ku, Tokyo 101-0051, Japan

First edition: March 2018

© 2011 by Igarashi Taro
English translation © 2018 by Japan Publishing Industry Foundation for Culture

All rights reserved.

This book is a translation of *Gendai Nihon Kenchikuka Retsuden* (Kawade Shobō Shinsha, 2011).
English publishing rights arranged with Kawade Shobō Shinsha.

Book design: Miki Kazuhiko, Ampersand Works

As this book is published primarily to be donated to overseas universities, research institutions, public libraries and other organizations, commercial publication rights are available. For all enquiries regarding those rights, please contact the publisher of the original Japanese edition at the following address:
Kawade Shobō Shinsha
2-32-2 Sendagaya, Shibuya-ku, Tokyo 151-0051, Japan
URL: http://www.kawade.co.jp/corporate/

Printed in Japan
ISBN 978-4-86658-021-0
http://www.jpic.or.jp/japanlibrary/

CONTENTS

PREFACE TO THE ENGLISH EDITION

■■
■■

This book is a consideration of contemporary Japanese architects from Tange Kenzō, who became the representative figure of the postwar decades, to Fujimoto Sou, Ishigami Jun'ya, and others of the generation born in the 1970s. Viewed from an international perspective, in the early Meiji period (1868–1912), Japan moved decisively away from a long period of national seclusion, adopting the architectural culture of the West, but it was Tange who refined a unique modernism in designs that could compete at the global level. His students Kurokawa Kishō and Isozaki Arata built international networks from the time of their debuts. Kurokawa published the Metabolist manifesto, *Metabolism 1960: Proposals for a New Urbanism*, which became the first major Japanese contribution to modern architectural theory. Isozaki developed many contacts overseas and engaged in a variety of cultural interventions through symposiums, competitions, and architectural projects. Born in the 1940s, Andō Tadao and Itō Toyoo tackled a number of international projects in the 1990s, and remain active as global architects, while the 1950s-born Sejima Kazuyo (of SANAA) and Kuma Kengo are also working on an increasing number of projects outside Japan. Atelier Bow-Wow and Abe Hitoshi, born in the 1960s, have exerted an influence internationally through their exhibitions, research, and teaching. And the 1970s generation of Fujimoto Sou and Ishigami Jun'ya has also built a strong network beyond Japan.

All of this activity has resulted in considerable international recognition. In the last decade, a number of Japanese architects have been awarded the Pritzker Architecture Prize, frequently referred to as the Nobel Prize of architecture. In 2010 it was awarded to SANAA, in 2013 to Itō Toyoo, and in 2014 to Ban Shigeru, known for his architecture using paper, particularly in the form of cardboard tubes. Before that, the prize was awarded to Tange Kenzō in 1987, to the Metabolist Maki Fumihiko in 1993, and to Andō Tadao in 1995. Thus, with six recipients, Japan is second only to the United States in the total number of winners—a significant accomplishment considering that historically the prize has focused largely on European and American architects. Japan has also done very well at the International Architecture Exhibition of the Venice Biennale, where the Japan Pavilion was awarded the Golden Lion in 1996 and 2012, with Isozaki Arata serving as its commissioner in 1996 and Itō Toyoo in 2012. Moreover, Fujimoto Terunobu's exhibition at the pavilion in 2006 was honored with a special mention by the jury as an outstanding contribution—tantamount to a second-place grand prize. And Itō Toyoo,

SANAA, Shinohara Kazuo, and Ishigami Jun'ya have all won Golden Lions for their individual work.

In 2016 the Museum of Modern Art in New York and in 2017–18 the Centre Pompidou-Metz mounted exhibitions surveying the history of Japanese architecture. Future historians may look back on contemporary Japanese architecture as the most vigorous of the early twenty-first century. Unfortunately, however, this view is not widely shared in Japan, where architects do not enjoy especially high status. One of my hopes for this book is that a positive response from overseas readers will bounce back to Japan. I might also mention that 2011, the year this book was originally published, was the year of the Great East Japan Earthquake. This disaster had an enormous impact on the world of architecture and, as suggested by the exhibition *How Did Architects Respond Immediately After 3.11—The Great East Japan Earthquake* that I curated in 2014–15, strengthened Japanese architects' commitment to collaborative endeavors. Contemporary architecture in Japan, which developed in the years after World War II, is once again standing at a crossroads.

Igarashi Taro
November 2017

PREFACE
A Genealogy of Contemporary Japanese Architects

■■
■■

This book is a series of profiles of contemporary Japanese architects. From Tange Kenzō, born in 1913, to Ishigami Jun'ya, born in 1974, I have grouped them by generation into five parts. The first chapter, "Tange Kenzō: A National Architect in the Era of Greater East Asia," provides an overview of social trends in wartime Japan and a discussion of how Japan's leading postwar architect arose from this context. It thus serves as an introduction to the rest of the book. Following this, we look at Kurokawa Kishō and Isozaki Arata, who started out in postwar Japan's devastated landscape and experienced its dramatic high-growth period; the generation of Andō Tadao, Itō Toyoo, and Sakamoto Kazunari, who carefully honed their talents during the downturn of the 1970s; the generation of Kuma Kengo and Sejima Kazuyo, who debuted during the economic bubble of the late 1980s; Atelier Bow-Wow, Abe Hitoshi, and others, who started their careers in earnest in the wake of the Great Hanshin-Awaji Earthquake in Kobe and the collapse of the bubble in the 1990s; and finally, the members of the new generation rising to prominence in the early years of the twenty-first century. As a result, this book offers readers a better understanding of the work of Japanese architects within broader socioeconomic trends in Japan.

While the themes of my previous books—such as *Shinpen: Shin Shūkyō to kyodai kenchiku* (New Edition: The New Religions and Monumental Architecture), *Sensō to kenchiku* (War and Architecture), *Kabōbi toshi* (The Overprotected City), and *Kenchiku wa ika ni shakai to kairo o tsunagu no ka* (How Does Architecture Connect with Society?)—are diverse, they have been consistent in focusing attention on the relationship between architecture and society.

The genealogical chart on the double-page spread following this preface should be a helpful reference as you make your way through the book. The chart presents an overview of the relationships among prominent architects in Japan since the beginning of the modern era, commencing with Josiah Conder, a British architect who worked as an advisor to the Japanese government in the late nineteenth century. For example, if we look at the lineages of the latter half of the twentieth century, we see that Isozaki Arata got his start in Tange Kenzō's research group; Isozaki's atelier was the nest that hatched Yatsuka Hajime, Watanabe Makoto (Shin), Watanabe Makoto (Sei), and Aoki Jun; and Inui Kumiko, Nagayama Yūko, and Nakamura Ryūji all debuted after working for Aoki Jun & Associates. Since it is impossible in a single brief volume to discuss, or even mention, all of the important architects in contemporary Japan, this chart is intended to provide supplementary information. Fundamentally, this overview is based on mentor relationships forged in universities and architectural design firms. In most cases mentors have exerted a strong influence—though it is probably true that at times rebellion against these relationships has provided creative motivation as well. In any case, it is extremely rare—exceptions like Andō Tadao notwithstanding—for an architect to establish an independent career without going to university or apprenticing for a time in someone else's office. The influence of the teacher or mentor is probably even more decisive in architecture than it is in other fields such as the visual arts or literature.

In writing this book I have drawn on a number of articles that originally appeared in collections of writings on the work of architects and interior designers (Iijima Naoki, Endō Shūhei, Fujimoto Sou, etc.) and as contributions to international periodicals or books (Kurokawa Kishō, Fujimori Terunobu, Nishizawa Ryūe, Tezuka Architects, etc.), but all have been significantly reworked and supplemented with material from other manuscripts, newspaper articles, and reviews. I am indebted to the editors of these publications. I have added information on the social context for readers who are not specialists in the field of architecture. I will be happy if this book makes some contribution to a greater understanding of contemporary Japanese architects, many of whom are now receiving global recognition.

Contemporary Japanese Architects: Profiles in Design appears as a volume in the Kawade Books series as a result of the proposal by and editorial labor of Fujisaki Hiroyuki of Kawade Shobō Shinsha. I would like to take this opportunity to express to him my deepest gratitude.

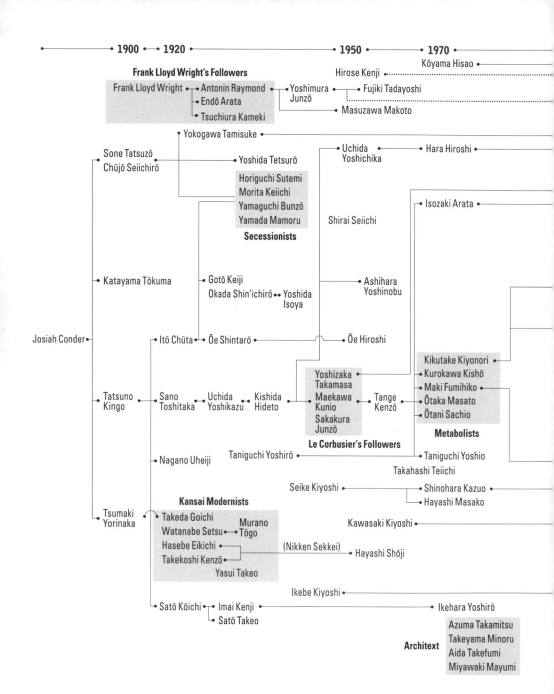

1900 — 1920 — 1950 — 1970

Kōyama Hisao

Frank Lloyd Wright's Followers

Hirose Kenji

Frank Lloyd Wright — Antonin Raymond — Yoshimura Junzō — Fujiki Tadayoshi
— Endō Arata
— Tsuchiura Kameki — Masuzawa Makoto

Yokogawa Tamisuke

Sone Tatsuzō
Chūjō Seiichirō — Yoshida Tetsurō

Uchida Yoshichika — Hara Hiroshi

Horiguchi Sutemi
Morita Keiichi
Yamaguchi Bunzō
Yamada Mamoru

Secessionists

Shirai Seiichi

Isozaki Arata

Katayama Tōkuma — Gotō Keiji
Okada Shin'ichirō — Yoshida Isoya

Ashihara Yoshinobu

Josiah Conder — Itō Chūta — Ōe Shintarō — Ōe Hiroshi

Kikutake Kiyonori
Kurokawa Kishō
Maki Fumihiko
Ōtaka Masato
Ōtani Sachio

Tatsuno Kingo — Sano Toshitaka — Uchida Yoshikazu — Kishida Hideto

Yoshizaka Takamasa
Maekawa Kunio
Sakakura Junzō
— Tange Kenzō

Metabolists

Le Corbusier's Followers

Nagano Uheiji

Taniguchi Yoshirō — Taniguchi Yoshio

Takahashi Teiichi

Seike Kiyoshi — Shinohara Kazuo
— Hayashi Masako

Kansai Modernists

Tsumaki Yorinaka — Takeda Goichi
Watanabe Setsu — Murano Tōgo
Hasebe Eikichi
Takekoshi Kenzō
Yasui Takeo

Kawasaki Kiyoshi

(Nikken Sekkei) — Hayashi Shōji

Ikebe Kiyoshi

Satō Kōichi — Imai Kenji — Ikehara Yoshirō
— Satō Takeo

Azuma Takamitsu
Takeyama Minoru
Aida Takefumi
Miyawaki Mayumi

Architext

Production assistance : Ichikawa Hiroshi
Chart design: Jinbo Yuka

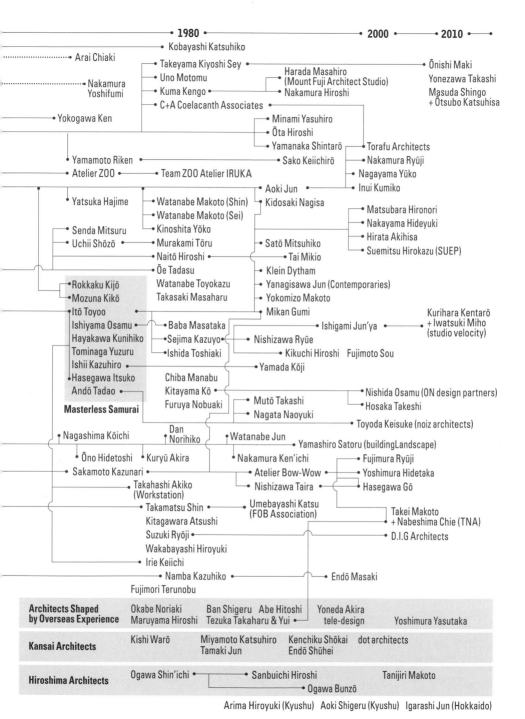

Arai Chiaki

Kobayashi Katsuhiko

Nakamura Yoshifumi

Takeyama Kiyoshi Sey ●
Uno Motomu ●
Kuma Kengo ●
C+A Coelacanth Associates ●

Harada Masahiro
(Mount Fuji Architect Studio)
Nakamura Hiroshi

Ōnishi Maki
Yonezawa Takashi
Masuda Shingo
+ Ōtsubo Katsuhisa

Yokogawa Ken ●

Minami Yasuhiro
Ōta Hiroshi
Yamanaka Shintarō
Sako Keiichirō

Torafu Architects
Nakamura Ryūji
Nagayama Yūko
Inui Kumiko

Yamamoto Riken ●
Atelier ZOO ● Team ZOO Atelier IRUKA ●

Aoki Jun ●

Yatsuka Hajime ●
Senda Mitsuru ●
Uchii Shōzō ●

Watanabe Makoto (Shin) ●
Watanabe Makoto (Sei) ●
Kinoshita Yōko ●
Murakami Tōru ●
Naitō Hiroshi ●
Ōe Tadasu ●
Watanabe Toyokazu
Takasaki Masaharu

Kidosaki Nagisa

Satō Mitsuhiko ●
Tai Mikio
Klein Dytham
Yanagisawa Jun (Contemporaries)
Yokomizo Makoto
Mikan Gumi

Matsubara Hironori
Nakayama Hideyuki
Hirata Akihisa
Suemitsu Hirokazu (SUEP)

Masterless Samurai

Rokkaku Kijō
Mozuna Kikō
Itō Toyoo ●
Ishiyama Osamu ●
Hayakawa Kunihiko
Tominaga Yuzuru
Ishii Kazuhiro ●
Hasegawa Itsuko ●
Andō Tadao ●

Baba Masataka ●
Sejima Kazuyo ●
Ishida Toshiaki ●

Ishigami Jun'ya ●
Nishizawa Ryūe
Kikuchi Hiroshi   Fujimoto Sou
Yamada Kōji

Kurihara Kentarō
+ Iwatsuki Miho
(studio velocity)

Chiba Manabu
Kitayama Kō ●
Furuya Nobuaki

Mutō Takashi
Nagata Naoyuki

Nishida Osamu (ON design partners)
Hosaka Takeshi
Toyoda Keisuke (noiz architects)

Nagashima Kōichi ●

Dan Norihiko

Watanabe Jun

Yamashiro Satoru (buildingLandscape)

Ōno Hidetoshi ●
Sakamoto Kazunari ●

Kuryū Akira ●

Takahashi Akiko
(Workstation)

Nakamura Ken'ichi ●
Atelier Bow-Wow ●
Nishizawa Taira ●

Fujimura Ryūji
Yoshimura Hidetaka
Hasegawa Gō

Takamatsu Shin ●
Kitagawara Atsushi
Suzuki Ryōji ●
Wakabayashi Hiroyuki
Irie Keiichi ●

Umebayashi Katsu
(FOB Association)

Takei Makoto
+ Nabeshima Chie (TNA)
D.I.G Architects

Namba Kazuhiko ●
Fujimori Terunobu

Endō Masaki

Architects Shaped by Overseas Experience	Okabe Noriaki Maruyama Hiroshi	Ban Shigeru Abe Hitoshi Tezuka Takaharu & Yui ●	Yoneda Akira tele-design		Yoshimura Yasutaka
Kansai Architects	Kishi Warō	Miyamoto Katsuhiro Tamaki Jun	Kenchiku Shōkai dot architects Endō Shūhei		
Hiroshima Architects	Ogawa Shin'ichi ●	Sanbuichi Hiroshi ● Ogawa Bunzō ●			Tanijiri Makoto

Arima Hiroyuki (Kyushu)   Aoki Shigeru (Kyushu)   Igarashi Jun (Hokkaido)

PART I

RISING FROM THE ASHES

The Prewar Generation

Tange Kenzō

A National Architect
in the Era of Greater East Asia

Wartime realism

In 1940, the Tokyo Olympics and International Exposition were canceled as the country committed more deeply to a wartime regime. What sort of architecture had been planned for these events? The prospectus for the 1937 competition to design the National Foundation Commemorative Hall, celebrating the 2,600th anniversary of the founding of the Japanese empire, called for a structure that would "serve as a dignified and heroic symbol of the Japanese spirit." The first prize went to a proposal for a building whose superstructure was reminiscent of a Shinto shrine—designed in a premodern style but built on a monumental scale made possible by modern architectural technology.

Nationalism in modern Japanese architecture has generally been associated with the so-called Imperial Crown style (*teikan yōshiki*). The architectural historian Sekino Masaru cites the Veterans Hall (Gunjin Kaikan, now Kudan Kaikan) and the main building of the Tokyo National

An example of the Imperial Crown style: Tokyo National Museum, 1938. (Photo by the author)

Museum as examples of the Imperial Crown style, and makes this observation: "Withdrawing from the League of Nations, Japan set itself on a path of aggression in East Asia. Ethnocentric and nationalist tendencies deepened and gradually began to exert an influence on architecture. The search for a 'Japanese-style architecture' veered toward monumentalism, rejecting internationalism and spurning rationalism in favor of the forceful promotion of a 'Japanese' imagination."[1]

The Rokumeikan, a grand hall designed by the British architect Josiah Conder in the late nineteenth century to house and entertain foreign guests, had become a symbol of rampant Westernization and national humiliation. When it was demolished in 1940, no one raised a voice in its defense. Yet as the cultural historian Inoue Shōichi has pointed out, unlike Nazi Germany or Fascist Italy, Japan never designated a national style in architecture.[2] No Japanese architect was tried as a war criminal, as Albert Speer was at Nuremberg, nor did any Japanese architects resolutely resist the war by going into exile, as Walter Gropius did.

Design-driven architects not only lost the opportunity to build in the pure aesthetic of transparent glass and steel modernism, they even found it difficult to publish their plans, as architectural journals shrank under wartime restrictions. In 1937 the government announced new regulations for steel-reinforced construction, forcing the suspension of a number of projects, including the Shin Marunouchi Building, a representative modernist structure that was planned in 1937 but not completed until 1952. Various other large construction ventures were also abandoned in the name of conserving limited resources. In 1943, elevators began to be reclaimed for their metal parts. Since steel was no longer available for construction, there were new experiments in wood-frame modernism, such as the Kishi Memorial Gymnasium (1941).

Also in 1941, a group led by the architectural planner Yoshitake Yasumi followed the lead of the Imperial Rule Assistance Association and published a manifesto advocating a "New Order in architecture" and calling on the national government to create an organization that would control all architectural enterprises. The following year they announced that the primary mission of architects in support of the new Greater East Asia was to build factories and offices to serve as centers of national industrial production, and that architects should move away from an emphasis on aesthetics and toward "a new rationalism." Also in 1942, the architectural planner Nishiyama Uzō argued that a new type of "residential architect" was needed for a national effort to build housing for the masses.[3] In other words, rather than mansions for the rich, what was needed was standardized housing for the general public. Moreover, housing should be planned scientifically, not designed according to the particulars of individual experience or background. After the war, Nishiyama would become widely known as a leftist academic, but the wartime drive to provide housing for the masses happened to coincide with his goals.

Rational planning was promoted for the most efficient use of materials and the standardization of space. For example, in order to save steel for use in the war effort, bamboo-reinforced concrete was touted as an alternative, and plans were put forward to conserve other essential materials by relaxing strict building codes. Slogans shifted as well: the "cultured housing" (*bunka jūtaku*) replete with modern conveniences that had been the prewar ideal now gave way to a minimal vision of "people's housing" (*kokumin jūtaku*). Even so, this new vision might be described as an economical version of modernism.

In the architectural world, air raid defense had emerged as a very real issue in the wake of World War I.[4] In 1939 the Military Secrets Protection Law prohibited photography from any high vantage point. And with aerial reconnaissance in mind, proposals for camouflage design for the defense of factories and the Diet building were presented, including methods of disguising the roofs of buildings to evade detection by enemy bombers. Wartime restrictions had led to a focus on structural engineering and efficient use of materials, accompanied by the sense that design didn't matter much. Camouflage design could be seen as a rather desperate attempt by architects to assert a new role for conceptual design in defense against modern weaponry. Moreover, Japan's cities were densely packed with wooden structures and thus, in comparison to the cities of Europe and America, had a fatal weakness in their vulnerability to fire. But resources were insufficient for this to be remedied by wholesale reconstruction, so a variety of other emergency countermeasures were attempted: forced relocation and thinning out of structures in specific urban neighborhoods, blackouts, bomb-proofing, air raid shelters, evacuation areas, and so on.

A vision linking Shinto shrines with modernism

Memorials and shrines to the war dead, intended to bolster the spirit of the nation, emerged as a new building type with immense social significance. In contrast to the Imperial Crown style, which amounted to little more than an exterior design affectation, these edifices were programmed as an embodiment of the shared duty to willingly give one's life for the nation. In 1939 there was a competition for the design of a war memorial on a monumental scale that would endure for millennia. One of the jurors was Kishida Hideto, who despised the Imperial Crown style, and stated that "the design should be straightforward and concise." This encouraged the participation of a number of modernist architects, and the submission of designs referencing styles such as Neoclassicism and Italian rationalism that eschewed ornamentation.

During these years, new shrines were being built to Japanese military leaders who had distinguished themselves in Japan's modern wars, such as General Nogi Maresuke and Admiral Tōgō Heihachirō, and Japan's expansion into continental Asia was accompanied by the construction of shrines to Japanese deities overseas. Shinto shrines were not a thing of the past, but a vital, viable contemporary form of architecture. Contemporary discourse on shrine architecture is also worth noting. In the final chapter of a history of Japanese architecture published in 1940, the historian Adachi Kō states that from the Meiji period (1868–1912) onward, Shinto shrines were being built in large numbers both in Japan and overseas, "inviting a golden age of shrine architecture," while conversely construction of Buddhist temples and monasteries was steadily declining.[5] It might be remarked in passing that if you open a textbook on architectural history today, you will not find similar passages claiming shrine architecture to be a powerful force in the modern era.

In *Nihon kenchiku no tokusei* (Characteristics of Japanese Architecture, 1941), Kishida makes the following observation: "If one searches within ancient Japanese architecture for examples rich in purely Japanese aesthetic elements, they are limited to structures that have not adopted the elements of Buddhist temple architecture, or have been little influenced by it."[6] Given that the adoption and assimilation of architectural styles and practices from the Asian mainland had been widely considered the primary influence on the development of architecture in Japan, this constituted a proclamation of the separation of Shinto and Buddhism in the sphere of design.[7] We may assume that it was the architecture of Shinto shrines that was being posited here as the ur-architecture of Japan.

This understanding may also inform Fujishima Gaijirō's criticism of the Scottish architectural historian James Fergusson for his dismissal of Japanese architecture as merely imitative of Chinese architecture, to which Fujishima, a professor of architectural history at Tokyo Imperial University, responded by calling for the "utter rejection of the vulgar opinion that Japanese architecture has overemphasized Chinese elements."[8] While it may be unsurprising that from a European perspective Japanese architecture was positioned as being a kind of ersatz version of Chinese architecture, according to Fujishima, it was the purity of Japanese architecture that had been sullied by continental influences. He was proud that Japan possessed what he described as "an architectural rationality rarely seen in the world," asserting that "in the East there is the Grand Shrine at Ise, in the West, the Parthenon." What the Greeks had built in stone, the Japanese had built in wood. Fujishima went on to divide the 2,600-year history of Japanese architecture into three main periods: an era of pure Japanese architecture, an era of continental influence, and an era of global influence. In *Kokusui Nihon kenchiku* (Ultranationalist Japanese Architecture, 1940), he argued that the influence of the West from the Meiji period onward must be purged, and that past influences from the continent had also disrupted Japanese architecture. If the negative foreign influences were eliminated, truly Japanese elements would arise. The 2,600th anniversary of the founding of the Japanese empire would mark the beginning of "a new millennium in architecture."

Kishida assessed temple architecture originating on the continent as overly decorative and criticized its curvilinear designs as un-Japanese; in contrast, he saw the simple rectilinear designs of Shinto shrines, unchanged since antiquity, as not only quintessentially Japanese but also, at the same time, connecting with modernism.[9] When the German architect Bruno Taut visited Japan in the 1930s, he contrasted the Ise Grand Shrine and Katsura Imperial Villa with the Tōshōgū mausoleum at Nikkō, positing two different stylistic lineages—the imperial and the shogunal. This contrast was now being described as an opposition between lineages of Shinto shrine architecture and Buddhist architecture. Kishida praised the design of Yasukuni Shrine—almost entirely passed over by architectural historians today—in almost fanatic terms. At Yasukuni Shrine, one was awakened to "the pure heart of Japanese architecture," with the "archetypical perfection of form and structure" embodied in "the beauty and sacredness of the torii gate providing us with a myriad revelations."[10] Kishida also personally drew up a proposal for the expansion of the shrine's precincts to celebrate the creation of a Greater East Asia. It is difficult for us to imagine today, but at the time, Shinto shrines were regarded as splendid examples of contemporary architecture.

Like Taut, Fujishima was critical of the kitschy Orientalism common in hotels that catered to foreign tourists as "unassimilated design," while at the same time assessing modernist architecture with virtually the same vocabulary he used in praise of traditional Japanese architecture. For example, in the essay "Shin sedai no kenchiku" (Architecture of a New Generation, 1940) he writes that the spirit of Japanese architecture from time immemorial has been "purity and simplicity" and praises the "inno-cent, pure, terribly plainspoken and honest architecture" of Taniguchi Yoshirō's Keio Yōchisha elementary school.[11] In other words, the language praising shrine architecture need not be confined to Japanese styles—it could be deployed in support of modernism as well. This was an acrobatic turn of mind that connected a pure Japanese sensibility purged of Chinese influence with the latest developments in modern architecture.

In his essay "Kinen kenzōbutsu no kenchiku yōshiki" (Architectural Styles for Monumental Structures), Fujishima touched on memorials for the war dead, saying this was an era that called for the construction of a variety of monuments to commemorate the national project, and arguing that "contemporary monuments must be suffused with a contemporary youthfulness. Our present time demands freshness, forthrightness, and simplicity. And it goes without saying that decorative elements display their true value only when used in moderation."[12]

An architectural style for Greater East Asia

The arrival of a new era led to serious discussion of architecture designed for Greater East Asia. In 1942, the Nihon Kenchiku Gakkai (Architectural Institute of Japan) chose structural plans for a Monument to the Construction of Greater East Asia for its annual engineering com-petition and exhibition. Kishida, who was one of the jurors, wrote an essay outlining his hopes for this project.[13] The competition called for propos-als "adequate to express the boldness of our determination to establish the Greater East Asian Co-Prosperity Sphere." This was architecture for a community that transcended the geographic boundaries of Japan—an important chance for architects who had lost opportunities for design work to express their ideas and aspirations. Kishida wrote, "I would like to see the architectural community in Japan clearly assert through the results of this competition that even in these times, architecture is not yet dead—architecture is alive and well. And I look forward with especially keen anticipation to the contributions of the rising generation of young architects."[14] The Monument to the Construction of Greater East Asia was a cry for attention to a state indifferent to design, a project to bring the fine art of architecture back from the brink of extinction.

Others expressed similar opinions. For example, the critic Kanba Toshio wrote an essay entitled "Dai Tōa bunka kensetsu no igi" (The Significance of Building a Greater East Asian Culture) in which he argued for the importance of the cultural sphere in addition to the usual focus on politics and economics.[15] And Nishiyama Uzō, despite the fact that his design was passed over in the competition, remarked that it was "an architect's dream."[16] The competition was a hypothetical exercise, not predicated on actual construction of the monument, so participants were given free range for their ideas. Kishida himself dreamed of monuments on the battlefields and in the major cities of the continent, monumental mountaintop towers, and Greater East Asia avenues in urban centers.

The Greater East Asia competition was not state-sponsored. It was really little more than a brainstorming session initiated voluntarily by a professional association—an event that normally would have drawn submissions from students rather than practicing architects. Yet it was being positioned within the context of an ambitious historical vision. As Kishida put it, "I feel deeply moved and very fortunate to be a Japanese architect born into this great era." In contrast to the "long past thirteen centuries" of influence by imports from the Asian continent, "Japanese architecture and technology are now poised to advance into and develop on the continent. Is this not the most splendid event in the entire history of Japanese architecture?" In other words, not only would a pure Japanese architecture be restored by ridding it of continental influence, its aesthetic and design practice would in turn be spread throughout mainland Asia. A crucial turning point in world history had arrived.

Kishida said that it was the advent of this new era that emboldened him to propose a monumental architecture. "To commemorate and celebrate our unwavering commitment and the auspicious path that lies before us, we should plan great monuments to be constructed in key locations throughout the Co-Prosperity Sphere, working to make permanent and indestructible the present glory and resolve of the peoples of Greater East Asia." The monuments of the past were for particular individuals or races. "They were not eternal monuments commemorating the glorious progress of many peoples united by the common goal of achieving coexistence and co-prosperity throughout a vast region comprising a quarter of the globe." This would be a different form of International Style, one that would express "a monumentality that is not passive in the slightest, but rather a completely active and positive monumentality." Yet at the same time Kishida had no interest in blindly following the styles of the past. A new architecture was necessary, one appropriate to this unprecedented utopia. "We must not depend upon preexisting notions of monumental architecture," he wrote, but work to create monuments "capable of contributing to a great leap forward for the architecture of Greater East Asia."

This competition occasioned considerable debate regarding what might constitute an architectural style for Greater East Asia. Let's review a few of the opinions expressed in the September 1942 issue of *Kenchiku zasshi*, the journal of the Architectural Institute of Japan.

In a roundtable discussion entitled "Dai Tōa Kyōeiken ni okeru kenchiku yōshiki" (Architectural Style in the Greater East Asian Co-Prosperity Sphere), Taniguchi Yoshirō, Horiguchi Sutemi, and others proposed an architecture unbound by formal conventions of the past, one that used new technologies and embodied the Japanese spirit while adapting to local conditions. Yamada Mamoru argued for the importance of "cultural architecture" in contrast to the "impermanent architecture" of the military. The war "would not bear fruit until a splendid architecture emerged." He also proposed surveys of the architecture of each ethnic group to guide the development of a Greater East Asian architecture. Itō Nobufumi said that the British Concession had created a zone of British style in Shanghai, and that this was an example of how architecture can "possess a profound significance, becoming a concrete symbol of the fact that a particular region is under the control of one's country." This led him to criticize Japan, saying that "as a matter of fact, we do not pay as much attention to architecture as other nations," and lamenting that a visitor to Seoul would scarcely realize that it was under Japanese rule. The Government-General Building (seat of the Japanese colonial government) was built in the Neoclassical style, and while Chōsen Jingū, the main Shinto shrine in Korea, was built in Japanese style, it was isolated from its surroundings. Itō argued that in order to convey that the era of a Japan-led Greater East Asia was different from the era of Western colonial domination, "we must construct an architecture that will serve as an emblem giving formal, external expression to the New Order in Greater East Asia." This is because architecture is a synthesis of the arts, possessing both quotidian and eternal elements, something Itō saw as "no doubt true for all peoples."

For Itō, it was "the architect's responsibility" to "research Greater East Asian architecture and propose a specific style." In that way the subjective elements of architecture (the quotidian) and the objective elements (environmental and cultural) might be distinguished, and investigation of a new style could proceed. Itō noted the parallel existence of three stylistic typologies—Shinto, Buddhist, and Western—suggesting that perhaps the Shinto style would be more appropriate to southern regions and the Buddhist style to the north, but also called for the creation of a unified style that could integrate all three.

A national architect with a world historical mission

The vision of an architecture for Greater East Asia could not be limited to simply foisting a Japanese style onto the peoples of the continent; it also encouraged a type of regionalism to sprout, though one aware of local climates and environments. Fujishima believed that the study of continental architecture would contribute to the birth of a new architecture. Yet in the special edition of *Kenchiku zasshi* discussed above, the most forthright opinion was that expressed by Tange Kenzō in response to a questionnaire. "We must conceive of a new Japanese architectural style, solemn and terse as a god, powerful and dignified as a giant. We would do well to ignore not only Anglo-American culture, but also the established cultures of the peoples of the southern regions. Singing the praises of Angkor Wat is the job of dilettantes. We must begin by having an unshakable confidence in the traditions and future of the Japanese people." In conceiving a new architecture for Greater East Asia, Tange believed that it was neither important nor necessary to take into consideration the architectural style of other cultures and traditions.

First prize in the competition was awarded to Tange, who had submitted a drawing in which Mt. Fuji rose symbolically in the background.[17] It was an astonishingly ambitious proposal, more on the scale of a massive civil engineering project than a simple architectural plan. It plunged into what was then a completely new dimension for architects, that of urban design. What Tange proposed was a Greater East Asia expressway and high-speed rail line paralleling one another from the

Tange Kenzō's first-prize entry in the competition for a Monument to the Construction of Greater East Asia. (*Kenchiku zasshi*, December 1942)

imperial palace at the center of Tokyo to the foothills of Mt. Fuji more than a hundred kilometers away, with a series of new urban developments distributed at intervals along the route: a "Greater East Asia political and economic core city," a "Greater East Asia cultural core," and finally a sacred precinct enshrining the spirits of the war dead. The layout of this memorial complex, integrating the natural surroundings with built structures along a broad pilgrimage route linking a shrine for the protection of the nation with a public square, anticipated the axial designs of Tange's major postwar projects, including his *A Plan for Tokyo 1960: Toward a Structural Reorganization* and the Hiroshima Peace Memorial Museum (1955). The architecture itself employed motifs from the Ise Grand Shrine, a further exploration of the ur-forms of shrine construction. What should be noted here is that he did not emphasize geometric volumes like the pyramid, but rather the performance of monumentality by encircling a sacred space.

Even Nishiyama Uzō, later strongly associated with the political left, participated in this competition. His entry, which was not selected, proposed the creation of a sacred space centered on the Yamato Sanzan—the Three Hills of Yamato, located in the Nara basin south of Kyoto, and closely associated with the origins of the Japanese state. His plan called for multiple complexes of buildings, including a symbolic tower, athletic fields and a festival ground, an altar and memorial hall for the war dead, a Greater East Asia museum, a stadium, a theater, a concert hall, and other public event spaces. Even so, this paled in comparison with the grandiosity of Tange's vision, whose overwhelming sense of scale seems to connect directly with Tange's concept, proposed in the 1960s, for a Tōkaidō Megalopolis interweaving urban areas from Tokyo to the Kyoto-Osaka area. Moreover, Tange's prize-winning proposal incorporated a fusion of the world of archaic form with the latest in concrete shell and railway technology, in what must be regarded as an outstanding expression of the effort to overcome Western-style modernity.

Responding to the results of the competition, the Architectural Institute of Japan published the "Report of the Committee on the Construction of Greater East Asia: Guidelines for Architecture in Southeast Asia" in the April 1943 issue of *Kenchiku zasshi*. It called for abandonment of "a world view based on the individual"; an emphasis on nature and the environment; and simplicity and clarity in design as opposed to Western manipulation of volumes and decorative elements. It is likely that the committee had Tange's proposal in mind. As opposed to the Western will to transform and visual approach to space, they stressed the Japanese sense of a natural environmental order and living space. In other words, while actual construction had declined during wartime, modernism had not simply retreated in the face of this challenge; it was continuing to evolve theoretically.

In 1943, a competition was held for the construction of the Japan-Thai Culture Center in Bangkok. Kishida again served as one of the jurors, and called for submissions "based on the simplicity and elegance of Japan's architectural tradition, but not swept into blind imitation of the past; brimming with individual creativity and capable of making this first grand hall to be built overseas something of which we can truly be proud." Tange Kenzō again took first place, with Maekawa Kunio coming in second. Both designs were modeled on traditional residential architecture. They were probably aware that Kishida had praised the Kyoto Imperial Palace for the simplicity and purity of its style. But Tange's submission also could be seen in certain respects as incorporating characteristics of shrine architecture.

Maekawa spoke boldly of the resolve architects should feel on the eve of a Greater East Asia. While critical of both "Japanist architecture" trapped in a traditionalist adherence to form and "structuralist architecture" guided by an abstract progressivism, he argued for the necessity of creating a national architecture that could be rated as one of the best in the world by refining its formal concepts through direct confrontation with the environment and a grasp of tradition, thus encouraging the uniqueness of Japanese reality to shine through.[18] He was searching for a third path, a new monumental style that did not emphasize external appearances. In a contemporary assessment, the architect Ikuta Tsutomu observed that in the transition from traditional to modern times functionality came to be valued over monumentality, and with regard to this competition, "Tange recaptures monumentality through a revival of the past, while Maekawa gives expression to a contemporary monumentality through a thick application of a functional palette."[19]

In "Nihon kokumin kenchiku yōshiki no mondai" (The Issue of a Japanese National Architectural Style), Hamaguchi Ryūichi evaluated Maekawa's and Tange's proposals for the competition while proposing a Japanese architecture oriented to action and space in contrast to a Western architecture oriented to materiality and structure.[20] He saw the issue as being one of overcoming modernity through an integration of modernism with traditional Japanese elements, without falling into classic monumental styles. He also argued for constructing a methodology at the level of layout and plan, not exterior design. This represents the culmination of architectural theory during the war. According to Hamaguchi, a Japanese architectural style would arise from the use of wood rather than stone as material, or from national character and sensibility.

Tange Kenzō's legacy for postwar Japan

The competitions for the Monument to the Construction of Greater East Asia and the Japan-Thai Culture Center in Bangkok were the most romantic expressions, in the face of wartime realism, of the dream of building a Greater East Asia. And both of these competitions were won by the young Tange Kenzō. Whether they would be realized or not, they were an effort—on a grand scale—to conceive a Japanese architecture that could bridge the traditional and the contemporary—a design for a new order in a world that had been reset. From today's perspective, this may seem to be an architecture founded upon pseudo-historical myth. But what was carried over from it into the postwar era was immense. It propelled Tange into the world spotlight as the architect who represented postwar Japan.

Tange was involved in two major events symbolic of Japan's postwar recovery: the 1964 Tokyo Olympics and Expo '70, the world's fair held in Osaka. Both were previously scheduled events that had been canceled under Japan's wartime regime. For the Olympics, Tange designed the Yoyogi National Gymnasium, with its dynamically suspended structure; for Expo '70 he conceived the master plan and also the massive space-frame roof for the Festival Plaza. With his projects of the 1990s—including the Tokyo Metropolitan Government Building (1991) and the Fuji Television Headquarters (1996) on reclaimed land in Tokyo Bay—a new Tokyo cityscape was born. His talent for shaping symbolic landmarks of this nature made him an architect whose work is imprinted in the mental landscapes of most Japanese.

With his brilliant designs, Tange provided a particularly apt response to the difficult issue confronting non-Western nations—that of integrating modernism with tradition. While keeping in mind Ise Grand Shrine and Katsura Imperial Villa, Tange led the 1950s debate on tradition in architecture, designing Yoyogi National Gymnasium to recall classic Japanese architecture with the sweeping curves of its roof. In other projects such as the Kagawa Prefectural Government Office (1958), Tange incorporated exquisite details suggesting the post-and-beam construction and exposed rafters of traditional wooden buildings. As a result, modern Japanese architecture was imbued with a unique mandate: not to imitate modernism, but to give a contemporary interpretation to traditional architecture. This orientation began with the Greater East Asia competition. Yet Tange also became Japan's first global architect, undertaking large-scale projects in Asia and the Middle East. And his research group at the University of Tokyo was the training ground for a number of prominent architects, including Isozaki Arata and Kurokawa Kishō, forming one of the main currents in the Japanese architectural scene.

In 1945, the country of the kamikaze became the first in the world to have an atomic bomb dropped on it. In Hiroshima, a city still bearing the stigmata of this trauma, a work of monumental architecture was born, centered on the eternal presence of the Atomic Bomb Dome. A site near ground zero of the blast was chosen for the most significant early project of Tange's postwar career: the Hiroshima Peace Memorial Museum, built ten years after the war ended.

Detail of Kagawa Prefectural Government Office, 1958.
(Photo by the author)

Kurokawa Kishō

Buddhism and Metabolism

Learning from the ruins

Even after entering the twenty-first century, the Tokyo megalopolis continues its astonishing transformations. For some time the architect Kurokawa Kishō has maintained his office on the eleventh floor of a building rising above the Aoyama Itchōme subway stop, in one of the city's most fashionable neighborhoods. When I visited his office to interview him, he looked out the window at the cityscape of Tokyo spread out before us and remarked that everything we could see had been built within the past sixty years. Buildings continued on as far as the eye could see; the horizon was invisible. While Western cities tend to have well-defined boundaries, the Kantō region, Tokyo included, is a single continuous urban sprawl. But when Japan was defeated in 1945, it was a barren expanse of scorched earth.

Born in 1934, Kurokawa was in fifth grade in 1945. He told me the following story from that time:

> I went to Shirakabe Elementary School in Nagoya until I was in third grade, but when the B-29 bombing raids began, we evacuated to where my grandfather was living, in Kaniechō, on the outskirts of the city. But I really did experience the urban air raids, because the

B-29s would pass over Kaniechō on the way to Nagoya, and lights had been set out in the rice paddies surrounding Kaniechō to create a decoy city. So the bombers would drop their bombs on this decoy Nagoya in the rice paddies of Kaniechō. We'd evacuated from the city only to become the target. There were incendiary bombs falling only a few meters away. . . . At the time Nagoya was a city of 100,000 or 150,000 people, and it burned for days on end. . . . My father was an architect, and less than a week or so after we'd heard the emperor's broadcast announcing the surrender, when the smoke was still rising over Nagoya, he went into the city to look for office space. At a time when everyone else was still stupefied by what had happened, my dad said, "Who do you think is going to rebuild our lost cities? Architects will have to do it!" Hearing my father talking about building cities, when all I could see around me was the distant mountains, was what made me first dream of becoming an architect. Because we were starting completely from zero."[1]

The American forces subjected virtually all of Japan's major cities to intense bombing raids. Out of this inconceivable devastation arose exceptional talents like Kurokawa. Yet he said he knew that the landscape of postwar Japan could also disappear in the blink of an eye. My generation, born amid already completed cities, might not be able to easily imagine how instantaneously these familiar landscapes could be erased. But he knew this from experience. He had lived through an era of radical change. After the war came the bullet trains and the spread of cars and TVs, and later mobile phones and the Internet became part of the fabric of everyday life. He experienced every stage in the social development of postwar Japan. And because of this, it was impossible for him to believe that anything would last forever. He has said, "Once upon a time, people thought that beauty was found in the eternal. But that sort of thinking has been exposed as a fraud. Real beauty is found in things that decline and fall, in things that change."[2] An aesthetics of transience. Not even love is eternal; beauty in human life comes precisely from the fact that we are all fated to die. The war experience had a major impact on many architects.

Kishida Hideto, professor of architecture at the University of Tokyo, said he looked out at the burnt-out ruins of the city and thought they were beautiful. The Tokyo cityscape had been a chaotic, ugly mess. Now he saw a chance to start over with a clean slate and set to work building a brand-new planned city in the European style. Tange Kenzō shouldered the burden of postwar reconstruction by creating monumental architecture, shrines that would serve as the face of the nation. On the other hand, Isozaki Arata, who was the same generation as Kurokawa, has made drawings featuring ruins and has spoken frequently of his experience of the war's devastation. Yet in his drawings the ruins, while crumbling, are sufficiently intact that one can still imagine the whole, and thus they retain a certain Western quality as images. In contrast, Kurokawa's images are of wooden houses obliterated almost without trace and already returning to nature, and might be said to be more Japanese. We might also say that while Isozaki speaks of ruins from an aesthetic perspective, Kurokawa apprehends the issue of destruction from a systems perspective. And in fact, when developing the theory of Metabolism, he explicitly included the question of how to destroy things within its purview. Here we might also mention another of the Metabolists, Kikutake Kiyonori, the son of a major landholder who lost most of the land in the postwar reforms—an experience that seems connected to his relentless pursuit of a vision of cities floating on the ocean waves.

The cycle of destruction and construction

Kurokawa recalls that when CIAM (Congrès internationaux d'architecture moderne), the organization that had led the modernist movement, fell apart at the end of the 1950s, he felt he'd lost the textbook on modern architecture. "But in addition to the unease this caused, it was also an era in which we really did not know what was going to come next, and thus was one full of hopes for the future."[3] Walking the fire-bombed streets, he had resolved to become an architect; now, with the ruins of modernist architecture in sight, he launched a new movement called Metabolism, and conceived the megastructures for cities of the future. Kurokawa believed that, confronted with a devastated and desolate landscape, one must not surrender to confusion or despair. Rather, one must respond with an unwavering light. Kurokawa's *Kōdō kenchiku ron* (On Active Architecture, 1967), a rare bestseller among books on architecture, contains the following line: "Tomorrow is another day,"[4] which reminds me of the last scene in the movie *Gone with the Wind*. The cycle of destruction and construction. Of nihilism and optimism. Kurokawa's thought cleaves to neither pole of such dualities, instead integrating yin and yang in a circular flow.

In Japanese cities development and destruction seem to proceed simultaneously. Sometimes urban areas are destroyed in an instant by earthquakes or typhoons, as in the 1995 Great Hanshin-Awaji Earthquake (or Kobe earthquake). But even when natural disasters do not strike, Japanese cities change at an astonishing rate; within a few decades large portions are completely rebuilt. In other words, a silent "invisible earthquake" is almost continually in progress. Kobe after the earthquake saw a spate of mini-developments like those that had sprung up all over the rest of the country. The catastrophe simply sped this change and made it more obvious. This recalls Rem Koolhaas's idea of the "generic city" in which no structures would last for more than thirty years. The megalopolis must be conceived beyond good and evil. In this attitude, Kurokawa anticipates Koolhaas.

The Metabolist group was formed by Kurokawa, Kikutake Kiyonori, Ōtaka Masato, Maki Fumihiko, and others on the occasion of the 1960 World Design Conference in Tokyo. The basic concept was of a modular design in which every element was interchangeable. Kurokawa's *Kōdō kenchiku ron* was something of a manifesto for the movement and sold explosively. Japanese architectural design is highly regarded overseas, but Metabolism is to this day the most famous theoretical movement in contemporary architecture originating in Japan and broadcast to the rest of the world. It marked the moment at which contemporary Japanese architecture stood on equal footing with that of the West, unclouded by Orientalism. The analogy to living organisms was seen largely in terms of the potential for replacement, proliferation, and transformation of their constituent cells, but we must not forget that these processes also include destruction. This is perhaps what most differentiates Kurokawa from the other members of the group. According to him, "Up to now, human culture has valued only 'creation'. . . . But we may now be entering an era of 'destructive culture.'"[5] A contrarian concept. He goes on to quote a biologist's prediction that the human race might meet extinction by burying itself in its own waste and garbage—and noting that a more fearful enemy than the hydrogen bomb lies nearer to hand. In this we can see at a very early stage an awareness of environmental problems that would lead to the recycling movement. From production to deconstruction and reuse. Time is perceived as circular.

When Frank Lloyd Wright's Imperial Hotel in Tokyo was torn down in the 1960s, engendering a debate on architectural preservation, Kurokawa argued for the coexistence of new and old, and proposed an idea for preserving the hotel's lobby as a partially underground structure with a high-rise tower built over it. The city is ever-changing; it does not let its arteries harden. When the city is governed by the consumer behavior of the masses, it must be continually destroyed according to their will.[6] At the time, Kurokawa observed that demolition often took place when the internal facilities and fittings aged faster than the structural framework of a building, and called for a theoretical investigation of structural ecosystems. Kurokawa was one of the first architects to propose a methodology of deconstruction engineering.

The helix and the structure of information

The most famous Japanese architect since the end of the twentieth century is the former boxer Andō Tadao, but in the 1960s it was Kurokawa, a young member of Japan's academic elite who had gone from Kyoto University to graduate studies at the University of Tokyo, who was the shining star. In those days, he made the cover of weekly magazines, billed as the "'Mighty Atom of the World of Architecture,' Who Has All the Coeds Swooning." His extensive social connections and marriage to the actress Wakao Ayako were the subject of much discussion. As Japan entered its period of high economic growth, it entrusted its dreams of the future to brilliant young architects like Kurokawa, who responded by designing not one but three pavilions for Expo '70 in Osaka while still in his thirties.

It was no coincidence that Expo '70 served as a crucial showcase for Kurokawa. Expo was an enormous event, calling into existence a deliberately time-limited city. It not only had to be built quickly; its deconstruction was already scheduled, and the architecture needed to be temporary. Because of this, Kurokawa claimed it to be a perfect testing ground for Metabolism. The Toshiba IHI Pavilion with its tetraframe structure and the Takara Beautilion with its accumulation of capsules were constructed of modular steel units designed from the beginning to be dismantled. As a result, they could simply be unbolted and taken apart quite cleanly and quickly. Kurokawa criticized other pavilions as primitive and inefficient, since they would eventually have to be demolished with bulldozers and wrecking balls.

This was not merely a technological argument. According to Kurokawa, in contrast to the European aesthetic of permanence, the Japanese aesthetic was deconstructive: "Through a continual process of dismantling, we sustain our identity."[7] And indeed, the materials of traditional wooden architecture could be reused when a building was torn down. The Grand Shrine at Ise is dismantled and rebuilt every twenty years. It is simultane-

Takara Beautilion under construction, Expo '70. (Courtesy of KISHO KUROKAWA architect & associates)

"Future Ruin" in the courtyard of the National Museum of Ethnology, 1977. (Photo by the author)

ously new and ancient. This unusual perception of time may also be seen in "Future Ruin," created in the central courtyard of the National Museum of Ethnology (1977), designed by Kurokawa on the former site of Expo '70. In it, traditional and contemporary materials coexist. Although they are newly constructed, its terraces and staircases call up associations with ancient shrines. The courtyard is intended as a central void within the structure. Kurokawa's Roppongi Prince Hotel (1984) incorporated a main bar called "Cosmic Ruin."

Kurokawa possessed broad interests ranging from ancient philosophy to contemporary technology, and skillfully linked them in his unique theoretical evolution—never still, ever moving, always changing. This was Kurokawa's fundamental worldview. He was prolific in the (re)invention of meaning in architectural design, and liberal in his use of metaphor in discourse. He was operating not at the level of things but in the dimension of transforming meaning. Among Western stylistic concepts, he was sympathetic to the Baroque, which, in contrast to the perfect ideal forms of the Renaissance, also delighted in movement and change.

"Architecture is the flow [of information], and cities make that flow visible in design."[8] This is not a statement by Itō Toyoo or Watanabe Makoto (Sei), conceiving of architecture in the age of computers. Remarkably, it is Kurokawa, writing in the 1960s. To discover beauty in movement itself, Kurokawa looked to the aesthetics of the early twentieth-century Futurists. The poet Filippo Tommaso Marinetti's *Manifesto of Futurism* praised the roar of the automobile as more beautiful than classical sculpture, and the architect Antonio Sant'Elia declared, "Each generation must build its own cities!" The city of the future, always renewing itself. Kurokawa, anticipating a new age, had already envisaged the fluidity that a data-driven world would demand. His urban design proposals from the 1960s onward still stand as a major achievement. Kurokawa's pathway to becoming a politician in his final years may seem quixotic, but it was his ultimate effort to realize the urban design he had pursued for more than forty years. He was adamantly opposed to the Tokyo-centric model of development.

If one focuses on movement, new structural forms are born. In the 1960s in France, the architect Claude Parent and the cultural theorist Paul Virilio were also influenced by the Futurists and praised the effects of sloping floors. They believed that the horizontal was a response to rural agriculture and the vertical to urban industry; in the postindustrial society to come, a third order must be evolved: "the function of the oblique." Meanwhile, Kurokawa, taking a hint from the helical structure of DNA, published *The Helix City Project: Tokyo 1961*, a proposal reminiscent of science fiction in which megastructures rise in twisting helical patterns from an artificial earth. Neither vertical nor horizontal, the helix represents the introduction of a new dimension. The dynamic contemporary city will not be constructed out of established concepts such as posts and beams and walls—we must examine the flow of energy and think in terms of completely different new structures. It is fascinating to note that the architecture of recent years, making full use of computers, has arrived at an almost identical logic. In any case, Kurokawa saw a helical conception of space as appropriate to the contemporary world. The helix, integrating both vertical and horizontal movement, would give birth to a new order.

Helix proposal (model) for Tokyo Plan 1960. (Courtesy of KISHO KUROKAWA architect & associates)

Rebirth as recycling

Kurokawa made frequent references to Buddhist thought. The cycle of creation and destruction and the fluidity of his worldview can be understood through the Buddhist concept of reincarnation, or transmigration. The linguistic root of this idea is the Sanskrit word *samsara*, which originally meant "to flow," and which took on the meaning of "wandering among various states of being," connoting the continuous cycle of birth and death.[9]

This is not a perception of linear time running straight from beginning to end but rather of circularity, of revolving. Therefore, Kurokawa wrote, for the Metabolist system to be adopted by society, "we have no choice but to throw ourselves into the continuous time of *samsara*, the cycle of rebirth, and grasp space in a more active way."[10] He goes on to say, "Before our very eyes we sense all around us the clattering collapse of beauty we believed to be eternal. . . . This is none other than a literal experience of 'hell.' But if this 'hell' is what is required to give birth to the next new realm for creative activity, then I positively affirm it."

According to Kurokawa, the Buddhist concept of the cycle of rebirth was rooted spiritually "in thinking of oneself as grounded in an eternity encompassing both birth and death."[11] We do not have only one existence. Architecture as well repeatedly recycles through birth and death. For Expo '85 in Tsukuba, he designed a pavilion for Toshiba which, with the lease in mind, was constructed of temporary scaffolding. When the six-month lease on the exhibition site was over, the building could be cleanly and efficiently dismantled, with zero waste. This developed into an even bolder version of rebuilding the entirety of Tokyo out of leased materials. When I spoke with him, Kurokawa elaborated on this idea.

> I thought the concept of leasing was even more intriguing than that of temporary structures. If you think about it, you might see human life itself as a kind of lease. . . . What we were fighting against from the time we first started talking about Metabolism was the European way of placing such an extreme value on the material, or on life versus death. But we had lived in a way that had always made neighbors of life and death. So I thought it would be interesting if we could rebuild such a balance once again.[12]

Here, too, we catch a glimpse of a Buddhist perspective on life and death. The observation that human life is like a lease also calls up the image of each human being as a prisoner in the cage of the self. Kurokawa's notion of the relationship between life and death no doubt reflects his personal experience. He retained a vivid memory of his younger brother's birth, near dawn at the house to which they had evacuated, and the experience of nursing his aging grandfather during the cold of that winter. It was a house in which life and death resided together. Relatives of theirs died from a direct hit in one of the air raids. "The Buddhist teaching of *samsara* is connected to a perspective that sees every living being—humans, animals, plants, buddhas—as being given life within an enormous existence that transcends birth and death."[13]

One might think it only natural for a Japanese architect to speak about

Buddhism. But in fact, with a few rare exceptions such as Shirai Seiichi, it is the rare exception and not the rule. Certainly many Japanese are nominally Buddhists, but Buddhist philosophy has not necessarily permeated the general culture. With regard to architecture, references to Greek philosophy and contemporary French thought are much more common. Thus Kurokawa's focus on Buddhism is noteworthy among Japanese architects.

Straight lines or curves?

However, there are certainly other instances in the past in which discussions of architecture in Japan have referenced religion. Modernism has frequently been discussed in connection with certain aspects of Shinto, particularly in prewar Japan, when State Shinto was a dominant force. For example, Kishida Hideto argued that Shinto architecture was simple and plain, with straight lines predominating; in contrast, the Buddhist architecture imported from the continent made liberal use of curves and was more decorative. This line of reasoning was not only a rejection of Chinese-influenced Buddhist architecture and a valorization of Shinto architecture as an expression of a purely Japanese character, it was also intended to link the latter with the modernist aesthetic. This was a nationalistic theory of architectural evolution promoting a shift from curves to straight lines.

Bruno Taut also made a contrasting classification of the Buddhist architecture of the shoguns with the Shinto architecture of the emperors, criticizing the baroque tendencies of the former as superficial and praising the simplicity of the latter as a world-class artistic accomplishment. The American postmodern architect Robert Venturi would later write that he avoided going to Japan for many years because the modernist image of classic Japanese wood-frame architecture promoted by Taut and others was so dominant. However, while Taut and Gropius praised the Ise Grand Shrine and Katsura Imperial Villa, Kurokawa focused attention on Himeji

Castle and the Tōshōgū at Nikkō as progenitors of postmodern style. And when Venturi did finally travel to Japan, he was delighted by the chaotic postmodern atmosphere of its cities. It is interesting that he designed the Mielparque Nikkō Kirifuri Hotel (1996), awash in kitschy signifiers, precisely because Taut had dismissed the Nikkō Tōshōgū as worthless trash.

In modern times Shinto operated as an oppressive and xenophobic ideology. In reality a polytheistic religion, at least in the world of architecture it was associated with the puritanical aesthetic of modernism. In response, Kurokawa rediscovered the undervalued possibilities of Buddhism and opened the way to postmodernism. But he did not phrase this in terms of a dichotomy in which Buddhism was good and Shinto evil. He was fundamentally critical of such dualistic thinking. Instead, he argued for avoiding such unproductive dualities, and pointed to the Mahayana Buddhist idea of "emptiness" as a third concept within which the other two might coexist. "Emptiness" is neither being nor non-being. Kurokawa aimed at an open and all-embracing philosophy.

It is interesting to note that Kurokawa's architecture makes extensive use of curves. Let's look at a few examples. In his K House Project (1960) and Kodomo no Kuni Central Lodge (1964), he used forms that suggest the curvilinear profiles of the roofs of ancient buildings. For a monument to the war dead in the city of Gamagori (1977), he designed a tower with two triangular columns rising in gentle curves from the base. The roofline of the Karuizawa Prince Hotel (1973) also describes a gentle curve melding with the natural scenery. Even in the design of Yamagata Hawaii Dreamland (1967), when he was referencing cellular imagery, the central void was not rectilinear but given rounded curves. The Saitama Museum of Modern Art (1982) and the Nagoya City Art Museum (1987) both employed a structural framework arrayed along a strict grid, but the introduction of contoured glass facades gave birth to the type of "intermediate zone" Kurokawa advocated. And in the National Bunraku Theater (1983) in Osaka, curved eaves extend over the entrance. In designs employing the

Saitama Museum of Modern
Art, 1982. (Photo by the author)

capsule (a standardized room module), like the Nakagin Capsule Building
(1972), round windows evoked a futuristic image. Circular motifs were also
used in the plans of the Hiroshima City Museum of Contemporary Art
(1988) and the Komatsu City Honjin Kinen Art Museum (1990).

From the 1990s onward Kurokawa advocated for what he called
"abstract symbolism," in which the abstract geometries constituting a
common aesthetic for the human race would give expression to symbolic
content—an architecture that could merge the global with the local, and
transcend dualism. For example, the cone could be interpreted as a European spire or steeple, a Chinese tower roof, the nose cone of a rocket, or a
Babylonian ziggurat. Cones appear with frequency in Kurokawa's works of
abstract symbolism, such as Melbourne Central (1991) and the Kuji City
Cultural Center (1998). He also applied fractal geometry to the design of
furniture (1996) and the Fujinomiya Golf Club clubhouse (1997), experimenting with pliable curves that would transcend the dualism of order and
chaos. He was adopting new geometrical concepts that might be discovered in the forms of the natural world.

In advocating for a rectilinear design aesthetic, Le Corbusier famously
stated that while "the pack-donkey meanders along" without purpose,
humans make straight paths with a goal in mind. Kurokawa countered
this by saying, "Humans discover their goals by wandering. Therefore their
pathways should be labyrinthian and twisting."[14] There is an interesting
anecdote concerning the period when Kurokawa was put in charge of

developing the transportation plan for Tange Kenzō's Tokyo Plan 1960 (1961). When he was handed initial sketches arranged along a straight axis, he did everything he could to bend them and round them off into cellular forms.[15] After he submitted the plans, Tange returned them to him with the lines straightened out again. Apparently this back-and-forth between the two repeated itself several times. A strong, linear central axis like that of the Hiroshima Peace Memorial Museum and Tokyo Plan 1960 was characteristic of Tange's work.

Metabolist architecture was predicated on change, and therefore had no completed form. This recalls what D.T. Suzuki observed in *Zen and Japanese Culture* (1959) regarding "the beauty of imperfection."[16] He wrote, "Where you would ordinarily expect a line or a mass or a balancing element, you miss it, and yet this very thing awakens in you an unexpected feeling of pleasure." Another characteristic mentioned by Suzuki is asymmetry. For example, he points out that in the layout of a Buddhist temple complex, not all of the structures align symmetrically along the central axis; some may be scattered about the grounds. Neither the Takara Beautilion nor the Nakagin Capsule Building possesses an axis of symmetry;

Nakagin Capsule Building, 1972.
(Photo by the author)

the volumes extend freely in every direction. Suzuki suggests that the totality is not superior to its constituent parts, but that part and whole embrace one another—which we might say is a very Metabolist way of thinking. Suzuki's *sokuhi no ronri* (the logic of identity through difference) encompasses duality through a simultaneous process of affirmation and negation.

Mediating difference

Kurokawa's "philosophy of symbiosis" had a particularly deep connection to Buddhism, with roots he himself traced to the teachings of the Consciousness-Only school. But neither did he confine himself to Buddhism; his thinking was fresh and broadly based, and overlapped with the biological concept of symbiosis. The philosophy of symbiosis was a significant mode of thought born out of modern Japanese Buddhism. In the 1910s, the scholar-monk Shiio Benkyō of the Pure Land Sect founded an organization called the Association for Symbiosis, starting a social movement that gathered strength in the late 1920s. He preached that liberation was to be achieved not by individuals, but socially, by perfecting genuine symbiosis—a doctrine he taught in the factories and farming villages as a solution to labor problems. He believed people must seek coexistence with all beings—other people, plants and animals, nature and the environment. After Kurokawa's proclamation of a "philosophy of symbiosis," Shiio's teachings at Tōkai Gakuen and the concept of "living together" (*tomoiki*) that arose in Buddhist circles in his day are now being rediscovered and re-evaluated.

Shiio was the principal of Tōkai Gakuen, where Kurokawa attended middle school and high school, and it was in Shiio's lectures that Kurokawa first encountered the concept of "symbiotic Buddhism." Apparently he questioned Shiio at one point, saying that if Buddhist doctrine taught that even plants possessed the Buddha-nature and forbade the killing of sentient beings, then wasn't vegetarianism a contradiction of the Buddhist teachings? Shiio responded that one should eat only what one needed, and that even vegetarians would eventually return to the earth, out of which would arise plants, which would be eaten by animals, in a great cycle of symbiotic relationships. Humanity is not a solitary existence. Life exists within cycles. This way of thinking clearly seems in tune with Metabolism. After the war, Kurokawa would keenly feel both a yearning for and an antipathy toward the overwhelming material culture of the Americans, which in his case occasioned an interest in Oriental philosophy that led him to study the Consciousness-Only school of Buddhism during his university years.

When he was a boy, he watched with mixed emotions as other children were given chocolate by the Occupation soldiers. But he also seems to have been quite impressed by the Jeeps the American soldiers rode around in—enough so that when he was finally able to buy a car for himself, he bought a Jeep. In *Homo movens* (1969), he predicted a more mobile society, inspired by what he knew of the American lifestyle and specifically the American trailer-park lifestyle.[17] America was the test-bed for the future. While Venturi explored the semiotics of roadside attractions as a new architectural vocabulary, Kurokawa sought to understand a new social system and proposed his theory of capsule architecture.

On the other hand, after encountering the historian Egami Namio's "horse-rider" theory—that an equestrian race (*kiba minzoku*) invaded the Japanese archipelago from the continent and played a significant role in shaping the ancient Japanese state—Kurokawa began to move in new directions. In the 1980s he published *Nomado no jidai* (The Age of Nomads), which superimposed the theme of *Homo movens* over an image of Japanese society in the Edo period (1600–1868).[18] He pointed out that Edo Japan had already become a highly developed information society, modifying his argument to encompass the realm of data processing in addition to that of the physical mobility he had focused on previously. It was a vision of an amalgam of American culture with the culture of

Edo—just as his own thought was formed through a mediation between East and West—essentially Baroque. The ideal form of the Renaissance was the circle, with its single center. But in the Baroque period this circle fissioned into an ellipse, surrounding two poles. It was a form pregnant with dynamic movement.

Looping space

From the 1980s onward, Kurokawa proclaimed his philosophy of symbiosis and experimented with design that would make it possible for different values to coexist simultaneously. While Isozaki Arata was writing essays on architecture read by intellectuals, Kurokawa's works—*Homo movens* (1969), *Kyōsei no shisō* (The Philosophy of Symbiosis, 1987), *Nomado no jidai* (The Age of Nomads, 1989), and others—proposed easily understood concepts for the present day, a type of architectural theory that businessmen could enjoy reading. Internationally the trend in architecture was also moving from an exclusionary modernism to an all-inclusive postmodernism. But Kurokawa did not simply import and adopt this mode of thought; he developed it into a unique vision integrated with the Japanese context. For example, the postmodernism of figures such as Michael Graves quoted classicism in an explicitly anti-modern stance, but never got beyond a self-referential Western perspective incapable of relativizing itself.

Kurokawa's efforts to deconstruct centrality promoted postmodern design with a constantly shifting series of keywords. For example, in the late 1970s he argued for a non-dualistic "culture of gray" and introduced the sense of a multivalent, ambiguous "Rikyū gray" (named after the famous tea master Sen no Rikyū) into his architecture. The Head Office of Fukuoka Bank (1975) inserts a large void (a central plaza under the overhang of the building) into the urban fabric, forming an intermediate space between public and private. Both it and the Ishikawa Kōsei Nenkin Hall (1977) were clad in Rikyū gray. For overseas projects as well, such as the Japanese-German Center Berlin (1988) and the New Wing of the Van Gogh Museum (1998), he took as his theme the symbiosis between new and old, between history and the future. And for the Kuala Lumpur International Airport (1998), he made a wooded central garden, aiming at a symbiosis of nature and high technology. A forest of columns support roofing units that describe gentle curves—contemporary industrial architecture that still manages to evoke associations with both traditional Islamic architecture and natural woodlands.

Just as Metabolism and the philosophy of symbiosis took inspiration from biology, the overall framework of the shift from modern to postmodern architecture signified a transformation from a simple mechanical model to a more complex biological one. At the same time, this was also a shift from a monotheistic to a polytheistic model. According to Kurokawa, monotheism is a worldview grounded in an orderly hierarchy. In contrast, Buddhism believes that the Buddha-nature is present in every leaf and branch, root and trunk—that there is no class, and all beings exist on the same plane as equal and autonomous values.[19] This is a system that is not like a tree with an axial trunk, but a rhizomatic network. Flat relationships. No center. Yet when the individual units are in motion, it is not random and completely disjointed. They are connected to one another. Translated into spatial terms, the form is that of a loop—a motif that recurs frequently in Kurokawa's work.

The National Museum of Ethnology (1977), built on the site of Expo '70, has a lattice-like structure of blocks with square plans that could be easily joined with new construction; each of these units has its own central courtyard, so that both the constituent parts and the whole building function as a system like that of the traditional Japanese stroll garden. In other words, wherever one goes, a looping movement occurs. This has been said to reflect the anthropological theories of the founding director-general of the museum, Umesao Tadao, who believed in relativizing the totality through observation.[20] According to Umesao, Europe is a monotheistic realm whose worldview is oriented to a fixed, single-point perspective. Even in polytheistic societies like India, the perspective was still fixed, with a panoply of deities unfolding before one. In contrast, Japan is pantheistic, with gods appearing everywhere, to be worshipped as one moved about. This mode of thinking—that there is no fixed center, and yet there is a rotating movement around it—conforms perfectly with the characteristics of spatial composition in the museum. In a 2004 interview, Kurokawa described his thinking:

> Levi-Strauss discovered the Other, and called that point of view "the savage mind." One might call this cultural relativism, but I believe there is something in this that is close to Umesao Tadao's *Bunmei no seitai shikan* (An Ecological View of History: Japanese Civilization in the World Context). This is why our discussions always focused on this question: How can we create a centerless architecture? . . . In other words, there is no inherent quality that dictates Europe should be at the center, and all around it are arrayed the more benighted cultures. Just because something is made in Japan doesn't mean Japan is the center of anything. Such a completely open structure— this is what I was trying to achieve in all my Expo pavilions as well, something eternally connected and eternally open.[21]

A structure without hierarchy has no front or back, no interior. It is a space that does not give birth to otherness. Various loops can be made to replicate, in a chain reaction. An urban structure of concentric circles, integrating such loops yet open to the sea and water, was used in the New Tokyo Plan 2025 (1987) and in proposals for urban planning in China. As early as his involvement in Tange's Tokyo Plan 1960, in which he was made responsible for the road system, Kurokawa had proposed what he called "cycle transportation" incorporating figure-eight loops and roundabouts. Rather than a square or plaza at the city center where crowds gathered, he envisioned roads on which cars were endlessly moving. If Metabolism signified circularity in the temporal realm, these were examples of circularity in the spatial realm.

Kurokawa's experience of the war and his study of Buddhism led him to expound a unique philosophy—one that was not limited to architecture. Because of this, he suggests an important direction for contemporary society. With the end of the Cold War and the stalemate between the Western and Eastern blocs, the world seemed poised to enter a period of diverse globalism. But after the 9/11 terrorist attacks in the United States, the world seemed to be losing its capacity for tolerating and imagining the Other. The dualities of good versus evil and Christianity versus Islam were emphasized, and the world appeared to be ready to polarize once again. This is why "the philosophy of symbiosis" and the questions it asks will continue to have great relevance, now and in the future.

Isozaki Arata

An Architect Torn Between Fiction and Reality

An unbuilt future

Unbuilt—that is, unrealized—architecture exists only in mediated form. It is architecture without physical reality. Such projects remain unbuilt for a variety of reasons. They may have been too purely conceptual, like Ledoux's eighteenth-century utopias. Or perhaps physically impossible and contradictory spaces are implied, as in Piranesi's meticulous etchings of imaginary prisons, or the prints and drawings of M.C. Escher. Then there are proposals defeated in competitions, like Maekawa Kunio's proposal for a Tokyo Imperial Museum (1931). Or those, like Buckminster Fuller's "Cloud Nine" spherical floating cities (1970), in which the technology outran the era's ability to produce it. There are cyber-architectural animations that exist only on the computer screen, yet carry out a limitless process of generation and transformation. In any case, we can neither visit nor touch any of these unbuilt works. They live and breathe in the conceptual realm of plans, drawings, models, and other means of conveying information.

These architectural renderings are an odd thing. The media used to represent architecture is never the actual material of building, yet through these media we can imagine a distant reality. A project may begin with a simple sketch, but once the building is completed, it becomes the original. Only unbuilt architecture—by inverting this relationship so that the media rendering becomes the original—is capable of clearing away the faint incongruousness that accompanies architectural monographs and exhibitions. These are forms of media as well, and thus appropriate for housing the unbuilt.

In the long history of architecture, it was the twentieth century in which media—including magazines, exhibitions, photographs, film, and video—came to exercise the most powerful influence. A single powerful image could travel to all corners of the architectural world almost instantaneously. An anonymous young architect with no actual buildings

Future City (The Incubation Process), a montage from the 1960s. (Courtesy of Arata Isozaki & Associates)

to his credit could suddenly be thrust into the limelight. Unbuilt architecture, in the sense that it cannot find expression in the real world, might be compared to dreams or the unconscious. Freud published *The Interpretation of Dreams* in 1900, and proceeded to analyze the structure of the unconscious as a determinant of human behavior, shaping the direction of twentieth-century thought. Similarly, in the twentieth century the unbuilt began to make inroads into the real world and influence actual buildings. Without speaking of the unbuilt, we cannot relate the history of twentieth-century architecture.

Nor is this just a twentieth-century matter. The unbuilt transcends time. It possesses an anachronistic quality that can summon up the architecture of antiquity while simultaneously embodying a vision of the future. At the time of his debut, Isozaki Arata proclaimed, "Ruins lie in the future of our city, and the future city itself will lie in ruins." This image was proposed in a drawing entitled *Future City (The Incubation Process)*, in which futuristic structures are collaged with Greek ruins—the very model of an unbuilt project. At a time when other architects were embracing rather simplistic aspirations for the future, Isozaki had selected an unusual strategy. From this point on, his works would display a fixation on the fictional. In dreams and the unconscious, normal time does not exist. In the same space, multiple times and structures can coexist. Isozaki was fourteen years old when Japan surrendered among the smoking ruins of its cities. Since the unbuilt will not be realized, it cannot be polluted by the real world and is eternally open to interpretation. His body of work presents a paradox: that the history/story of architecture is composed of timeless things.

Isozaki Arata's words are always ironic. The "counter-architecture" of which he used to speak was an ideal of what architecture should be. At the end of the twentieth century, the critic Asada Akira predicted that "counter-architecture will be the architecture of the next century," and it might be that we could replace "architecture" in this formulation with "architectural history." In other words, only "counter-architectural history" can be called architectural history.

Isozaki Arata began his career in the late 1950s and early 1960s, when the rapid proliferation of the media brought the idea of linear progress to an end, and time seemed to begin to fold back on itself. Out of his more than forty years of work, let's consider his most representative unbuilt projects, checking in at ten-year intervals. In Isozaki's dreams, a craving for self-replicating networks violently collides with a will to control them by structuring them as architecture. Perhaps this reflects the trauma of cities consumed in the fire unleashed by a nuclear chain reaction. But these are not merely dreams. These works still possess intensity because underlying them was a new system of architecture.

In *City in the Air* and *Future City (The Incubation Process)*, created by Isozaki in the 1960s, core groups of vertical towers rise high into the air above the 31-meter limit mandated by the building codes, linked by horizontal projections extending freely in every direction—raising the self-replicating growth of urban functions and density to the maximum. Isozaki also contributed proposals based on similar technology to Tange's Tokyo Plan 1960, in which he was responsible for the design of office buildings.

In the 1970s, *Computer Aided City* (1972) envisioned the use of advanced information systems to reconfigure existing building types, melding them into a single continuous space. Although this in some ways anticipated the amorphously dispersed "convenience store" city, it also showed the limitations of the period in its rather antiquated science-fiction image of the controlling, centralized mainframe computer.

His 1980s *Plan for New Tokyo Metropolitan Government Offices* (1985), while incorporating Platonic solids such as spheres and pyramids, is overlaid with other archaic geometric forms that can be interpreted from the perspective of feng shui. This plan proposed offices arranged in a dispersed network and an enclosed public square to promote democracy. By rejecting the specifications of the competition, which called for a super-high-rise structure, Isozaki essentially dared the judges to reject his design. The present Tokyo Metropolitan Government Offices were designed by his mentor, Tange Kenzō, who won the competition.

In the 1990s Isozaki conceived *Haishi: The Mirage City* (1995) and *Shenzhen International Trade Plaza* (1995). Staged in an Asia in which temporal and spatial distance has been compressed, the former experimented with various models for the networked city in the era of information capitalism, while the latter was a project subject to the chal-

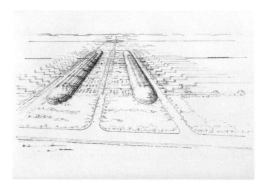

Computer Aided City,
isometric perspective drawing.
(Courtesy of Arata Isozaki & Associates)

lenges that the system of rapid growth is presenting China. The *Mirage City* exhibition was an experimental project utilizing the Internet to create a virtual city on an artificial Asian island.

By the time the next millennium arrives a thousand years from now, the architecture of the twentieth century will have almost completely vanished. In that distant future, how will historians look back at the twentieth century? Few actual buildings will remain. They will rely on mediated information. Isozaki does not discriminate between built and unbuilt, deliberately making his ideas clear through wooden models that are built to last, and if the original built structures are eventually lost, then the difference between built and unbuilt will all but disappear. There are actually examples of wooden architectural models from the Renaissance that have survived for more than five hundred years. It may be that the people of the future will discover the first stirrings of the architecture of the twenty-first century among Isozaki's unbuilt plans.

Realized buildings—ahead of their time

Now let us consider Isozaki's career from the perspective of his realized buildings. Isozaki Arata and Kurokawa Kishō, born in the 1930s, were both enrolled in Tange Kenzō's research group at the University of Tokyo, and from their student days were cosmopolitan in their activities, with many friends overseas. Both of them have engaged in many projects outside Japan, from high-rise buildings to museums. Kurokawa reached overseas audiences not only through his leading role in the Metabolist movement but also through his theories of design based in Buddhist thought. On the other hand, Isozaki used the universal language of logic to convey the appeal of Japanese architecture.

Over more than forty years, Isozaki published an enormous number of written works as a critic at the leading edge of architectural thought— all while practicing as an architect, developing his expressive style with an acute sensitivity to the changing times. He has also engaged in collaborative projects involving other architects and artists, and served as a commissioner of the International Architecture Exhibition of the Venice Biennale and of Kumamoto Artpolis. As a juror for major competitions, he has supported the discovery of young talent and the realization of challenging works, including those for La Villette Park (Paris), Hong Kong Peak, and Sendai Mediatheque. From his early days he has maintained a wide web of relationships with artists and other cultural figures, breaking the rigid mold of the architect to create venues for broad-ranging discussion in the opinion magazines *Hermes* and *Hihyō kūkan* (Critical Space) and in the ANY series of international architecture conferences, where he joined the critic Asada Akira in facilitating interdisciplinary and cross-border dialogues.

In the 1960s Isozaki created dynamic designs emphasizing powerful masses of concrete, such as the Ōita Medical Hall (1960) and Ōita Prefectural Library in his hometown of Ōita. Fascinated by the directions technology was taking, from the late 1960s onward he began to shift his focus from static physical forms to more interactive information environments, and he began to articulate concepts such as "invisible cities" and "soft architecture." His *Electric Labyrinth* (1968), an installation for the Milan Triennale, incorporated curved panels that rotated in response to the viewer's movements. Isozaki was responsible for the two giant entertainment robots, Deme and Deku, deployed in the Festival Plaza that Tange Kenzō had designed for Expo '70 in Osaka.

As the 1970s began, Isozaki announced a withdrawal from the metropolis and proclaimed a methodology that was more interested in the pursuit and manipulation of pure geometric form than in the relationship between society and design. For example, the Gunma Museum of Modern Art (1974) was constructed as a complex framework of connected cubes, while the Kitakyushu Central Library (1974) extended semicylindrical vaulted ceilings along curved pathways to define the structural space. In both cases he was exploring the possibilities of unique architectural forms as his design theme. This style took off from the formalist tendencies then current in overseas architecture.

In the 1980s, responding to the currents of global postmodernism, Isozaki experimented with quotations from historic architecture. The Tsukuba Center Building (1983) stirred much discussion for its bold sampling and repurposing of fragments of Western architecture dear to Isozaki—such as Michelangelo's Piazza del Campidoglio and Ledoux's column motifs—applying them despite their lack of any particular relationship to the Japanese public facility he was designing. He also produced drawings of the Tsukuba Center Building as a ruin. The Los Angeles Museum of Contemporary Art (1986), which incorporated proportional systems based on both the European golden ratio and Oriental yin-yang cosmology, marked the full-scale commencement of Isozaki's career outside Japan.

Art Tower Mito (1990) could be called a unification of all of Isozaki's styles up to that point. It quotes freely from a range of classical elements—the work of European architects such as John Soane of eighteenth-century England and Bernini of seventeenth-century Italy, the theaters of Shakespearean England, and so on. Second, it relied heavily on the use of geometric forms in composition: a tower of tetrahedrons rising from a triangular base, a rectangular main gallery topped by a pyramid, a concert hall whose plan was a hexagon enclosing a circle, a theater combining cylindrical and cubic forms, and a meeting hall

Elevation drawing of Art Tower Mito, built in 1990. (Courtesy of Arata Isozaki & Associates)

with a plan based on semicircles and a square. Third, the glistening silver exterior of the tower, clad in titanium, provided a futuristic image and expressed a technological topology. The 100-meter tower, commemorating the centennial of Mito's incorporation as a city, functions as a symbol of the municipality.

Following this, Isozaki kept changing, staying with no fixed style. Other buildings of the 1990s included the Nagi Museum of Contemporary Art (1994), the design of which was intimately connected with the goal of providing site-specific installations for particular works of art, and Nara Centennial Hall (1998), with its graceful elliptical exteriors. From the 1990s onward, along with the growing impact of globalism, Isozaki did an increasing amount of work overseas, from the colorful Team Disney Building (1991) in Orlando, Florida, to the CAFA (Central Academy of Fine Arts) Art Museum (2008) in Beijing. With the advent of the twenty-first century, forms exploiting the potential of computer-aided design became especially noticeable in his designs.

This recent body of work supported Isozaki's pronouncements as practical realizations of his innovative architectural theories; he is always staying ahead of the times and providing stimulus to his contemporaries. Isozaki is always the best interpreter of his own work. Yet a portion of his early work has already been demolished; unlike Europe, the "scrap and build" ethos is extremely powerful in Japan, and architecture has a difficult time surviving for long.

Isozaki has actively displayed his work in a series of exhibitions, including *Arata Isozaki Architecture 1960–1990* (1991), a major retrospective; *Ma: Twenty Years On and Iki: Espace-Temps du Japon* (2000), an international traveling exhibition of *Ma: Space-Time in Japan* (1978), which had debuted in Paris and made a final triumphal return to Tokyo; *Arata Isozaki: Unbuilt* (2001), focusing on his unrealized designs; and others. In them, Isozaki employed a variety of media in an effort to suture together a body of work torn between reality and fiction and position it in history.

PART II

BREAKING OUT
OF THE BOX

The Generation Born in the 1940s

Andō Tadao

Geometries of Concrete, Reflecting the Environment

The opposing mirrors of East and West

Andō Tadao was born in Osaka in 1941, the same year that produced other rising stars, such as Itō Toyoo. It was a generation that Maki Fumihiko would later call "masterless samurai of peacetime." But what made Andō unique was that he had a career as a professional boxer and studied architecture on his own. In the 1960s he toured all of Japan and made two trips to Europe, experiencing a variety of architecture. He established his architectural practice in 1969, and in 1976 his Row House in Sumiyoshi was completed, winning the Architectural Institute of Japan Prize. Inserting a windowless facade of raw concrete into the downtown milieu, this small residential structure enveloped a surprisingly rich interior space—a small universe. Itō Toyoo's White U (House in Nakano Honchō), also built in 1976, was a similarly introverted dwelling. Andō's basic design might be described as an inheritance from modernist architects such as Le Corbusier and Louis Kahn. At the same time, the Row House in Sumiyoshi sparked discussion by devoting a full third of its very limited building site to a courtyard garden, requiring the use of an umbrella on rainy days simply to go to the toilet. In other words, while the design employed modern materials ordered by geometric principles, the lack of an efficient traffic flow might be seen as an experiment in overcoming modernity.

In the 1980s, projects such as Rokkō Housing I (1983), an apartment complex set into a steep hillside, and Times I (1984), a commercial building following the bank of a river, achieved a skillful harmonization of architecture with the natural setting that established an unshakable position for Andō. His early work centered on private residences and small commercial buildings, but by the late 1980s he began to undertake the design of larger public facilities such as the Hyōgo Children's Museum (1989) and the Himeji Museum of Literature (1991). As a result, the scale of his work increased, and his design, previously limited to smaller structures, developed an almost Baroque dynamism—bold cutouts, dramatic effects using light and water, grand staircases, underground chambers. Awaji Yumebutai (1999) can be regarded as a kind of museum of Andō's accumulated styles and techniques. While Itō Toyoo apprenticed in the offices of Kikutake Kiyonori (1928–2011) and was interested in the latest technology, pursuing an articulation of space using the lightest possible materials, Andō was building robust, solid structures.

Times I, 1984. (Photo by the author)

Andō's trademark is probably his spartan use of unadorned raw concrete. It is interesting that this should call up—for Westerners—the very image of Japanese minimalism. There are even foreign critics who have linked it with Zen and Shinto in their analyses. From Bruno Taut onward, traditional Japanese architecture has frequently been praised for its commonalities with modernist design, and Andō has succeeded with using modern materials to evoke the spirituality present in traditional buildings. The architectural critic Kenneth Frampton sees in Andō's work an embodiment of the Japanese sensibility, and gives it high marks—especially for the way in which it continues the project of modernist design while simultaneously evoking the nature of specific sites. Frampton positions Andō as a practitioner of the kind of "critical regionalism" Frampton himself champions, and reads in him a Japanese sensibility. When Western critics write about Andō, the Japanese tradition is often mentioned. This is true not only for works using wood construction but for his concrete buildings as well, associating Andō's design with Zen gardens, tea rooms, *sukiya*-style architecture, and Shinto shrines.

Luciano Benetton, a co-founder of the Benetton Group and a client of Andō's, remarks, "I was completely taken with the Oriental simplicity of his architectural style, so different from Western architecture." And the artist Richard Serra has spoken of Andō's work as most representative of traditional Japanese architecture.

But from my perspective, Andō's architecture is extremely Western. For example, the towering vertical walls of bookshelves lining a central void that feature in the Shiba Ryōtarō Memorial Museum (2001), Toyosaka City Library in Niigata (2000), and Andō's own Atelier in Ōyodo (1990–91) are rare in Japan but bring to mind such bibliographic temples as the British Museum Reading Room in London and the former Imperial Library in Vienna, or the work of Gunnar Asplund, the great Swedish architect. In projects like the Sayamaike Historical Museum (2001), the exterior staircases and water garden resemble, if anything, the geometries of Western formal gardens. Andō, who was born and raised in the Kansai region, recalls that he had ample opportunity to acquaint himself with traditional architecture, but the trips to Europe he managed to make during his youth in the 1960s must also have exerted a major influence. Andō's approach to space is imprinted with a Western sense of composition.

It would seem that both the Western critics and I discover in Andō's architecture something missing in our respective cultures. As a mirror, Andō offers an inverted image. The Chinese artist Cai Guo-Qiang says that Andō's architecture acknowledges both harmony and conflict with nature, and possesses both Eastern and Western aspects—or neither. If this is the case, then perhaps the universality of Andō's work resides precisely in its ambiguity—that it feels Eastern from a Western perspective, and vice versa. It is impossible to build a global presence as an architect merely on the exoticism connected with being Japanese.

The potential of wooden architecture

Generally speaking, Andō is regarded as an architect who works in concrete, but from the 1990s onward he has also made extensive use of the most traditional of Japanese building materials—wood. And in doing so, he has pursued a variety of the expressive possibilities of this medium.

His first major wooden structure was the Japan Pavilion (1992) at Expo '92 in Seville. Laminate wood post-and-beam construction supported a Teflon-membrane roof, while the dramatically upswept curve of the facade was clad with horizontal wood siding. The scale of the structure—60 meters wide, 40 meters deep, and 25 meters high—placed it among the largest wooden buildings in the world. One of the outstanding features of traditional Japanese architecture is the beauty of the wood joinery employed in the block-and-bracket systems (known as *tokyō* or *masugumi*) used to support the roof on posts or columns. Although it used laminated materials, the Japan Pavilion in Seville gave visitors a sense of the structural beauty of the joinery characteristic of classical Japanese architecture. And this was not simply a matter of design aesthetics—the practical aspects were equally important. Use of standardized materials permitted extensive prefabrication and a rational, systematic approach to construction. Concrete requires considerable drying time, which lengthens the period needed for construction. Projects like Expo '92 had to be completed quickly, so wood was a better choice from this point of view as well.

Prior to Expo '92, Andō had experimented with the use of wood in several temporary projects. In 1990, he created a four-day temporary theater installation called *Alternative Museum* at the P3 Gallery in Tokyo, which used darkly painted layers of construction scaffold planking to define an elliptical space. For the Shitamachi Kara-za (1988), a temporary theater built for playwright and director Kara Jurō, metal pipe scaffolding was used to create a structural system that could be readily assembled and disassembled, though Andō initially considered a timber-framed, towerlike structure. The final overall plan was for a dodecagon 40 meters in diameter and 23 meters high, with exterior walls clad in black wood siding, and a red tent—Kara's trademark—for the roof. Regardless of whether the framing was timber or aluminum pipe, the basic concept was the same: to use standardized units for the structural framework.

In the Nara period (710–794), when it became necessary to construct the immense Tōdaiji temple in a limited time frame, a new construction technology using standardized units was employed, which later came to be called *daibutsuyō* ("great Buddha style"). This style, which dramatically exposed the underlying framework, with an almost infinite number of vertical and horizontal members intersecting one another high above the ground, was echoed in Andō's designs for the Japan Pavilion in Seville and the Museum of Wood.

The Museum of Wood (1994) was a project that began with a request to relocate the Seville pavilion to a site in Japan. In the end, legal and other

Museum of Wood, 1994. (Photo by the author)

issues led to the abandonment of this idea, but the basic style of framing, supported by columns grouped in sets of four, as well as the exterior cladding of wood siding, was shared by both buildings. The concept of the Japan Pavilion had been carried forward. However, while the Japan Pavilion had arranged its columns in straight lines around a rectilinear plan, the Museum of Wood had a circular plan that required sixteen sets of columns to encircle a central void with a diameter of 22 meters. As one ascends the sloping path that transects the building, this central void offers a delightful view of the sky through a central circular opening resembling the oculus of the Pantheon in Rome. Thus the Museum of Wood is not merely an exhibition space; it's also a shrine to the spirit of wood. Entering the central space and looking up, one is amazed at the sense of volume conveyed by the massive square columns, measuring 18 meters high and 50 centimeters a side. Although they are made of laminated Japanese cedar, they possess a dynamism that recalls the thick columns of old-growth timber used in ancient Japanese architecture.

The Japan Pavilion and the Museum of Wood represent Andō working with wood on a heroic scale; he also undertook more delicate wooden architecture. One of his initial designs for the Church of Light (1989) envisioned it as a wooden structure—apparently referencing the minimalist aesthetic of Shaker design. His Minamidera (1999), on the island of Naoshima in the Inland Sea, is a simple rectangular box whose exterior is clad in vertical charred cedar boards (*yakisugi ita*), but unlike his concrete buildings, it features projecting eaves.

Nangakuzan Kōmyōji (2000), a Buddhist temple Andō designed to replace an aging 250-year-old structure, emphasizes the refinement rather than the power of its lines. The four layers of rafters supporting the roof inherit the stately, ordered beauty of *kiwari*, the traditional Japanese formulas used to determine proportional relationships in timber construction. Another typically Japanese feature is the use of parallel rafters (*heikō-daruki*) that project from the building at right angles to form eaves. On the other hand, the membrane-like exterior walls are formed by thin columns alternating with vertical strips of glass at 15-centimeter intervals—a perfectly contemporary design. The traditional joinery of the rafters and the innovative forest of columns establish lovely linear harmonies. The interior is graced by the structural interplay of the beams with the supporting columns made of laminated Douglas fir. Concrete is hard, but malleable until it sets. Like clay, it can be freely shaped and molded. Andō's architecture applies a geometric order to the fluidity of concrete, but wooden materials are cut out of their natural context and reassembled. His wooden structures have been designed with an acute awareness of the nature and personality of this material.

Architecture for urban revitalization

From the late 1990s, Andō began to win prestigious international design competitions, such as that for the Modern Art Museum of Fort Worth (2002), and rode the wave of globalism to initiate a series of overseas projects in France, Italy, the United States, and the Middle East. In addition, he attracted attention by serving as a visiting faculty member at Yale, Columbia, and Harvard universities, and was appointed to a professorship at the University of Tokyo in 1997. Projects such as the Hyōgo Prefectural Museum of Art (2002), with its massive projecting eaves and concrete internal structure enveloped in glass curtain walls, and the International Library of Children's Literature (2002) in Tokyo's Ueno Park, which bisects an existing early twentieth-century building with a contemporary glass box, indicate new directions in his work, utilizing combinations of quite different materials to enhance one another's fundamental qualities.

Andō is also one of a handful of architects with influence on the society at large, beyond the world of architecture. Through outspoken appearances on NHK television and other mass media, after the Great Hanshin-Awaji Earthquake in 1995 (also known as the Kobe earthquake), he was instrumental in initiating and promoting Green Network, a movement for the greening of urban areas—acting as a social activist and not simply a designer of buildings. In the wake of the 9/11 terrorist attacks in New York, he submitted a proposal for a memorial at the site that rejected the idea of rebuilding the high-rise structures that had stood there, envisioning in their place only a circular earthen memorial mound resembling an ancient burial tumulus. In *Regeneration: Surroundings and Architecture*, an exhibition at Tokyo Station Gallery in 2003, Andō located the sites of projects or proposals of his on large maps of cities such as Paris, Kobe, and New York, giving viewers a sense of his awareness that buildings should not be thought of as independent entities, but in terms of their continuity with the surrounding urban environment.

International Library of Children's Literature, 2002. (Photo by the author)

The salient characteristic of Omotesandō Hills (2006), a commercial complex that rose on the former site of the Dōjunkai Apartments in Tokyo, was its astonishing length—a continuous facade of some 250 meters, something exceptionally rare in Japanese architecture. In China it is relatively common to develop entire city blocks as units, but it is quite unusual in Japan. This was the largest-scale project Andō had built in Tokyo. Yet at the same time, he restricted the height of the building to harmonize with the zelkova trees (*keyaki* in Japanese) lining the avenue along which the building is situated. The facade is finely articulated with regular divisions that recall the scale of the apartment complex that had previously occupied the site. The main structure is set back from the slope of the hill traversed by the boulevard of Omotesandō, with a six-story atrium enclosed by a spiral ramp that echoes the slope outside. Such large atriums have existed since the appearance of major shopping arcades and department stores in the nineteenth century, but what characterizes Omotesandō Hills is the way it is set into the slope on which it is sited. Because of this, there is no clear demarcation between the first and second floors; once inside you can continue to take pleasure in the feeling of walking along a sloping street lined with shops—an interior extension of the boulevard outside: another Omotesandō. Favorite Andō motifs, such as broad staircases and underground spaces drawing light from above, are also used to advantage here.

Omotesandō Hills, 2006. (Photo by the author)

The Omotesandō district of Tokyo has preserved its greenery and retained its image as a center for incubating and disseminating the latest culture. The Dōjunkai Apartments were built in 1926–27 by the government to provide housing after the 1923 Kantō earthquake; Omotesandō Hills has taken up the challenge of creating a new urban landscape while preserving their memory. At one end of the complex is a building that recreates the facade of one of the Dōjunkai buildings. Harmonization of the architecture with its surroundings was also achieved by incorporation of roof gardens and allowing vines to grow along the exterior walls.

Fukutake Hall (2008), built for the University of Tokyo Interfaculty Initiative in Information Studies, incorporates research facilities and a cafe in a long, narrow site extending along Hongō-dōri between the university's landmark Akamon (Red Gate) and Main Gate. As a result, the structure encloses a long and narrow volume: 15 by 95 meters. But the building never reveals itself completely, encouraging visitors to imagine the parts of it they cannot see. A long wall runs along the facade of the building facing the University of Tokyo Library, which was built in 1928, bisected along much of its length by a narrow horizontal slit that creates a sense of tension. From the inside, this same slit provides a narrowly framed view of the campus quite different from what one might normally encounter.

Andō designed a similarly long, narrow structure for the Creative Hall at Aomori Contemporary Art Center (2001), but the volume of Fukutake Hall is half sunken below ground level, moderating its impact on the surroundings. The open space fronting the two basement floors takes the form of a staircase dug into the earth, recalling the stepwells of India that Andō experienced during his travels as a young man. The University of Tokyo is already graced with a number of historic buildings, but the attention to the surrounding environment and the powerful sculptural intelligence of Andō's architecture infuse it with new presence.

Opened to coincide with the 2009 Venice Biennale, Andō's Punta della Dogana stands on a point of land opposite the Piazza San Marco. It is a museum housing the contemporary art collection of François Pinault, a French entrepreneur. From the exterior, it is difficult to see any evidence of the geometric raw concrete walls or other elements characteristic of Andō's design—because this project transformed the Venetian Republic's original customs house into a contemporary art space. Andō took a similar approach to another renovation project in Venice for the same client, the Palazzo Grassi.

For the interior of the museum, Andō respected the fundamentals of the original plan, which was laid out as a series of narrow rectangular warehouses, but with a few significant interventions of his own. New flooring was laid throughout the interior and a traffic flow established that skillfully employed ramps and stairs to direct visitors along a single continuous path through the exhibition spaces in a restrained and understated design. Andō showed his architectural hand most plainly in the central area of the museum with the introduction of a rectangular atrium. Here alone, raw concrete clad the walls to a height of two stories, providing a strikingly fresh contrast between old and new. Of course, this was intended as an exhibition space, but in a sense, these concrete walls could also be seen as a massive minimalist art installation inserted into the heart of the museum.

On the second floor of the Punta della Dogana, one can enjoy the view of the cityscape of Venice through arched windows. Here, the exhibition rooms are not limited to the display of artworks alone. The view from the tip of the building is spectacular; the museum's triangular plan projects into the waters of the surrounding canals like the prow of a ship, taking full advantage of the topography of Venice. The *Andō Tadao Exhibition 2009: City of Water—Osaka vs. Venice* at the Suntory Museum in Osaka was a proposal for how to make the city of Osaka more attractive by offering Punta della Dogana and other projects of Andō's involving the relationship between architecture and water as examples. One of the most impressive aspects of the exhibition was the panoramic view of Osaka

Bay from the fourth- and fifth-floor galleries of the museum—which was designed by Andō. The potential for a City of Water was demonstrated, not just by models and drawings, but by the landscape unfolding before the visitors' eyes. In Omotesandō, Venice, and elsewhere, Andō has set his hand to important works of architecture that confront the weight of history embodied in urban spaces and play the role of connecting it with the future.

Itō Toyoo

A New Architecture for the Information Age

A primal landscape of water

Born in 1941, Itō Toyoo spent his youth along the shores of Lake Suwa in the mountains of Nagano prefecture. His design for the Shimosuwa Municipal Museum (1993) describes a broad and gentle arc like that of a boomerang, its tubular form extending horizontally along the shores of this lake. This building marked a shift in Itō's style in the 1990s away from strictly defined forms rooted in modernism and toward a more fluid design aesthetic. The Matsumoto Performing Arts Centre (2004) also occupies its long, narrow site with a form defined by long, sinuous curves. When I visited Lake Suwa, I could not help but feel that these indeterminate forms, reminiscent of flowing water, must have drawn inspiration from the primal landscape of Itō's boyhood. He saw the lake every day on the way to school. Yet it was not

Shimosuwa Municipal Museum, 1993.
(Courtesy of Toyo Ito & Associates, Architects)

in his early years as an architect, but much later, when he was in his fifties, that this new direction flowered in what seems like a return to his roots.

It is interesting to compare Itō's career with that of another architect from the same prefecture, Fujimori Terunobu (b. 1946). Fujimori had already won renown as an architectural historian when he began to actually design buildings. His debut work, the Jinchōkan Moriya Historical Museum (1991) in his hometown of Chino in Nagano prefecture, has astonishingly eccentric design elements, such as columns that thrust straight through the eaves. Fujimori's 6-meter-high teahouse Takasugian (2004) would eventually be built on a plot of family land behind the museum, and Hikusugi-an ("Too-Low Teahouse," 2017) was recently dug into a neighboring vacant lot. In contrast to Itō's horizontality, Fujimori stresses the vertical. Fujimori may have been influenced by the Onbashira Festival of the Suwa Grand Shrine, not far from where he grew up. The Moriya family served as priests and celebrants at Suwa Grand Shrine for countless generations, and the Jinchōkan Moriya Historical Museum contains exhibits on the history of the shrine's festivals. Fujimori's architecture, like the rough-and-tumble Onbashira Festival itself, in which enormous logs are felled and ridden down steep mountainsides, brings the primal energy of antiquity to life in the contemporary world. In addition, through his historical research, Fujimori had become familiar with the standing stones and tree worship of deep antiquity, which may also have influenced his sensibility.

Another religious ritual connected with Lake Suwa, known as *omiwatari* ("the god's crossing"), has been practiced since at least the fourteenth century. In winter the surface of the lake freezes, and with the repeated expansion and contraction due to the nighttime and daytime temperature differential, the ice cracks and buckles with a deep, audible groan. An upthrust of ice—like a miniature mountain range from 30 centimeters to almost 2 meters in height—runs across the lake from shore to shore, forming a landscape reminiscent of the "land art" of contemporary artists such as Robert Smithson and Michael Heizer. At Lake Suwa this is called *omiwatari* and is said to be the traces left by the male deity of the Upper Suwa Shrine Takeminakata no Mikoto as he visits the female deity of Lower Suwa Shrine, Yasakatome no Mikoto. The first two lines to form running north-south across the surface of the lake are known as the first and second crossings, while the first east-west line to cross these is called the Saku crossing. The ritual involves the examination and reading of these three intersecting lines by a Shinto priest to divine whether the year's harvest will be bountiful or not.

Growing up near the shores of Lake Suwa, Itō Toyoo would have observed how the irregular lines produced by a natural phenomenon—ice cracking and buckling—gives birth to unforeseen beauty. It would seem that the dynamic ice sculpting on Lake Suwa may have influenced Itō's architecture and his quest for new geometries.

It might be pointed out that an almost liquid fluidity has characterized not only Itō's designs but his architectural practice. Rather than acting as a strong-willed autocrat, he has instead surrounded himself with skilled people, eliciting their broad range of talents to form a kind of creative whirlpool out of which his architecture emerges. At his worksites, communication among many people has established a new form of architecture. The journalist Takiguchi Noriko has written a book documenting the work of Itō and Rem Koolhaas, calling them the two most important contemporary architects of the era of globalism, but saying that they are a study in contrasts: "The aggressive Koolhaas, and the passive Itō, who catches falling water and diverts it into different channels."[1] Here as well we see the image of Itō's fluidity. Itō himself says, "I always attend to the comments and criticism of others, and stop for a moment to consider whether I should change my mind. . . . I always think about whether my own way of thinking might evolve by incorporating the opinion of others."[2] If Koolhaas is a kind of fierce carnivore, then perhaps Itō is a gentle herbivore.

Beyond the crisis in architecture

Itō's 1989 manifesto, written at the height of Japan's bubble economy when postmodern architecture was all the rage, was titled "There can be no new architecture without submerging in the sea of consumption."[3] He was convinced that architecture had entered a period of crisis. "And so my concerns converge on the question of whether architecture can survive as architecture in this era. No matter how much we may try to enjoy the game of architecture in this consumption-oriented society, this is the one issue we absolutely cannot avoid. We face a situation in which architecture has been almost completely assimilated into fashion, and it has become almost impossible to distinguish architects from interior designers, or even graphic designers and copywriters. Precisely because of this, I have come to feel that it is necessary to question the possibilities for establishing architecture in the midst of a consumer society."

Itō felt that it was fruitless to simply adopt a conservative stance and mourn the loss of authenticity in an era in which architecture had become a commodity. "It seems to me that reality is not something that exists prior to consumerism, but only far above and beyond it. And so I think there is nothing for it but to submerge ourselves in the sea of consumption that stretches before us, hoping that we will discover something when we reach the other shore." He was not suggesting that we should drown in the sea of consumption, but rather that we should confront it, and "thoroughly question the possibilities for establishing architecture" as we do so. Indisputably, Itō swam through the sea of the bubble economy, succeeded in charting a new course, and arrived at a "new reality" when he reached the other shore.

By replacing the phrase "consumer society" with "information society," we can describe the situation since the 1990s as well. When architecture fell into crisis with the advent of the Information Age, new possibilities for architecture began to be explored. In the 1990s computers began to invade design studios and architectural offices, and suddenly we were discussing "virtual" or "cyber" architecture—playing with the shape-shifting possibilities of images on digital monitors. As convenience stores evolved into mini distribution centers linked by computer terminals, and large information screens began to appear in major commercial facilities, the whispers that architecture was on the verge of extinction began to seem almost plausible. Apparently, visualizing what was being called cyberspace was difficult. New technology would kill architecture. This was the crisis of architecture. Victor Hugo once observed that the new medium of the printed book killed the cathedral; would the new technology of the computer render the art of architecture obsolete?

As if combatting this challenge, Itō introduced the possibilities offered by the computer into his design process, and instead gave architecture a rebirth. The benchmark project for this—the Sendai Mediatheque—opened with impressive timing. The countdown to the twenty-first century began just before midnight on December 31, 2000, and when zero was reached, the glass doors opened and crowds poured into the building. The opening thus took place on the first day of January of a new millennium—as if symbolizing a new era for architecture.

The genesis of the Sendai Mediatheque

A single sketch set the project in motion. Itō was sitting in an airport when an idea suddenly came to him. He immediately sketched it and faxed it to his office. And this was the beginning of the Sendai Mediatheque.

This sketch, dated January 23, 1995, was of a rectangular box divided by six horizontal lines.[4] Within this clear box danced six sinuous columns of varying circumference, almost as if they were wavering or flickering. At a glance it looks less like a sketch of a building than of a tub of water. And in fact, Itō's notes on the sketch say that the image he had in mind was of seaweed floating in a tub. In other words, plant life was a source of inspiration. The notes written on the sketch are fascinating. "Absolutely flat slabs,

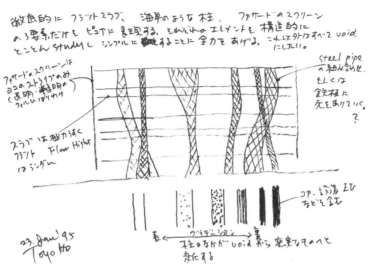

Initial sketch for Sendai Mediatheque, 1995.
(Courtesy of Toyo Ito & Associates, Architects)

columns like seaweed, a screened facade. These three elements only must be purely expressed. All our energy must go into an exhaustive structural study of these elements and how to simplify them. Everything else should be a void." There are then comments on the slabs, columns, and facade. "The slabs should be extremely thin and flat. Floor heights should be random." The columns should be "an assemblage of steel pipes or perforated steel plate." Their interiors should fall along a gradation "from void to solid," permitting core systems and amenities, including elevators, to be housed within them. "The screen for the facade should consist only of horizontal stripes (application of clear or translucent film)." The essential features of what would become the Mediatheque had already been enumerated.

In March 1995, Itō Toyoo won the international competition for the design of the Sendai Mediatheque. A breathtakingly beautiful acrylic model had been constructed for the competition. The professional modelmaker responsible for it said he sensed right away that this was a project incorporating a different dimension from any that he had worked on previously.[5] Convinced the project would win, he was not at all surprised when Itō's office called with the news it had taken first place. Isozaki Arata, known for favoring radical proposals, had served as the head of the jury for the competition. He played a key role in naming this facility the first mediatheque (multimedia library) in Japan, and had challenged the participants in the competition to propose a totally new archetype for public facilities in the Information Age.

Itō's winning entry shocked the architectural world. Many people, while acknowledging how innovative the proposal was, probably wondered whether it could actually be built. The structural engineer Sasaki Mutsurō, after first seeing the sketches, was said to have felt it "was probably unrealistic."[6] But he agreed to participate in the project, his imagination stimulated by the powerful lyricism of the drawings. He then proposed "constructing transparent tubes by arranging thin steel pipe into a hyperbolic paraboloid latticework shell, and having these tubes serve as the main structure . . . as well as using a structure of sandwiched steel plates to form the thinnest floors possible."

Six years after the competition, the Sendai Mediatheque finally opened. The building fronted on Jōzenji-dōri, a major artery in the city of Sendai, and its other sides faced parking lots and smaller buildings, so there was no plaza. Instead, the ground floor of the Mediatheque itself was presented as a public space. The Mediatheque's most salient feature was that where ordinary architecture is composed of slabs, columns, and walls, the main elements of this new structure were plates, tubes, and skins. Its structure was as follows: each of the six floors is formed by a 50-meter-square steel plate. The entire building is an enormous box, clad in a glass skin. A set of thirteen vertical tubes pierce each of the plates.

The facade is varied. Three of the sides have gigantic glass screens. On the south face, the skin is doubled. On the north and east faces, glass and aluminum are used in combination. On the west face and the roof, there are arrays of steel louvers. It is a structure with many faces, capable of a variety of expressions. The height of each floor is different. The Sendai Mediatheque avoids repetition, even commissioning furniture for each of the floors from different designers, including Karim Rashid and Sejima Kazuyo. On each floor the finish of the ceiling, the color palette, and other aspects of the interior design are also different. Because of this, each floor can be thought of as a separate world unto itself.

What the tubes created

Instead of vertical columns or posts, the Sendai Mediatheque uses twisting tubes. In Baroque architecture, twisting columns of the same size normally repeat in an orderly series and keep to a strictly vertical orientation. In contrast, the tubes of the Mediatheque all differ in size and proportions and are positioned seemingly at random. The largest is 9 meters in diameter, the smallest 2 meters. And they twist and bend. They carry light, air, water, electricity, people, and information throughout the structure, and can be seen from the exterior. In other words, this is see-through architecture. Areas normally concealed from view, such as loading docks, are in plain sight. And through the tubes one might sense the activities taking place on floors above or below—achieving a transparency not only in the horizontal axis but in the vertical as well. The tubes were a new architectural element, like thick columns, but with hollow interiors that created another interior space.

At first glance the plan and elevations of the Sendai Mediatheque resemble those of Jean Nouvel's Galeries Lafayette Berlin (1995). There, too, a number of hollow cones oriented either upward or downward vertically pierce a series of horizontal slabs. In Nouvel's design for this major department store, a cone that reflects its surroundings like a gigantic kaleidoscope is set into a central atrium, and this is the only cone open to the public as commercial space. Other, smaller cones are in areas with no public access. But in Itō's Mediatheque, all of the tubes are visible and open to the public, and the space itself is more decentralized and fluid.

When completed, the Sendai Mediatheque drew a great deal of comment, with some people criticizing it for being less radical than the initial images and others remarking that the first floor felt a bit like an auto showroom. It is true that in the process of realizing the project, a number of changes had been made. Initially the thirteen tubes were distributed in an almost random arrangement, but this was modified. And because those in the four corners were enlarged, the design drew somewhat closer to ordinary architecture. Some of the tubes also ended up being clad in glass—to prevent falls, conduct air, or for other reasons. Because of the way the glass overlapped with the framework of the tubes, the transparency effect is somewhat diminished and the underlying concept obscured.

Let's look at this in the context of Itō's personal history. After graduating from the University of Tokyo, he worked from 1965 to 1969 in the architectural office of Kikutake Kiyonori, one of the leaders of the Metabolist movement. One might point to the fusion of dynamic structure and design in Itō's work as something inherited from his mentor. After leaving Kikutake's office, in 1971 Itō established an independent practice with Tsukio Toshio, called URBOT (Urban Robot)—a name redolent of the technological optimism of the 1960s. Yet at first he undertook a number of residential projects that turned their backs on the outside world. The House in Nakano Honchō (1976), affectionately known as the White U, had a U-shaped plan with a central courtyard; designed for his recently widowed older sister and her daughters, it is regarded as a classic example of what was dubbed "introspective" residential architecture. In Back to Black (House in Sakura Josui, 1975), House in Chūō Rinkan (1979), and others one can see the influence of Shinohara Kazuo (1926–2006). At the time, Itō was friendly with members of Shinohara's research group at Tokyo Institute of Technology and the critic Taki Kōji, who led him to an

White U (House in Nakano Honchō) 1976. (Courtesy of Toyo Ito & Associates, Architects)

interest in "dry" architecture, devoid of depth or hierarchy.

In the 1980s, he began to pursue an architecture more open to the city, and design involving the concept of membranes. His own home, the Silver Hut (1984), was a succession of light, barrel-vaulted roofs. Tower of Winds (1986), clad in perforated metal, houses water tanks serving the air conditioning for an underground mall. At night it functions as a mixed-media sculpture outside the west entrance of Yokohama Station, transforming changes in the sound and wind around the station into patterns of light and color. In the 1990s, the focus of Itō's practice shifted to public buildings, such as Nagaoka Lyric Hall (1994), and he became involved in projects all over Japan. The work that created these opportunities was Yatsushiro Municipal Museum (1991), which buried much of the huge volume of the structure in an artificially created mounded landscape, making the visible portions appear as light and airy as possible. The efforts Itō had been making to achieve lightness in domestic architecture were thus successfully applied at the scale of a major public building.

Itō's style had changed dramatically, yet interestingly enough, the Sendai Mediatheque retained a continuity with his earliest work—a point I was able to confirm in an interview with him.[7] His first commissioned project, Aluminum House (1971) has a vertical cylinder at its center, which Itō conceived not just as a light well but as an information conduit as well. In

Yatsushiro Municipal Museum, 1991.
(Courtesy of Toyo Ito & Associates,
Architects)

other words, the central cylinder of the Aluminum House was a precursor of the tubes of the Sendai Mediatheque. It may be said that his architecture has always featured vertical as well as horizontal transparency. And the Kasama House (1981) shows that Itō was already demolishing hierarchy and exploring a flat space in which fragments of form appear to be floating, raising fundamental questions about the significance of form in architecture.[8]

Architecture for the body electric

I n 1985, Itō designed an installation called *Pao: Dwelling for the Tokyo Nomad Woman*, which consisted of an airy tent with a bed and a few other simple furnishings for women; a dwelling of cloth that billowed in the breeze. This was not a masculine architecture like that of the Doric order of classical Greece or the powerful forms envisioned by Le Corbusier. But neither was it voluptuous. It evoked a light corporeality like that of a girl skipping off to the convenience store. Sejima Kazuyo, then a young architect working in Itō's office, served as the model for this project. This was not modernist architecture, conceived as a corrective for creating healthier bodies. The new body was conceived as fluidity. It is interesting that in the era of Art Nouveau, the body was imagined with a similar softness and femininity, as something organically fusing with nature. Perhaps it is because the information environment has emerged as a new "nature" that these two different periods share similar imagery.

The model for Sendai Mediatheque recalls Le Corbusier's model for Maison Dom-ino, because it expresses so clearly the underlying architectural principles at work. But in contrast to the orderly geometries of Maison Dom-ino, the Mediatheque leads toward a physics of disorder. Le Corbusier's Maison Dom-ino is the prototype for an age in which machines served as the model for architecture. On the other hand, Itō's Mediatheque is a new Maison Dom-ino for the Information Age. It is a Maison Dom-ino that trembles and vibrates. And underlying this is Itō's concept of the layered body.

Itō believes that we have a body as our lived experience, and another body that is trying to break free of the first. The standardized spaces of modernist architecture were a response to this situation, but they are no longer adequate to contemporary needs. The body augmented and expanded by digital communication is different from the strictly defined body of modernism. For Itō, the digitally mediated body is labile, and must remain unbound by any specific space.

In the 1960s Marshall McLuhan spoke of clothing and shelter as extensions of our skins, but Itō has said that architecture should be a "media suit" with a soft and fluid membrane. "Architecture is expanded clothing, an expanded media suit … and wearing their transparent media suits, people will inhabit a virtual nature, a forest of media. They will be Tarzans of the media jungle."[9] In other words, he envisions an architecture for digital nomads. In any case, the crucial concept linking the new human body with architecture is fluidity, which is completely at odds with traditional architecture. And to give expression to this fluidity, Itō uses his organically shaped tubes, referencing botanical imagery such as seaweed.

Plants as metaphor

Why plants? At the end of the twentieth century, the astonishing development of digital technology transformed our thinking about space, and some even argued that the information revolution would render architecture unnecessary. This was because, unlike machines, which are assemblages of functional parts, we cannot really visualize cyberspace. Information is not a physical object; it is weightless; it is an invisible network.

So it is interesting that plants are used in the Mediatheque as a conceptual guide toward envisioning architecture for the Information Age. According to Itō, the Mediatheque possesses a spatiality that is more like a forest than a work of architecture. Welded steel pipes form mesh tubes resembling trees, which harmonize with the zelkovas lining the avenue in front of the building. Pillars arranged on a grid apply order to a space, but the tubes break up such a standardized spatiality. In the Mediatheque, Itō was attempting, through the creation of a natural space, to bring into being a variety of different spaces. In a forest, space is defined by the trees in relationship to each other, and no two spaces are alike. So nature becomes an important metaphor. Itō writes, "Sendai Mediatheque is a multilayered urban forest. It is an intelligent architecture, an intelligent forest."[10] In other words, at the turn of the twenty-first century, nature gave inspiration to the architect, and gave birth to a new design.

Iidabashi Station on Tokyo Metro's Ōedo subway line also opened in December 2000. It is the work of digital architect Watanabe Makoto (Sei), known for his use of computer-aided design, and interestingly enough, it also employs plant imagery throughout the entire structure. Strange petal-like forms overhang the subway entrance, like gigantic metallic flowers madly blossoming, up to the height of a four-story building. Underground, weblike frameworks of tubular steel, painted bright green and resembling the roots of plants, overhang the escalators, extending in some areas of the station for as much as 120 meters. The design of this underground portion was not drawn by the architect but generated automatically by a computer program. In this case, the architect input parameters in advance, defining areas where the web should proliferate and other areas that it should not invade; these were like the initial conditions defining the growth of plants: good or poor light, soil, nutrients. And in fact Watanabe explains his design as a process of planting "architectural seeds" and watching them bud and grow. In Paris a century before Watanabe's Iidabashi Station, the Art Nouveau architect Hector Guimard also decorated the entrances of the Paris Métro with lovely botanical motifs. Although separated by a century, these two subway projects share similar backgrounds and a common design approach.

In 2000, at a lecture Itō was giving at the Netherlands Architecture Institute in Rotterdam, one of the audience members remarked that the Mediatheque seemed to resemble the architecture of Antoni Gaudí.[11] I was there, and I have to admit that, at the time, I found the comment strange. The more I thought about it, however, the more I came to realize that Gaudí's organic, curvilinear forms—overgrown with decorative elements while at the same time pursuing structural possibilities—awaken a physical response. But the overwhelming transparency of Itō's design gives a decisively different feeling. We might note in passing that Gaudí was an architect of the Modernisme movement—Spain's Art Nouveau.

Sendai Mediatheque expresses the image of the Information Age. Yet this is also an extremely architectural architecture. That is to say, it does not abandon architecture in order to convey the image of information; instead, it uses the methods of architecture to bring it to a new level. Or perhaps it would be better to say that it uses the methods of architecture to erase traditional architecture. As information technology threatened architecture from without, Itō pushed back. This is why it is so fascinating to compare the Sendai Mediatheque, born on the cusp of a new century, with the Art Nouveau architecture of Europe a century before—and the use of botanical imagery by both.

Digital Art Nouveau

A rt Nouveau made its appearance as an avant-garde movement break-ing with the past. It was a quest for a literally "new art," without dependence on past styles. Yet it had to reference something, and so it drew its inspiration from the boundless life energy of nature and the plant world—in fact, it was also known as the "flower style." If you examine the details, you will frequently find direct floral or botanical references in many of the patterns and motifs. Utilizing the relative malleability of wrought iron, beautifully sinuous forms were achieved. But this was before moder-nism formalized the design methodologies of architecture. Art Nouveau enjoyed only a brief existence, yet its swirling, fluid motifs penetrated every aspect of daily life—not only architecture, but clothing, jewelry, textile designs, wallpaper, furniture, tableware, and even the arrangement of food.

Art Nouveau was born at a time of architectural crisis. The architecture of the late nineteenth century seemed about to be left behind by techno-logical progress—mechanization, and developments in materials such as steel, glass, and concrete. Let's review the history of nineteenth-century architecture. At that time, mass production of steel and glass had become possible, and a new architecture utilizing these new materials to replace the traditional architecture of stone and brick seemed imminent. But the architects of the time, without any experience in how to make use of these new conditions, clung to the catalogue of past styles and preoccupied themselves with ringing the changes on these established forms. Their academic training assured them that if they mastered these forms, their works would be regarded as having artistic value.

So the bridge to the formal vocabulary of the twentieth century was provided instead by technicians who had not received formal education in architecture—Joseph Paxton, designer of the Crystal Palace (1851), for example, or Gustave Eiffel of the Eiffel Tower (1889). Paxton was a builder of greenhouses, and Eiffel an engineer of bridges and railways; neither were designers of "architecture" adhering to a particular set of decorative conventions. Nowadays, any textbook on architectural history you care to open will speak of their works as the beginnings of modern architecture, but contemporary architects would probably not have acknowledged it as artistic. The antipathy of the intelligentsia of the era to the Eiffel Tower is well known.

So the architectural world of the nineteenth century bifurcated into architects wedded to an outmoded architectural tradition on the one hand, and on the other, engineers who were beginning to utilize new materials. Art versus technology. Between the two opened a gulf that was difficult to span. Certainly the architects of the nineteenth century proved incapable of coming up with designs on their own that were appropriate to a more modern style of life—although there were certain architects, such as Eugène Viollet-le-Duc in France, with his rationalist approach, who prepared the intellectual groundwork for modern architecture. In any case, architecture as art seemed on the verge of extinction. With the disappearance of formal orders and styles from architecture, and all forms derived from calculations, the artistic element seemed lost. Buildings would continue to be built, but they would no longer be works of art.

Then along came Art Nouveau. The importance of this style was not simply its rejection of the past but its interest in how to use steel, and particularly its characteristic malleability. Art Nouveau also responded to the modern system of production and its ability to reproduce and reiterate. As the critic Walter Benjamin observed, Art Nouveau "represents the last attempted sortie of an art besieged in its ivory tower by technology."[12] In other words, while Art Nouveau introduced new technological possibilities, it also sought to revive artistic architecture from the brink of death. This formulation also seems to pertain to the situation at the end of the twentieth century.

In the 1980s postmodernism was all the rage with its plethora of quotations from the styles and forms of the past. But Itō rejected such historicist design, with its references to Palladio, Ledoux, and others, and instead focused on the botanical, as Antoni Gaudí and Art Nouveau had done when distancing themselves from the rigidly formal architecture of the nineteenth century. At the end of the twentieth century, as the waves of the Information Age roiled the world of architecture, the very concept of space was radically transformed by the rapid development of digital technology. Watanabe's Iidabashi Station goes beyond mere formal resemblance to reference plant life at the level of design programming, breathing new life into architecture. And Itō's Sendai Mediatheque, like an architectural Big Bang, gave birth to a new universe of geometry.

Dissolving space

Itō frequently speaks of convenience stores. According to him, the ubiquity of these stores, where one can easily procure almost all the essentials of daily life, has made it possible to live in homes without much of anything in them. Many people now want to live in simple one-room apartments, and the functions of family and household have disintegrated. But he does not view the convenience stores negatively, nor does he argue for a return to the way things used to be. Instead, he considers this situation an opportunity for new architecture.

Itō calls Sendai Mediatheque "a convenience store for media." Just as a profusion of products are arranged on the shelves of the convenience store, a variety of media are housed in this facility. Artwork, books, digital resources, and all other items are treated as being of equal value, and equally accessible to all visitors. In short, the convenience store is seen as creating a positive momentum toward the dissolution of discriminatory hierarchies. Once upon a time, in the era of modernism, it was the factory as a functional facility that served as the model for the new architecture; now, the convenience store has become the model for public institutions in the age of information.

Since the establishment of an institution such as the Sendai Mediatheque was unprecedented in Japan, a program committee (Taki Kōji, Suzuki Akira, and Onoda Yasuaki) was organized to prepare a set of guidelines. The "Mediatheque Charter" proclaims the following three points:

1. Deliver a cutting-edge spirit (and services).
   Respond flexibly to the demands of users.
2. Nodes, not terminals.
   Leverage the advantages of the network to the maximum.
3. Barrier-free in every respect.
   Transcend all barriers between healthy and handicapped, users and managers, different languages and cultures.[13]

Certainly, these guidelines might conjure up the image of convenience stores—or perhaps a superflat society. Nowadays convenience stores are not just for youth prowling the night. We live in an era in which some convenience stores have even begun to offer home delivery of meals for the elderly. It makes sense for our old-school public institutions to try to learn from the latest commercial ventures. Itō has said that, in the future, museums, galleries, libraries, and theaters will all become a single contiguous space. They will merge into one. The resemblance of public facilities to the convenience store will no longer be merely symbolic. Existing institutions will be reorganized, and dissolve into the fabric of the city.

However, libraries in Japan have not yet shed their established image. Galleries remain conventional, and digital archives are not yet fully developed. Unfortunately, in comparison to many other countries, we have not excelled in creating networked environments—nor with creating public facilities that high schoolers might use as places to do their homework. But people working from within the bureaucratic system have actually succeeded in removing many barriers. Now it is the users' turn to exercise their imaginations.

Itō aims at an architecture with flexible boundaries. Sendai Mediatheque rejects a distinct relationship between program and venue. Modern architects believed that each room of a building should have a specified function. But Itō liberates the room from functional constraints, transforming a defined space into a space of probability. Architecture is not a closed space—it should be part of the fabric of the city. It should have "blurry" boundaries, responsive to the surrounding environment.

Itō has pointed out that modern architecture is based on the concept of division. The total volume is an assemblage of functionally differentiated elements. Human activity is simplified, and then classified according to function. Because of this, the architect is continually called upon to produce a skillful arrangement of functionally defined rooms. Itō resists this modernist architecture by proposing the following five directives for producing continuous spaces:

1. No joints.
2. No beams.
3. No walls.
4. No rooms.
5. No architecture.[14]

Architectural details are determined with reference to these directives. With the most advanced shipbuilding technology and seamlessly welded steel, joints are eliminated. Beams require a grid or modular structure, but honeycomb slabs make beams unnecessary. Remove walls, and a fluid space is born. Fixed rooms demand specific uses, but replacing them with tubes creates a variety of spaces. As a result, people can freely choose spaces appropriate to what they want to do. Ordinarily, management decides what a facility is to be used for, and users must follow the rules. But at the Mediatheque, the goal is a freely usable space, like the streets. These tubes enclosing a continuous space became a favorite motif of the architectural world in the 1990s. And in that sense, they have come to symbolize the Sendai Mediatheque.

The fifth directive—"no architecture"—would seem to be a self-negating pronouncement for an architect. How does Itō overcome this dilemma? Itō uses scrupulously architectural methods to deconstruct "architecture." In one lecture, as he showed slides of the completed Sendai Mediatheque, Itō confessed that he actually did not want to install the glass cladding.[15] The model built for the competition did not have glass set into all its faces. For Itō, glass is not simply transparent; it possesses a materiality that is overly powerful in some situations. But it was not practical to complete the actual building without using glass. This was not a resolvable dilemma. So the Mediatheque exists in the midst of its contradictions.[16] It stands at the juncture between an individual's dream and social reality. But it is precisely this situation that may convey most vividly the difficult relationship between architecture and information at the present time.

After Sendai Mediatheque

But Itō's thinking did not stop here. It continued to transform. This is perhaps the most amazing thing about his activity after Sendai Mediatheque.

In 2004, when I was organizing a series of symposiums called "Alternative Modern," Itō spoke in his lecture about the ways in which concepts of function, abstraction, production, and time had changed, and cited digital functionality, self-generating geometries, agricultural production, and nonlinear processes as the principles of a new architecture. In his formulation of this discourse, I sense that Itō is not only an heir to the modernist tradition but is also possessed by a powerful will to transcend it. The keywords he proposed had less to do with architecture than with a kind of garden-like realm midway between nature and human culture. The most impressive aspect of his lecture was a sense that Itō had been liberated from all constraints, or perhaps had achieved a kind of satori. Collaboration with engineers, a freedom of form, an acute sense of color, an animal sense of space that drew attention to physicality—what stood before us was an architect who had actively thrown himself into the processes of transformation through his interaction with others.

The phrase "alternative modern" is my own coinage, based on the premise that some of the previously unrealized possibilities of modernism are just now emerging. If postmodernism was a rhetorical manipulation of existing architectural forms, "alternative modern," while possessing a variety of diverse tendencies from Art Nouveau to expressionism, is an attempt to liberate the potential of modernism from the strictures of the International Style. Itō is probably situated at the epicenter of this, sometimes employing new geometries that realize complex spaces through simple rules, and sometimes proposing new decorative elements that are simultaneously structural. Itō's office has produced a roster of outstanding next-generation architects, headed by Sejima Kazuyo, rivaling the mother lode of talent cultivated by Tange Kenzō and Itō's own mentor, Kikutake Kiyonori.

In the twenty-first century, Itō ranged far beyond Japan to engage a global practice that included projects in Spain, Belgium, the United Kingdom, France, Singapore, Taiwan, and the United States. Moreover, though it would not have been unusual for him to take a bit of a breather after the completion of a major work like the Sendai Mediatheque before making his next move, he immediately began to break new ground, delivering a series of works at the cutting edge of contemporary architecture like a man possessed: the Serpentine Gallery Pavilion (2002) in London, whose pattern of cutout shapes followed the trajectory of a single continuous line; his proposal for a pavilion in Santa Cruz Park in Coimbra, Portugal, with its plantlike mesh; Tod's Omotesandō Building (2004), clad in a forest-like concrete exoskeleton; and the National Taichung Theater (2014), which evokes images of the organs of living things.

Let's take a closer look at several projects. In an interactive educational facility themed on flowers and greenery called Grin Grin (2005), designed for Fukuoka Island City Central Park, curvilinear concrete structures emerge from the earth in a complex series of double folds. This would be easy enough to accomplish as a sculpture or architectural model, but Grin Grin is a fully realized building. The shapes of these structures recall the chrysalis of the tree nymph butterfly, which is one of the exhibits on display in the facility. There are large openings in the roofs to admit light into the interior of Grin Grin, which functions as a greenhouse. If you follow the prescribed route through the exhibits, you suddenly find yourself emerging from the interior and walking on one of the roofs, which are covered in sod and other plantings. It is a space in which interior and exterior are linked in a sort of twisting continuity.

The structural engineering for the project was handled by Sasaki Mutsurō. After Itō had sketched out a basic design, a computer program was devised to analyze the physical loads and stresses and make subtle, self-correcting adjustments to the structures. In other words, the architect's intuition was fused with the latest techniques of structural analysis. This produced a rational modeling of forms that were optimized in terms of structural dynamics—a process similar to the natural forces shaping

Interactive educational facility Grin Grin, Fukuoka Island City Central Park, 2005. (Courtesy of Toyo Ito & Associates, Architects)

the development of the shells and carapaces produced by living organisms. The exterior of Grin Grin is covered in greenery, blending in almost completely with the surrounding park. The architecture disappears into its natural environment, evoking the imaginative worlds of animator Miyazaki Hayao. So not only is the design process itself similar to natural systems, but the results harmonize with the natural landscape.

The Tama Art University Library (2007) is a forest of the kind of arches typically shunned by contemporary architecture. Yet it is not a simple revisiting of the past. This is because the design, which incorporates arches in a variety of sizes, would have been unthinkable from the perspective and norms of classical architecture. Neither does it veer into an expressionist sensibility. The skewed facade is punctuated by what appear to be a host of well-lighted caves. The floor of the ground level gently rises to follow the slope of the land on which it is sited. The incorporation of the almost natural topography of the site into the design in this fashion stimulates visitors from the soles of their feet. Itō's solo exhibition *Itō Toyoo: Architecture—A New Real* (2006) did not stop with displaying drawings and models; the installation also appealed to the corporeal senses with a landscape-like modification of the floor into gently rolling waves.

This exhibition was not a retrospective—it was an introduction to his

Tama Art University Library, Hachiōji campus, 2007. (Photo by Ishiguro Photographic Institute)

recent work through the bold structural experimentation characteristic of Itō's practice from the Sendai Mediatheque onward. In other words, it was a snapshot of Itō's present: an unprecedented and intense outpouring of imaginative design. When I served in 2007 as moderator of a symposium linked to the touring *New Real* exhibition, I almost felt as if time itself was flowing at a different speed in Itō's vicinity as I listened to his lecture and sensed the rapidly accelerating pace of his evolution.[17] No time for reiteration. A commitment to constant change. This presents a major challenge to the critic. Anything written about him is left behind by the "new real" to which he has already transitioned. You are then forced to revise your own position and argument. Even the aforementioned corporeal imagery seems to be shifting in the direction of something overflowing with vitality and responsive to the joy of materiality.

From the present vantage, the Sendai Mediatheque, which emerged on the cusp of the new century, seems almost like ancient history.

Sakamoto Kazunari

Free Architecture, or the Construction of Overlapping Systems

A system of overlapping decisions

Sakamoto Kazunari's House SA was completed in 1999, when he was fifty-six. In 2002, when the Gallery Ma exhibit of Sakamoto's work, *House: Poetics in the Ordinary*, traveled to Aichi Shukutoku University in Nagoya, I was invited to be the moderator for the lectures, and was fortunate enough to have the opportunity to visit it—a breathtaking experience. One reason for this is that while his residential architecture rejects easy comprehension and clear-cut explanation, on another level it is governed by a thoroughly refined theoretical position. What does this signify?

As far as I am concerned, a major criterion for determining whether a particular building should be regarded as a work of architecture is whether or not it is governed in its totality by a consistent theoretical orientation. This does not necessarily mean the creation of spaces that are pleasant to inhabit—though it would be preferable if these goals were compatible. Once certain rules have been established, the details are determined almost automatically. One might say that this is a basic condition for outstanding architecture. This is true, for example, of the projects of Norman Foster, the dean of British high-tech architecture. And no matter how fantastic and decorative his work may appear, the fact that it was backed by solid structural theory makes Antoni Gaudí an architect—while we may judge that Hundertwasser was not an architect, but a painter.

Yet House SA is a work that demolishes the hypothesis I have just outlined. No clear rules govern it overall. But neither is it arbitrary. It is an expression of an architecture in which multiple logics coexist simultaneously. All of the interior spaces are on different levels, but connected in series, while there are no rooms as such. The level changes correspond to the height of a conventional three-story building, but the floor height varies continuously on each level and there are no staircases. Or perhaps the entire structure is a staircase. A house without stairs: this alone would be enough of a concept for a standard work of architecture. But House SA does not want to be inhibited by such clarity of expression.

Difficult architecture

The defining feature of House SA is that it is structured so that if you circulate to the right from the entrance you rise, and descend if you go left. So it is possible to describe the continuous space in formal terms as a helix. But Sakamoto does not express this overtly. The exterior of the portion corresponding to the second floor emphasizes discontinuity with the first, and is set askew atop the first floor at an apparently random angle. From the shapes of the exterior walls and roof there is no easy way to perceive the helical interior. In the initial proposal, around 1995, the helical structure clearly began from a parking space immediately in front of the entrance. But in the final plan, an axis was established leading straight to the garden from the parking area, cutting across the helix and complicating the layout. As a result, the helical motif became more difficult to discern. Sakamoto says he changed his design in order to avoid making the layout too obvious.[1] In other words, the difficulty was intentional.

Sakamoto frequently uses the term "anti-typology" to express an attitude unbound by established forms. The helix or spiral is an established spatial typology. Examples include the spiral staircases of Baroque archi-

Interior of House SA, 1999.
(Photo by Honma Takashi)

tecture, or the double helix (referencing the structure of the DNA molecule) used by Mozuna Kikō in his Kushiro City Museum (1984). Frank Lloyd Wright's Guggenheim Museum employs a bold spiral form to establish the traffic pattern for viewing the exhibited works. In short, the helix or spiral has strong connotations as a form, and this is the reason Sakamoto is trying to avoid it. Instead, he would seem to prefer to see the unintentional or natural eruption of a helical slope into the interior of the house as merely an extension of its sloping site.

House SA is Sakamoto's personal residence. When an architect builds his own home he in effect becomes his own client. Unburdened by the taste and demands of a client who is not a professional architect, he is thus free to make of this work a kind of manifesto, a straight expression of his own design philosophy. Many architect's homes have been experimental designs that served as important stepping stones in their careers, such as Kikutake Kiyonori's Sky House (1958) and Azuma Takamitsu's Tower House (1966). But here we also encounter something odd. Descriptions of House SA never clearly state that it is Sakamoto's home. I was unaware of this fact myself until I visited it, and Sakamoto himself showed me around and confirmed that he lives there. He said that House SA was designed to meet the following demands: "The client is very capricious, and not only demanded a house larger than the available site—but also didn't want a second or third floor. [Laughs.] How could I resolve this conflict? Then it occurred to me that I could achieve greater area by overlapping a series of one-story houses."[2] The client of which Sakamoto speaks is actually his wife. It seems to me that an architect's home is where his personality is most likely to be displayed. The storyline is clear: This is how I think, so this is why I designed it this way. But if the client is his wife, even his home is not a free exercise in self-expression, but something derived from or determined by external conditions.

In a review of Sakamoto's book *Taiwa: Kenchiku no shikō* (Dialogues: Architectural Thinking, 1996), I previously wrote:

> I must confess that my impression of Sakamoto Kazunari was of an architect difficult to understand. His stance of rejecting easy understanding probably arises from the fact that he was not carried away by the wave of postmodern architecture that swept Japan in the 1980s . . . because he remained committed instead to an extremely restrained design aesthetic. And Sakamoto is not an architect (like Isozaki Arata) who serves as the best interpreter of his own work.[3]

Even now, my fundamental perception of Sakamoto has not changed. This is because his architecture does not aim at being easily understood by the mass media, nor is it especially photogenic. I doubt anyone has hired him based on seeing his work in an architectural magazine. Sakamoto himself says, "I don't think anyone would look at my work in a magazine and feel they wanted to build it."[4]

But House SA did not suddenly emerge from nowhere. It is the culmination of thirty years of architectural practice. Because of this, before spending more time analyzing this residence, I would first like to trace the history that led up to it.

From closed to open

The title of the lecture accompanying Sakamoto's exhibition was "From Closed to Open, Toward Liberation." As this suggests, a major trend in his work reflects a shift from closed to open structures.

Early works such as House in Sanda (1969), Machiya in Minase (1970), and Kumono-Nagareyama House (1973) turned their backs on the polluted urban environment, sealing themselves off from the outside world. At that time, Sakamoto made the following observation: "We might say the 'closed box' is a fortress against the contradictory and chaotic cultural realm of contemporary society."[5] An internal order is created in response to external chaos. This perception is not unrelated to developments in the world of architecture from the 1960s into the 1970s. In the 1960s, Tange Kenzō, Kurokawa Kishō, Kikutake Kiyonori, and others proposed a series of futuristic urban projects, and actual large-scale urban development proceeded at a frantic pace. But after Expo '70 and the oil shocks, architects began to design hermetic private residences rather than engaging with the city.

Andō Tadao's Row House in Sumiyoshi and Itō Toyoo's U-House (in Nakano Honchō), both completed in 1976, are excellent examples of this trend. Both confronted the surrounding urban environment with sheer walls of concrete, largely unpunctuated by openings. Eventually, however, their architecture began to open to the outside world. In the 1980s, Itō started to make use of perforated metal or all-glass facades that dissolved the structure, aiming at a space of blurred boundaries with no clear demarcation between interior and exterior. Andō also began

Machiya in Minase, 1970. (Courtesy of Atelier and I, Kazunari Sakamoto Architectural Laboratory)

experimenting with more open designs in which the concrete box no longer formed the exterior walls of the building but was instead enclosed with glass. This shift from the weight of concrete to the transparency of glass as a material for the facade is easy to understand. In contrast, in Sakamoto's case the transition from closed to open is less clear. For one thing, the House in Sanda, Machiya in Minase, and Kumono-Nagareyama House had exteriors that were punctuated by relatively large openings and therefore might not be considered closed boxes.

But here we must remember that Sakamoto was not as concerned with the style of the facade as he was with the basic architectural layout. What he called the "closed box" was a spatial organization based on nested boxes, or the ways in which the layout of rooms might enfold itself. So even if the houses mentioned above had windows, they might be described as apertures that did not directly connect the interior with either the exterior or garden. There were no floor-height windows or sliding doors set at the level of the garden, linking interior and exterior on the same plane, as in a traditional Japanese house. Instead, the openings appeared to be more like interior alcoves that had expanded to the exterior, more like small rooms than windows. In the Sanda house, these protruding windows were designed from the beginning to be outfitted with shoji screens of translucent paper, admitting light but not intended to be looked out of. From the outside, they appear as blind windows drinking in light from the exterior. According to Sakamoto, the difference between open versus closed is "not a dimension defined by the presence or absence of openings, or their number. The way in which the distribution of space handled is crucially involved."[6]

Eventually the "closed box" acquired more of the external appearance of an ordinary house; by shifting to an arrangement of the rooms in adjoining sequence, the aim was to open it up. The turning point was Machiya in Daita (1976), completed the same year as Andō's Row House in Sumiyoshi and Itō's White U. The street-front facade was punctuated by a single tiny window and an opening into the garage. The main entrance was concealed around the corner to the left, to the rear of the side wall, which gave the house a "closed" appearance. A low concrete wall dividing the parking space from a courtyard garden behind it prevented direct entry but allowed for visual continuity between the two.

Sakamoto began to question the use of functionally specific terminology such as "living room" to refer to and relativize the interior spaces of a house, and instead started using labels on his plans that emphasized spatial relationships: "main room," "intermediate rooms 1 and 2," "outer rooms 1 and 2," "rooms 1 and 2," and so on. Later, when Sakamoto's architectural plans appeared in various publications, even such designations as "main room" and "intermediate room" were omitted. From an ordinary perspective, this might seem a bit unfriendly, an obstacle to understanding the interior spaces and what they were to be used for. And in fact, we tend to think we are reading a plan when in fact we are using the labels as clues for how to conceive of the spaces and their use. But by unmooring the spaces from their names, Sakamoto brings the layout itself to our attention. This is probably because he has serious reservations regarding the concept of functionally specific rooms.

But change was not linear. House in Nago (1978) returned to the nested-box layout. Sakamoto's style progressed in a more ruminative fashion, rather than through dramatic breaks. Essentially the same pattern was used for House in Sakata Yamatsuki (1978) and House in Imajuku (1978). Common House in Sanda (1981), an

Common House in Sanda, 1981.
(Courtesy of Atelier and I, Kazunari
Sakamoto Architectural Laboratory)

apartment building, had four intersecting gables, which made it look more like a single-family dwelling. But House in Soshigaya (1981) broke with the conventional house format, altering it with combinations of geometric forms such as the triangle and semicylinder. This was the era of postmodernism, in which mannerist tendencies were strong, and incongruities between the exterior and the underlying structure were rampant. In the 1980s, Sakamoto moved away from the conventional "house" format to begin exploring the roof as a form of spatial enclosure.

Sakamoto's postmodernism

The critic Taki Kōji has described the phases of Sakamoto's activity as follows.[7]

First was the period in which, while overwhelmingly influenced by Shinohara Kazuo (1926–2006), Sakamoto attempted to free himself by designing residential housing. If Shinohara was about creating dramatic spaces in pursuit of beauty, Sakamoto would suppress that aspiration. Shinohara, an idealist, created memorable symbolic spaces even when he was designing houses and not religious edifices. According to Taki, Shinohara was also a romantic, whose architecture sought to achieve a spiritual climax, while Sakamoto aimed instead at anticlimax. This was something that Sakamoto had learned by working in Shinohara's research group, encountering failure, and realizing he was never going to be like Shinohara. Sakamoto saw that when Shinohara divided space, it always created a clear distinction between interior and exterior, front and back, and he became interested in this relationship. Not in order to spotlight one or the other, or to create a drama of light and shadow. Rather than trying to create a climax, he was more interested in questioning the composition of this mutual relationship.

Second was a period in which Sakamoto, confronting the commodification of housing in consumer society as represented by real estate ads in the mass media and elsewhere, carefully studied the image and conventional form of the house. But this was not in order to use it as a postmodern semantic motif that would be meaningful to the general public. Quite the opposite: in his academic research, Sakamoto analyzed the social conditions that were running completely counter to his own position, thereby throwing it into relief. If Aida Takefumi's Toy Block Houses employed triangles semiotically and Aldo Rossi's architecture used them as pure geometric forms, and Naitō Hiroshi incorporated gables for structural reasons, Sakamoto saw the form of the house as essentially a problem of layout—and as a device for integrating a space. When he used gables, he avoided a Gothic verticality or an appealing expansiveness—his refusal to create semiotic meaning was quite deliberate.[8]

The difference between design for a consumer society and architectural design is frequently spoken of in terms of a dichotomy between commodity and creative expression. But Sakamoto questioned such an easy formula. He pointed out that while ordinary people in thrall to consumer society tend toward kitschy images of the home, residential works by architects rejecting such trends ran the risk of elitist exclusivity. He says, "Even if one cannot completely affirm the consumer society that constitutes our reality, neither can one deny it. . . . We must realize that our fundamental image of what it is to live, or our aspirations for how we want to live, can only be realized through an appropriate subversion of our image of the home. At this point I can't think there is any point of departure for us other than such a perception."[9]

These words recall Itō's pronouncement that "there can be no new architecture without submerging in the sea of consumption."[10] In the 1970s both Sakamoto and Itō frequented similar circles, such as the groups surrounding Shinohara and the critic Taki Kōji, so it is not surprising that their perceptions of the times were similar. And their migration from "closed" works in the 1970s to more "open" styles in the 1980s paralleled one another. Itō sought light and airy shelters, like the tents of nomads.

But the opening up of Sakamoto's architecture expressed itself in a different way.

Sakamoto says that in an effort to grasp architecture in terms of its relationship to the wider world, he began to develop an interest in problems of form. But he realized that there was no fundamental relationship between form and society—that such relationships were arbitrary—and this drove him in the direction of architecture as composition. "If we may provisionally refer to the postmodern manipulation of forms as design, then design itself is no more than a passing whim of society at a particular time. It is crucial for the architect to conceive of the composition that is the antecedent of design."[11] Thus he avoids the semiotic approach to design advocated by the critic Charles Jencks in his influential work *The Language of Post-Modern Architecture* (1977). The social meaning evoked by forms cannot be anything other than arbitrary.

Moreover, Sakamoto says, "I also feel that the pursuit of novelty in appearance has nothing to do with one's program. That's why, as far as commercial architecture is concerned I became somewhat less resistant to the eccentric forms produced during the period of the economic bubble."[12] In other words, he was more interested in composition and program than in the superficial aspects of design. Nor was he interested in symmetry or other potent signifiers of power. But he says that he was influenced by other postmodern tendencies, notably the "inclusive" way of thinking advocated by Robert Venturi—not an exclusive, either/or choice, but rather a wider net that allowed for the incorporation and overlapping of diverse elements.

Designless design

Sakamoto is not a prolific architect. Even in the superheated bubble years of the late 1980s, he completed only House F (1988), and had no commercial projects backed by major capital investment. He was not an outsider; he had a position at a university and did teaching and research. But clearly he had also distanced himself from the trends of the times. He took a different direction from the madding crowd of postmodern design. Here I'd like to quote a somewhat lengthy but revealing statement regarding his position.

> [Architecture] stimulates our imaginations, and becomes a work of architecture by providing us with beauty and meaning. . . . But even so . . . my hopes for architecture do not lie in "architecture in the positive sense," the formal or spatial beauty that stimulates the above-mentioned images and touches the sources of our emotions, and empowers architecture itself. More than this . . . I am interested in a free and lively "architecture as environment." . . . By engagement with specific spatial forms we achieve freedom and give rise to new activity. I would like to call the way in which architecture engages people through such forms "architecture as form." . . . The themes of such an architecture are not predicated on what is called architectural design.[13]

In House F, a cluster of steel columns sprout smaller branchlike pipes supporting a roof that covers the structure, both inside and out. The conventional form of a house has been completely deconstructed, and the roof has an almost topographic feeling. There is no overall unifying shape to the house; its forms are scattered. The four facades are all different, and there is no strong frontality. The relationship of enclosure does not produce a sense of completion; it is a house that rejects wholeness.

In the 1990s, Sakamoto undertook several collective housing projects, including Makuhari Baytown Patios No. 4 (1995), a portion of a much larger new town project, in which he struggled against design guidelines based on traditional western European townscapes. Taki classifies this as Sakamoto's third period, one in which he was forced to fight against social conditions. According to Taki, Sakamoto's ascetic tendencies were opposed to the excesses of capitalism, and in the course of a withering critique, he "pared structural composition down to a form that could confront capitalism."

Common City Hoshida (1992), although built on a hillside, avoided the terraced lots normally used in such cases, opting instead for a sloping development of the land that scatters the units on the hillside to achieve spatial continuity. The result is a labyrinthine streetscape recalling that of an ancient town. According to Sakamoto, "This chaotic, abstruse quality is not natural to newly built modern towns."[14] There is no clearly defined master plan unifying the whole. Sakamoto was now applying what he had experimented with at the level of individual structures to the scale of entire urban developments. Also, the concept of not creating divisions within Common City Hoshida is something shared with Itō's Sendai Mediatheque, albeit on a different scale. An awareness of the uncertainties of society and of deconstructed, elusive corporeality in the 1990s—and the search for a new architecture in response—was something both architects had in common.[15]

In the apartment building Egota House A (2004), each floor has an L-shaped plan that is rotated with each floor so the orientation along the longer axis is different from the next floor. For example, the long wall dividing the third floor runs east-west, while on the fourth floor it runs north-south. Moreover, the units are configured as bilevel maisonettes, linked on the vertical axis by atriums. This means that as you ascend a staircase from a level with a long east-west axis you

Egota House A, 2004. (Courtesy of Atelier and I, Kazunari Sakamoto Architectural Laboratory)

emerge into a space with a long north-south orientation. The result is that each of the maisonettes has views in all four directions. In each of the four corners of the building is an external private entrance staircase for each of the units, leading directly to its terrace and entry. Rather than common hallways that would create the need for privacy screening, this arrangement creates visual privacy while permitting an open feeling. This is a design made possible by the layout of two-story maisonettes spread over four floors. Egota House A is like a three-dimensional puzzle constructed of L-shaped blocks. But this internal spatial arrangement is not directly expressed on the exterior, which has been given different rules. Using color, materials, and plantings, each of the four faces of the building has been given a different expression, creating a disjuncture with the interiors. In other words, while it is an "open" structure, it is far from simple, possessing the complex relationships characteristic of Sakamoto.

Sakamoto does not particularly care for the expression "architectural work," because this use of the term "work" has artistic and authorial pretentions. His buildings have been called "designless" by some. When he received critical comments on his Takuma Housing in Kumamoto (1994) regarding the absence of what was perceived as design, he was pleased with what he considered a positive assessment. In this context one might recall the debate over the concept of "anti-author" in architectural circles in the late 1990s. This is not accidental: the debate was triggered by the Mikan Gumi collective, whose members were students of Sakamoto. In a conversation with the architectural historian Fujioka Hiroyasu, Sakamoto made the following statement:

> I've tried as much as possible to rid myself of individuality that seeks the best situation for itself, of the sense of self that produces strong messages, as we all float amid the currents of society. Fujioka-san, you've just spoken about the death of the author, and if it were possible, I'd be in favor of it. But I think it's totally impossible. Not only

that, but conversely, the harder you try to erase the authorial voice, the more dire the results. I think you can see what I mean by looking at the vernacular design today, or the state of the really vulgar realms of architecture.[16]

Sakamoto is speaking of authorship as a matter requiring a very delicate balance. Influenced by Roland Barthes's *Writing Degree Zero* (1953), he had sought a zero degree of meaning, but eventually came to think that was impossible. In this sense, while still taking an anti-authorial stance, he differs from Mikan Gumi. Sakamoto fears that the erasure of the authorial intelligence will produce vulgar, kitschy design. Yet at the same time, he is not in favor of strong individuality. He stretches meaning as thinly as possible. Although both engage in undramatic architecture, Mikan Gumi thinks of it as an extension of quotidian reality, while Sakamoto seems to be pursuing an alternative quotidian. This leads to an exploration of free spaces, liberated from any system. But this quest is not necessarily accompanied by dramatic and revolutionary change. A parallel quotidian peeps out from the corners and crevices of everyday life. The following passage aptly expresses Sakamoto's thinking:

I have continually wanted to free architectural space from a variety of different frameworks. I've sought an as yet undiscovered free space. . . . This space is not something attached to a special place or time; I've thought of it as a perfectly ordinary everyday place, a continuance of normal time. . . . Can we not glimpse an alternative quotidian between the cracks of everyday life? I feel that beyond the normal, obvious everyday there exists an as yet unseen world of freedom. But in the arrangement and configuration of unremarkable everyday objects and things, neither special nor extreme, and in the relationship among these elements of composition, or in their reconfiguration, there is a poetics that can function as the rhetoric connecting us with an alternative quotidian. . . . It is with this hope that I have sought an architecture of free space by achieving within that most quotidian of spaces, the home, an alternative quotidian.[17]

House SA as a summation

Let's return to House SA. This building is one in which multiple logics are at work, irreducible to a single one. Sakamoto has factored in an overload of external conditions, the manipulation of which creates a complexity that is not demanded by, and cannot be compared to architecture based in simpler ideas. If we use the metaphor of a computer, it is like the vast computational power that might be available a couple of generations in the future. Personally, this density of manipulation reminds me of the ornate spaces of the masterpieces of mannerist architecture by Michelangelo.

The shape of the floor plan largely follows the boundaries of the site. The walls are formed by a framework of evenly spaced 2-by-12-inch boards. This type of wall treatment probably influenced House Asama (2000) and D.a.S. House (2002) by Atelier Bow-Wow. The roof of House SA is built around an array of south-facing rectangular solar panels by OM Solar, with the remainder of the roof divided into seven faces, adapted to the irregular plan. Four of these faces are curved, their framing bending them into hyperbolic paraboloids. The distorted geometry of the roof is not an aggressive expression of authorial intent but rather a response to the conflict between various conditions imposed by the nature of the site, the type of solar panels used, and so forth—which result in an assemblage of planes that resembles natural topography.

This roof is clearly a further development of the roof of House F (1988), with an even greater formal complexity. The decisive difference is that while each of the different roof planes of House F are supported by branching steel supports rising out of the floor, House SA has no supporting columns for the roof or walls dividing the rooms, creating a vast open space completely separating the roof from the continuous floor. The forest-like system of supporting members in House F, by making structural connections between each roof plane and its columns, cannot help but create a hierarchy. But in House SA, the various elements pursue their own parallel logic, without aiming toward a unified space.

Sakamoto wanted to create a continuous space made up of a chain of slightly different parts. By employing the helical form in House SA he created spatial continuity while deconstructing the concept of separate rooms and even of separate floors. He transformed the entire structure into a single space, doing away with rooms altogether and creating an enormous, open, liberated space—more like an artist's atelier than a traditional home. In the floor plan published in the August 1999 issue of *Kenchiku bunka* (Architectural Culture), there are no labels for rooms—only numbers indicating the differing heights between levels. This is quite unusual for an architectural journal. In the same issue, only the plan for Kawanishi Camping Cottage B (1999) by Atelier Bow-Wow—both of whose principals, Tsukamoto Yoshiharu and Kaijima Momoyo, studied with Sakamoto—also omits room labels. *Gendai jūtaku kenkyū* (Studies on Contemporary Residential Architecture, 2004), by Tsukamoto and Nishizawa Taira, rigorously pursues this stylistic convention for architectural plans.

The continuous space of House SA may be interpreted as the application of techniques for building on a slope, first developed in the Common City Hoshida project, to the interior space of a home. The gradually rising floor continues in the same way both inside and out, creating a sense of receding perspective that invites one from the parking area into the garden. House SA, standing in a sloping residential neighborhood, looks through a latticework of FRP (fiber-reinforced panel) in the garden toward the distant hills. The translucent green tint of the FRP harmonizes well with the greenery of the hillsides.

If architectural manipulation is carried to an extreme of complexity, as in deconstructivism, the floors and walls tilt violently, making for a queasy spatial atmosphere. But there is none of that in this house. Instead, it has a comfortable quality that makes you want to settle in and stay. The other interesting thing is that, filled with the furniture and possessions of the owner, it presents an even more pleasing interior prospect than when it was just completed and empty. Architect's homes are usually presented in publications with staged photos in which everything has been cleared away to present the building in the best light (open houses usually operate on the same principle); they tend to become less attractive the more they are lived in and become filled with the owner's belongings. Yet even considering the fact that this is the architect's own home, and presumably designed with a sense of the amount and nature of his own possessions, it is worth noting the capacity this house has to be so full of things and yet still not feel chaotic. Sakamoto took stock of the furniture he owned and calculated the space carefully. Quico Jingumae (2006), one of Sakamoto's rare commercial projects, used the spatial model of House SA and proved that it can work quite well for product displays. Nishizawa Taira points out that House SA uses a remarkably diverse set of proportional scales. This kind of careful attention to detail may be why the architecture and the things it holds do not conflict with one another, making for a highly accepting space.[18]

Sakamoto says, "I think recent projects such as House SA or Hut T have a noticeably unfinished feeling, and I am keenly cognizant of it. What I mean by an unfinished feeling is that they exclude completion; or perhaps it's a matter of time—something with an unfinished feeling seems to me something that implicates and involves time."[19] In other words, he resists the idea that architecture alone completes a space. And that is free architecture.

Toward another type of "flat" architecture

If ordinary architecture is governed by a single overarching system, then we might say that House SA is a multi-focused architecture involving a variety of interacting systems. Fujioka Hiroyasu provides us with an apt analysis of the aim of this kind architecture: "It avoids a principle or system that controls the whole, creating a realm in which parts and whole relate smoothly, with the parts being allowed a certain independence. This is also a way of thinking that accepts the absence of consistent rules or hierarchy, as well as the absence of purpose (ideal) or center (climax)."[20]

Compare that with the following statement by the artist Murakami Takashi, proposing his concept of "superflat" art: "There is no camera eye. No depth. No stratification. No interior. No human presence. But the gaze is full. Everything is in focus. There is a network. There is movement. And there is 'freedom.'"[21] House SA is an architecture that might be quite adequately understood within the superflat context. Superflat is a useful concept in explicating 1990s design, which in the case of architecture was characterized by an emphasis on flat facades and an absence of hierarchy.[22] I previously thought that the simple, clear-cut work of architects like SANAA were the best representatives of a non-hierarchical architecture, but House SA proposes a distinctly different type of flat architecture: open network architecture. It doesn't have the transparency of the 1990s, but as Sakamoto has observed, simply cutting a bunch of openings in buildings "seems like a pretty superficial sort of openness."[23] As noted previously, this is because the issue is one of spatial composition.

House SA has been interpreted as a heteronomous semi-lattice model of partially overlapping and polymerizing relationships. Sakamoto writes, "In House SA . . . the interior space is formed by the arrangement and distribution of parts responding independently to differing external conditions. Because of this, it can be said that the individual parts do not become stratified, but run parallel and coexist with one another as fragments, without being unified in any particular direction, presenting themselves as an unfinished form."[24] Considering this from the superflat perspective, architectural theorist Sakaushi Taku has an interesting observation. He points out that a common characteristic of Sakamoto's principal projects—from House in Nago (1978), with its interior unified by the use of lauan (mahogany) veneer panels, to Hut T (2001)—is an "all-over" finish giving a similar appearance to the entire structure. Sakaushi writes: "The all-over treatment . . . thus becomes radically polycentric. In the House in Nago, for instance, the fact the furnishings are all built-ins means that our gaze refuses to be drawn to any particular place. One might say that the viewer's effort to extract meaning from what is seen is being rejected."[25] This quality of not determining or limiting the gaze is the essence of superflat.

Hut T (2001) is a structure imbued with a sense of floating and transparency. Walls formed by a lattice of 2-by-10-inch lumber and the flat roof are equivalent presences, serving, along with sliding door and window panels, to achieve an "all-over" effect. The fixed relationship between interior and exterior is broken down, aiming at a melding of the two into a single open space. More than House SA, this conveys an easily understandable 1990s sensibility. Yet in a sense this is a photogenic architecture that really seems somewhat unlike Sakamoto.

Sakamoto, both university professor and architect, does not draw much—he communicates with his students verbally, and sets them to work on plans. Powerful sketches quickly become a fixed style, inhibiting further creativity. In extreme cases students simply fall into copying the master, and never advance beyond mere reproduction. Yet by avoiding this, one can also avoid falling into repeating oneself and, by dismantling previously established methodologies, sustain a constantly shifting train of thought. No doubt this can also have a significant educational impact. Needless to say, it is significant that his personal residence is an outstanding work as well.

As a result, Sakamoto has had enormous influence on the architects affiliated with Tokyo Institute of Technology. Here is a list of some of the people who have been involved in his projects: Takahashi Hiroshi; Okuyama Shin'ichi; Kamo Kiwako, Sogabe Masashi, and Uehara Yūshi of

Mikan Gumi; Tsukamoto Yoshiharu and Kaijima Momoyo of Atelier Bow-Wow; Ogawa Jirō; Terauchi Mikiko; Mimura Daisuke; Kuroda Junzō; Kuno Yasuhiro; and Yasumori Akio. Fujimura Ryūji, born in 1976, also probably falls within the range of talent born out of experience in the design groups at Tokyo Institute of Technology. Sakamoto has sown many seeds for a type of design that cannot be consumed merely as style. A new generation of architects who have inherited his approach—how he poses a variety of problems—are evolving their own methodologies in response, and creating brilliant work. Architecture since the 1990s begins with students who trained under Sakamoto.

Fujimori Terunobu

The Incomparable Architect(ural Historian)

A contemporary Itō Chūta?

Fujimori Terunobu makes unusual architecture. Many people, unable to categorize it, are confounded by it. But that is his aim. When he began his career as a practicing architect, Fujimori, who had been active as a historian and critic of contemporary architecture, avoided the derision that would greet him if he diligently studied and clumsily imitated anything resembling existing models, and chose instead to create an architecture that resembled nothing else. Because of this, it is impossible to evaluate him by the standards of modernism or postmodernism. It is Fujimori style. Or perhaps it might be more accurate to say that Fujimori has focused his attention on traditional architecture that no one else has referenced. For example, he is not interested in temples, shrines, and teahouses, but in structures such as the farmhouses of northeastern Japan capped with *shibamune*—a thatched roof with grass growing along the ridge. This is a historical architecture that even the Japanese have largely forgotten. But Fujimori has created contemporary versions of it (complete with irrigation systems) for his own home, Tanpopo House (1995), and for Nira House (1997), built as the residence of his comrade-in-arms, the avant-garde artist Akasegawa Genpei.

Ordinarily, architectural historians do not design buildings themselves, or if they do, they keep it quiet. They don't want to be attacked for not

Nira House, 1997. (Photo by the author)

Jinchōkan Moriya Historical Museum, 1991. (Photo by the author)

living up to what they've said about the work of others. But Fujimori is not like that. I'm told that when his debut work, the Jinchōkan Moriya Historical Museum (1991), was written up in the newspapers, he distributed copies of the articles to the students in his seminars. He loved it. Or rather, he loves making things. He closes his afterword to *Nihon no kindai kenchiku* (Modern Architecture in Japan, 1993) with the statement, "Now that this book is completed, I hope that I may turn my hands to something that from childhood I preferred to writing: the work of actually making things." And so he became an architect.[1] With Fujimori, the word is father to the deed. He says that his childhood love of building things was what set him on the path to becoming an architect. And this interest in handiwork has something in common with Fujimori's approach to architectural history, which eschews metacritique and ideological analysis and focuses on the concrete details of things.

He's a rare individual. There are, from the opposite standpoint, radical architects acutely conversant with history, such as Horiguchi Sutemi, architect and scholar of teahouses, or Isozaki Arata, who quoted extensively from European architecture. But there is almost no other example of someone who began as a historian and then became active as an architect. Except for one man, Itō Chūta (1867–1954), who virtually created the field of Japanese architectural history and also pursued an influential career as an architect. His Earthquake Memorial Hall (1930, now Tokyo Memorial Hall), and Chōsen Jingū (1925) recall historic shrines and temples; Kanematsu Auditorium (1927) at Hitotsubashi University is an example of Romanesque Revival; and the Tsukiji Honganji temple (1934) traces Buddhist architecture back to its sources in India and references them extensively. This is what might be called mainstream architectural history. In contrast, Fujimori draws his inspiration from vernacular architecture overlooked by standard architectural histories. This is what gives him his incomparable strength.

It's a brilliant strategy. Fujimori says, "Even the avant-garde isn't really that interesting," and "things that are called beautiful" are no good.[2] If you do modernism, your sense for the niceties of proportion and the quality of finishes is questioned; on the other hand, period styles like Gothic or Renaissance are impossible in this day and age. And the acceptance of postmodernism by future generations is unclear. So he decided to create a new arena for architecture, unbound by the existing context. This is connected with the rejection of art with a capital A that characterizes his involvement with Akasegawa Genpei and the Roadway Observation Society, which prowled the streets of Tokyo collecting and enjoying found objects—taking pictures of manhole covers, discovering "pure stairways" that led upward but had lost their original function of actually connecting with an upper floor.

Something that Fujimori has in common with Itō Chūta is the commitment to fieldwork coupled with a global sensibility. Fujimori's charts of the Anglophile and Francophile factions in *Modern Architecture in Japan* bear a certain resemblance to the evolutionary architectural typology conceived by Itō. For example, Itō believed that entasis—the slight convex curve of the Classical Greek column in structures such as the Parthenon—had been transmitted to Japan and used in temples like Hōryūji (607), and he set out to prove this theory by following the route of that transmission across Asia. Fujimori, after thoroughly familiarizing himself with modern

Japanese architectural sites, began collaborative research in the 1990s with scholars in other parts of Asia, and observed that there were both westward and eastward flows of transmission around the globe.[3]

The veranda on Western-style buildings was transmitted eastward from the European colonies in Asia, while clapboard siding traveled westward from Europe and across America. Japan was the terminus of both routes. This conception of Japan as the terminus of world culture is something else that Fujimori shares with Itō Chūta.

The historical vision of Fujimori Terunobu

In the recessionary 1970s, Fujimori had time on his hands; he formed the Architectural Detectives, prowling the streets investigating modern architecture. Born in 1946, he grew up, like Itō Toyoo, in the town of Suwa in Nagano prefecture, and attended Tōhoku University during the era when Japan was caught up in enthusiasm for the 1964 Olympics and Expo '70 in Osaka. In the architecture course there, he was a classmate of Oda Kazumasa of the folk-rock band Off Course. By the time he advanced to graduate studies at the University of Tokyo in 1971, the architectural boom of the 1960s was over. But he soon found "joy in discovering the odd things scattered about the streets, unnoticed by others."[4] He was in tune with the times. In the 1980s a lively discourse arose on the urban culture of Tokyo; meanwhile, the wave of postmodernism inspired a re-evaluation of decorative design. Fujimori's popularity has of course been aided by the verbal dexterity you might expect from someone making a living by writing, but that was not all: he could move from discussions of ornament to semiotics to biographical detail with equal facility. An example is his discovery of the design motif on the capitals of the columns of the Imperial Agricultural Association (1930), "in which a peasant sows seeds, guarded by an eagle, a symbol of power, with its wings extended," which he interprets as signifying fertility.[5] Discussions of architectural structure and composition can be difficult, but Fujimori's writing is accessible, even without specialized knowledge.

Nor was Fujimori interested only in pursuing oddities. His doctoral dissertation, published as *Meiji no Tōkyō keikaku* (1982), was an orthodox study of urban planning in Meiji Japan, a straightforward analysis of the red-brick district of Ginza and the plan for the concentration of government ministries and agencies in central Tokyo as expressions of how the state, highly conscious of foreign opinion, wanted to shape the appearance of the Japanese capital.[6] As Fujimori himself has said, "I felt like I'd suddenly gone from being an architectural detective to being installed as chief of police," and "was looking down on history from someplace high above."[7] One of his most ambitious books was *Tange Kenzō* (2003), a major scholarly monograph on the architect who gave postwar Japan its image, in projects such as the facilities for the Tokyo Olympics and for Expo '70.[8] Fujimori unquestionably has an eye—or two: one prowling the ground like a dog's, the other soaring overhead, providing a bird's-eye view.

These interests may seem divergent. But unbound by convention and precedent, they allow a certain romanticism in which personal dreams may flourish. Fujimori was interested in Meiji Japan because it was an era in which an individual could still propose grand schemes; by the Taishō era (1912–26), urban planning had already become bureaucratized. Tange operated as an architectural genius, a larger-than-life figure who cut a wide swath. The architectural historian Doi Yoshitake writes of Fujimori that "he is an anti-historical historian, and the pleasure in reading him lies not in his ideas, but in his quest to discover the wellsprings of creativity in the individuals he writes about."[9] In fact, Fujimori says he hates order and systems with a passion. There are things that cannot be contained—above or below—by the world governed by social institutions and economic principles. Things like Meiji schemes for the development of Tokyo, or the vernacular modern architecture of its streets.

I'd like to reference the writer Milan Kundera, who seems to hold a view of history exactly the opposite of Fujimori's. Born in 1929 in Czechoslovakia, Kundera went into exile in France in 1975. Fujimori, born in Nagano in 1946, was a beneficiary, in Tokyo, of Japan's postwar economic miracle. According to Kundera, modern architecture is none other than the institutions of modern society—the police, the courts, high finance, the military.[10] This typological view of buildings as facilities or institutions, prioritizing systems over things or people, is a perspective Fujimori would probably dislike. In Kundera's novels, the individual is relentlessly spun about in the whirlpool of history. Politics cannot be purged even from the love interest. But Fujimori, living in the capitalist world, was able to maintain an apolitical demeanor. He began his fieldwork in a Japan in which history had been suspended by the Cold War. And the architecture he designs is so eccentric that it rejects interpretation as a widely applicable social critique.

Their perception of nostalgia differs as well. Fujimori says that the sentiment of nostalgia does not exist in animals, only in humans, and that "architecture is the greatest vessel of nostalgia."[11] Nostalgia is a bond that allows humans to be humans, by helping them preserve their faith in the stability and continuity of their world. Therein lies the significance of both history and architecture. It might be called a form of total affirmation. In the preface to his first novel, *The Joke* (1967), Kundera wrote: "Yesterday's action is obscured by today, and the strongest link binding us to a life constantly being eaten away by forgetting is nostalgia. Remorseful nostalgia and remorseless skepticism are the two pans of the scales that give the novel its equilibrium."[12] Although he lost relatives in the concentration camps, he sees a book by Hitler and is surprised to find himself recalling nostalgically the lost days of his youth. Nostalgia as reconciliation. "For how can we condemn something that is ephemeral, in transit? In the sunset of dissolution, everything is illuminated by the aura of nostalgia, even the guillotine."[13] Negative memories of brutality render the sentiment of nostalgia into something more complex.

A new Jōmon and Yayoi

Fujimori has led a loose group of nonprofessional volunteers with an interest in architecture and construction, dubbed the Jōmon Architecture Team, in the design and production of a number of unusual architectural projects. Jōmon refers to a prehistoric period in Japan; the name means "cord-marked," a reference to the lively patterns decorating the earthenware characteristic of the period. The popularity from the 1990s onward of modernist glass and steel architecture made the group's rough-and-ready approach all the more remarkable. Fujimori has said, "The first aspect of our 'Jōmon style' is the strong presence of columns."[14] And indeed, this produces a completely different sense of space than the transparent glass walls of modernism. For example, in the Jinchōkan Moriya Historical Museum (1991), four columns made of unfinished tree trunks pierce the roof at one end of the building, creating an ominous atmosphere. It's a novel structural treatment, yet it somehow seems familiar. I've pointed out previously that it is reminiscent of the house of Medama Oyaji (Daddy Eyeball) in the ghost-story manga *Gegege no Kitarō*, but Takasugi-an (Too-High Teahouse, 2004), built as a treehouse, resembles it even more.[15]

The philosophical underpinnings of this eccentric approach to design may be seen in Fujimori's *Jinrui to kenchiku no rekishi* (The History of Humankind and Architecture, 2005). This is an oddly unbalanced history. In fact,

Takasugi-an, 2004. (Photo by the author)

most of the content is devoted to prehistoric veneration of standing stones and pillars; the treatment of topics from antiquity to the present is a bit sketchy. Fujimori is more interested in the roughly vigorous monoliths and dolmens that predate Western classicism and even the concept of "architecture." Fujimori's own home, Tanpopo House, like Jinchō-kan Moriya Historical Museum and Takasugi-an, does not really look like

Tanpopo House, 1995. (Photo by the author)

a human habitation. Perhaps this sensibility is a continuation of the motivation behind the Architectural Detectives—a delight in the "strangeness" and "difference" embodied in historic Western-style buildings in Japan.[16] We might add that Itō Chūta was known to be a lover of ghost stories and fairy tales.

An intriguing debate on tradition arose in the architectural world of the 1950s—initiated by the claim that the spare minimalism of the Katsura Detached Palace and Ise Grand Shrine originated in a style imposed by the ruling class of the Yayoi period—the period that followed the Jōmon—and that it was the rougher and more powerful populist forms of the Jōmon period that contemporary architecture should seek to inherit. The architect Shirai Seiichi questioned this fad for "Jōmon things" but was critical of the standard interpretation of modernism associated with Bruno Taut's discovery of Katsura Detached Palace. Of course, the work of abstract artist Okamoto Tarō and the popularity of Brutalism were also part of the context for these discussions. Jōmon versus Yayoi—the debate continued fiercely in the architectural journals of the day. Now, more than a half century later, it would seem these two contemporary reinterpretations of traditional Japanese architecture are being reproduced once again, albeit in somewhat different form. Fujimori, it goes without saying, represents the new Jōmon. And we might posit Kuma Kengō as representative of the new Yayoi.

Kuma Kengo (b. 1954) debuted as a postmodernist architect in the 1980s, but from the latter half of the 1990s onward began to use minimalist design to express a Japanese sense of space, preferring to work with wood and bamboo. For example, for his Great (Bamboo) Wall (2002) in Beijing and the Main Gate of the Lake Hamana Flower Festival (2003), bamboo was chosen as the primary material. On the other hand, Fujimori also loves to use natural materials, but says he doesn't like bamboo because it is too "glossy and shiny," and confesses that "I just can't get on with 'Yayoi-style things' that come from bamboo. . . ."[17] In other words, he means that the proportions of bamboo are too slender, and as a material it seems too elegant and refined. It represents a different aesthetic from one that would plant shepherd's purse on the ridge of a thatched roof or cover a roof in dandelions or leeks.

Kuma's Nakagawa-machi Bato Hiroshige Museum of Art (2000) is a simple gable-roofed structure that makes extensive use of local cedar and Japanese paper. The entire structure is clad in louvers made of extremely thin cedar timbers, spaced 12 centimeters apart, said to be inspired by the fine lines that Andō Hiroshige used in his ukiyo-e woodblock prints. These cedar louvers have two layers, inner and outer, with a layer of either glass or metal sandwiched in between for a total of three layers in all. This layering also took its inspiration from Hiroshige's prints, in which two dimensions are given three-dimensional depth through the skillful use of multiple layering. Kuma's lovely, delicate design might be seen as Yayoi style. Yet at the same time, the facade of repeating cedar strips reads almost like a barcode. It does not make use of traditional woodworking techniques, and might be described as digitally processed wooden architecture.

Fujimori describes the style of his own work as *yaban gyarudo* ("barbaric guard"), a play on the word *avant-garde*. It is an architecture with a rough-hewn charm, the opposite of interchangeable. While it touches on the past, it does not indulge in nostalgic reference, displaying a bare-toothed wildness that is utterly new. If there is any nostalgia to be felt here, it is probably because the primitive mode of expression employed in Fujimori's work suggests structures that might have been built in the past—but weren't. On the other hand, what makes Kuma's work an example of new Yayoi style is its transparency, and its potential for computer-aided manipulation. In other words, at present the Jōmon versus Yayoi dichotomy has taken on new significance as wild versus digital.

Nonexistent places and times

Fujimori's architecture, because of its use of natural materials, is frequently characterized as New Age or ecological, but it's not as simple as that. It is a contemporary experiment in reviving the ancient powers manifested in traditions such as the Onbashira Festival in Suwa, a wild and dangerous event held every six years. Giant fir trees are felled high on the mountain slopes above Suwa Grand Shrine; participants ride the logs down the mountainside, where they are used as pillars in the renovation of the shrine. At the same time, Fujimori does not reject modern technology altogether. He is not completely fixated on traditional wooden construction; he has also used steel and concrete in his structures. According to the architect Chō Umihiko, when the participants at the Takayama Architecture School, a summer program, got excited about catching brook trout, Fujimori quickly constructed a small dam, trapping the fish and making them easier to catch. So he is not a simple rustic—he does have modern tendencies.

Fujimori is critical of the glossy, uniform surfaces produced by contemporary technology; he sticks to a rough, Brutalist finish for his work. For example, he chars timber and then uses a rock drill to give it a rough surface texture, reminiscent of rustic design in the West. Although his work is grounded in modern structural technology, Fujimori uses natural materials to achieve surface treatments that give his architecture a unique texture and feel. This privileging of the sense of touch over the sense of sight may bring to mind the critical regionalism proposed by Kenneth Frampton. But if the latter is a strategy for giving birth to a regionalism that remains grounded in modernism, Fujimori's architecture displays a powerful primitivism that does not derive from any specific locale. It may arouse feelings of nostalgia, but not for any identifiable place. This is why Fujimori himself calls it "international vernacular."

As suggested by his proposal to build a super-skyscraper covered in dandelions, Fujimori is not merely an architect drenched in nostalgia for the past. He has also proposed a Tokyo Plan 2101—a critical response to the legacy of Tange Kenzō's Tokyo Plan 1960—that envisions a Tokyo inundated by rising seawaters unleashed by global warming, out of which rise wood-framed skyscrapers and the lonely ruin of Tokyo Tower.

As one might expect of an architectural historian, Fujimori is a skillful interpreter of his own position. He says there have been plenty of architects who return to the ground of tradition to complain about the present, but that what he's done is to find a fresh way of looking at the ground of the present by running full tilt in the opposite direction. And it does seem that an architecture fusing contemporary structural technology with finishing materials of the past has somehow elicited a vision of the future. Even the sleek and shiny architecture of our present, abandoned for long enough, will return to the earth and be covered with plant life. One recalls the science-fiction worlds of Miyazaki Hayao's films *Nausicaä of the Valley of the Wind* or *Laputa: Castle in the Sky*, in both of which technology is overgrown with greenery in the ruins of future societies. As he runs backwards against the ground of the present, Fujimori fast-forwards time—creating an architecture that spans past, present, and future.

The architectural detectives go to Venice

In the autumn of 2006, Fujimori Terunobu served as the commissioner for the Japan Pavilion at the 10th International Architecture Exhibition at the Venice Biennale. The largest in scale of regular international architecture exhibitions, it featured everything from art installations to displays of valuable research materials, but in the midst of it all, the Japan Pavilion stood out as unusual. Normally the commissioner works as an organizer and curator, selecting the work of others, but remarkably, Fujimori chose to display models and photographs of his own unique architectural creations, from his graduation project to the Takasugi-an teahouse, as well as exhibiting the discoveries of the ROJO Society (Roadway Observation Society).

Fujimori was already famous in Japan but comparatively unknown overseas. How was this exhibit received? The first thing to note is the smiles on the faces of visitors to the Japan Pavilion. The photos of bizarre objects collected in the Tokyo streets by the Roadway Observation Society elicited grins from viewers. The entrance to the exhibition also created a sense of relaxation and fun: after removing their shoes, visitors passed through a half-height portal, like the *nijiriguchi* of a traditional teahouse, requiring them to bow as they passed through into an anteroom floored in mats woven from wisteria vines. His Hamamatsu City Akino Fuku Art Museum (1997) employs a similar concept, but this was even more effective in Europe, where people are used to wearing shoes indoors—allowing them to experience a public space with a sense of intimacy. Since the overall theme of the 2006 exhibition was urban issues, many of the national pavilions adopted a somber and serious approach—like the United States pavilion, devoted to recovery planning in the wake of Hurricane Katrina—so the lighthearted friendliness of Fujimori's Japan Pavilion provided some welcome relief. In the past the Japan Pavilion at the Venice Biennale had featured exhibits that amazed overseas viewers—*City of Girls* (2000); *Otaku* (2004), themed on the culture of Akihabara, Tokyo's

Akino Fuku Art Museum, 1997.
(Photo by the author)

electronics and pop culture district; and *Fractures* (1996), which exhibited fragments of buildings destroyed in the 1995 Kobe earthquake—but this exhibition of Fujimori's world made them marvel at aspects of Japan they had never encountered before. From the country seen as synonymous with high tech, they were confronted with a primitive wildness in the form of models made from logs carved with chainsaws and a small theater installation constructed of rough rope stretched over a framework of split bamboo. Perplexed by how to interpret Fujimori's architecture, more than one visitor pronounced it to be "bizarre." But that was, in part, his aim.

Japanese people are also startled by Fujimori's buildings. The first time I visited the Jinchōkan Moriya Historical Museum, I was flabbergasted. The following observation by architect Takahashi Teiichi is an apt response to Fujimori's position: "I don't feel threatened looking at Fujimori's work. Because he is not my rival. I couldn't do work like that even if I stood on my head, so he's not invading my territory. So I can always get along with him peacefully. I think everyone feels that way." Fujimori's strange vernacular—odd buildings that look like they might exist someplace else in the globe, although they have never been seen before—has charmed the world. In 2010 Fujimori was invited to participate in an architectural exhibition at London's Victoria and Albert Museum (V&A) entitled *1:1 Architects Build Small Spaces*, and built a small teahouse out of charred cedar.

Fujimori did important work as a scholar of modern architecture, and after writing a valuable survey history, *Modern Architecture in Japan*, started a career as a practicing architect. He's made the leap from observer to leading actor on the main stage of architectural history.

Iijima Naoki

At the Boundaries of Interior Design

Between architecture and interior design

Although architecture and interior design share certain similarities, they are fundamentally different. As a critic I specialize in the former, and I find writing about the latter rather difficult. Architects speak in the media of the ideas and philosophy behind their work, and the work itself often has strong formal properties. In other words, even if you cannot make out the finer details of the actual building from photos in a magazine, the plans and concept provide quite a bit of supplementary information that can then be verbalized. In a trade journal like *Shōten kenchiku* (Commercial Architecture), by contrast, not much space is devoted to plans or drawings. There may be attractive photos, but interior design prioritizes the atmosphere created in the actual space, which is hard to reproduce in other media. These conditions are probably what makes criticism so difficult as well. On the other hand, with interior design there is a clear index of commercial success—does it attract customers?—that is even more rigorous than that normally encountered by architecture.

Koizumi Kazuko, an expert on furniture design, has observed that in traditional Japanese domestic culture, furnishings have been considered part of the architecture, and furniture in the Western sense has scarcely existed. She also notes that since very few Japanese scholars have studied the history of interior design and furnishings, encouraging younger scholars to engage this discipline has been challenging. Even though it is a related field, interior design has attracted virtually no historical analysis, not even research focused on work since the twentieth century. In the MESH Environmental Seminar, an interior design study group that has met more than seventy times since it was established in 1998 in Nagoya, the first time that the relationship between interior design and architecture was set as a theme for discussion was in a session I attended in 2011. In fact, as I was preparing for my talk, I was reminded how sparse the basic documentation and information on the history of contemporary interior design was. Information and knowledge shared by people in the industry have not been put in written form that can be accessed by people in other fields. Serious dialogue across the divide between architecture and interior design still lies in the future.

Even so, in the architectural world, after the collapse of the bubble economy, renovation began to attract attention as an alternative to the scrap-and-build approach in place since the 1990s. In other words, rather than completely replacing the existing structure, the idea was to work inside the box with interior interventions. Then, in the early 2000s, young architects who could find little other work began to publish outstanding interior designs as positive representations of their talents—a development the industry could not afford to ignore. In addition to Aoki Jun, who had formerly written interior design criticism for *Shōten kenchiku* with Iijima Naoki, and other members of Aoki's design office such as Inui Kumiko and Nakamura Ryūji, there were a number of cutting-edge architects moving into the field of interior design. This was why, when I was editor-in-chief of *Kenchiku zasshi* (Journal of Architecture and Building Science), we did a special issue in 2009 on interior design—remarkably, the first on this topic in the more than 120-year history of the journal.[1] This indicates the depth of the gap between the two fields. I for one had been bothered by how little was being said about interior design and wrote a piece dubbing

Morita Yasumichi's style—typified by his hanging a crystal chandelier over a toilet—as "Yankee Baroque."[2]

Morita debuted in the late 1990s with design imbued with a semiotic gorgeousness that even nonprofessionals could understand—which was precisely why he flew completely under the radar of critics who saw designers like Kuramata Shirō as the epitome of good taste. In other words, Morita, who was born in 1967, behaved as if there had been no previous generation of designers like Uchida Shigeru or Iijima Naoki who had been influenced by modernism to reject a more pedestrian, feel-good design sensibility. You might say he defiantly asked: What is wrong with superficial decoration? And it happened that in the first decade of the twenty-first century, the architectural world was engaged in a re-evaluation of decorative elements, though this was not a matter of the semiotics of decoration but of using decoration to create site-specific place experiences of spaces.

Kuramata Shirō as a milestone

Kuramata Shirō (b. 1934) was accorded a special status in the interior design business. He was also a figure respected in the world of architecture.[3] An extraordinary number of articles have been written about him.[4] His playful sense of form and colorful palette created a fresh tendency distinct from functionalist modernism. *Begin the Beguine* (1985), for which he wrapped a Joseph Hoffman bentwood chair in steel wire and set fire to it, preserving only the metal wrapping, was not merely a beautiful piece of design but a plunge into the realm of avant-garde art. He also employed decorative elements with impeccable taste. For example, in the late 1980s his work often featured plant motifs. Just in Time (1986) was a clock that used twigs as the hands; Panacea (1989) was a woven carpet with a motif of candies in the shape of fruit. For the interior design of Bar Oblomov (1989) and the shop Spiral (1990), as well as Laputa (1991), a bed, he made effective use of artificial flowers. Hatsuki (1999), a vase, was embellished with glass flowers. His use of these plant motifs expressed an image of ephemerality.

Perhaps his most famous piece is Miss Blanche (1988). This is a stunningly beautiful chair with a clear acrylic body in which float a number of artificial roses. According to Kuramata, the rose motif was inspired by the corsage worn by Vivien Leigh, who played the character of Blanche in the film version of Tennessee Williams's play A *Streetcar Named Desire*. In studies for the chair, Kuramata's team collected just about every variety of artificial rose they could find in Japan, and experimented repeatedly with how to make them appear to float in the air. When the chair entered production, acrylic resin was poured into the mold in stages, with the staff holding the roses in position with tweezers as it hardened. During this process, Kuramata is said to have called the factory every half hour or so, insisting, "You have to make them float!"

What is interesting is how Miss Blanche appears in cross-section. In other words, when you look at one of the arms of the chair from the top down, refraction of the light causes double images of each rose, which then replicate in mirror-image recession. The result is an image of floating roses far more numerous than the number actually embedded in the piece. Flowers have been used for decoration since ancient times, but whether Classical or Gothic, or some other style, they have been treated either three-dimensionally as sculpture or two-dimensionally as surface decoration. But Kuramata's roses are simultaneously real and imagistic. Yet they are also not real, but artificial. This ambiguous relationship between reality and fiction is extremely contemporary.

Detail of Miss Blanche chair, 1988, by Kuramata Shirō. (Photo by the author)

The *Kuramata Shiro / Ettore Sottsass* exhibition at 21_21 Design Sight in Tokyo Midtown in 2011 took as its point of departure the year 1981, when Kuramata joined Sottsass's Memphis project, which had such an impact globally as an exponent of postmodern design. The exhibit introduced the work of both men from that time onward and chronicled the deep friendship between the Italian and Japanese designers during their lifetimes, but if anything it was weighted toward Kuramata Shirō and his work. The exhibition design, by Kuramata's protégés Kondō Yasuo and Igarashi Hisae, did a beautiful job of eliciting the strengths of the works on display, as might be expected from individuals so familiar with their mentor's style. The exhibition revisited Kuramata's work, twenty years after his death in 1991 at the age of fifty-six, and in light of subsequent developments in both architecture and design, visitors were struck by how prescient he was.

Kuramata's weightless, transparent design sensibility was on display surprisingly early, in work from the late 1960s and 1970s such as his interiors for the headquarters of Edward's (1969), a men's fashion company—work that still seems fresh, even today. He was clearly ahead of the curve in terms of trends in architecture from the 1980s onward. The light and airy feel of his furniture and his interiors that used expanded metal were also very much in synch with 80s architecture. And Twilight Time (1985), a glass table whose legs are tapered tubes of expanded metal, anticipates the much larger tubes of Itō Toyoo's Sendai Mediatheque (competition 1995; completed 2000). Moreover, it should be pointed out that his orientation toward design creating a quality of lightness was a direct influence on Sejima Kazuyo of SANAA and an atavistic throwback affecting young architects who came to prominence in the early 2000s as well, including Ishigami Jun'ya and Nakamura Ryūji. Of course, architects took the sort of design that Kuramata had arrived at through taste and intuition, and grappled with the engineering issues it presented on a structural level.

On a personal note, I recall going to the Kuramata exhibition at the Hara Museum of Art on its closing day in 1995, and giving up on seeing it because of the long lines of people waiting to get in. I think coming to grips with his work rather late, after so many years have passed, has actually provided me with a chance to more deeply appreciate the enormous impact he has had on the industry. It was too early to assess his historical significance so soon after his passing, because it was as yet unclear how trends in design would develop after that. Because the 2011 exhibition was mounted after the times had finally caught up with Kuramata, his significance was highlighted.

The architectural mind of Iijima Naoki

Born in 1949, Iijima Naoki was of the generation shaped by the counterculture of the 1960s.[5] He rejected the established approach to doing interior design, based on feel or subjective sensibility. The design firm Super Potato, where he worked from the 1970s to the 1980s, also pursued a formalist aesthetic aimed at shedding the idea of interiors as mere decoration. This was a highly self-conscious approach to interior design. For example, Super Potato utilized a grid system, similar to an architectural technique. The 1960s Italian architectural collective Superstudio had also proposed using a standardized grid, replicated at different scales, to achieve an overall design encompassing everything from furnishings and interior design to large structures. Conversely, the postmodern architect Hans Hollein's early work focused on the interior design of small shops inserted into the existing fabric of the streets of Vienna. It was an era in which the boundaries between architecture and interior design were breaking down.

The work done by Iijima after he went independent in the mid-1980s resembles installation art, objects that possess a strong formal presence. Sonia Rykiel Nagoya (1986), with its accumulation of lines colliding at acute angles in a bleached white space, or The Wall (1990), a restaurant featuring assemblages of geometric shapes, are good examples. These designs resonated with the postmodernist and deconstructivist tenor of

Sonia Rykiel Nagoya, 1986.
(Photo by Shiratori Yoshio)

the times, stressing their presence as things, as structures within the larger structures of the architecture containing them.

In contrast to interior design, which is seen as more sensual or intuitive, architects like to speak logically. But Iijima's thinking is architectural. For example, he explained what he called the "dialectical design" of Club Dios (1998), in the Kabukichō entertainment district of Tokyo, in the following way.[6] Because it was a "host club," thus inverting the usual male-female relationship in the world of nightlife, he used black for most of the interior to make the dark suits of the men disappear, but the seating was done in blue "to give the place a touch of glamour." Backlit glass was used behind the booths in order to spotlight the women as principal guests and the focus of attention. The curving lines of the seating also provided visual privacy for guests without dividing the space into separate box seats. This type of thought process is architectural.

From the 1990s onward design manipulating spatial relationships rather than objects came to the fore. For example, in the Japanese-style restaurant Wayo (2000) in the Ikspiari mall at Tokyo Disney Resort, Iijima took his cue from the fictional nature of the theme park, and created a scene dimly lit by flickering flames of candles set between glass screens with water flowing down them and the mirrored walls of the interior.[7] For the beauty salon Afloat (2000), the salon mirrors were also set into a glass screen with flowing water.[8]

In response to a questionnaire in *Shōten kenchiku* concerning the relationship between architecture and interior design, Iijima said that he was seeking "an airy framework" and explained this in the following terms:

> I definitely have not wanted to think of refinement in terms of sensuality. I believe that design is about relationships, not about feeling. The German movement *Neue Sachlichkeit* (New Objectivity), which was popular at the beginning of the twentieth century, appeals to me. I have always disliked half-baked, superficial, decorative interior design and have desired some kind of framework that was not superficial and decorative. But that framework is different from the framework of a building; it does not actually exist. It is a peculiar thing, deriving from the atmosphere of a place, mediated by the interior surfaces and their effects . . . an airy framework or structure.[9]

This would seem to exist somewhere between architecture and interior design.

For Baccari di Natura (2002) in the Shunkan restaurant complex in Shinjuku and the Star Jewelry + Workshop (2003) in Roppongi Hills, Iijima created interior spaces that were designed to look like cityscapes, using large glass

Baccari di Natura, 2002.
(Photo by Satō Shin'ichi)

screens with warped and twisted sections to create an optical phenomenon that lends a sense of volume. Although separated by a transparent wall, a conscious connection between interior and exterior is formed. The warped glass creates distorted landscape, making one aware of the walls of air separating us. The Shin Bungeiza (2000) in Ikebukuro, a cinema renovated as part of a complex shared with a pachinko parlor, was a project that was probably unforgettable for Iijima, a movie fan. In the lobby, vending machines, bookshelves, and a cafe were all set into the walls, carving out a clean L-shaped void.

Between the movies and interior design

Perhaps interior design overlaps with the aesthetic realm of the movies more than architecture does. Basically, if you can control what is visible, you don't have to worry about the external shell or structural issues. For example, Nakamura Kimihiko started in the movies as a set designer and then, when his design for commercial spaces began to attract attention, he opened his own interior design studio in 1971.[10] His best-known work as an art director for films includes Nijūshi no hitomi (Twenty-Four Eyes, 1954) and Arashi o yobu otoko (The Man Who Raised a Storm, 1957). While he was designing sets of bars and clubs, he began to be asked to design real interiors. But he had this to say about design for film: film prescribes the movements of the actors, but it is camera-centric, and in order to position the camera and secure its sightlines, the walls or ceilings of sets are frequently eliminated. Unlike with interior design, a real living space is not being created—the main goal is to capture an image on film. Another key to design for film is conveying a sense of the passage of time.

Iijima's love of the movies is clear from his essay, contributed to the series "Sōzō no gensen" (Sources of Creativity) in Shōten kenchiku, which introduces a number of his favorite films and books.[11] He says that he learned from the writings of Hasumi Shigehiko how to look at movies from a theoretical perspective. "We tend to look at movies as narrative, but if you don't, another world opens up in which you can enjoy a purely visual experience—'the sensuality of the image' as a succession of frames appearing before our eyes on the screen." It is true that Hasumi's methodology produced a film criticism quite different from that based on ideology or content. When this way of thinking is applied to interior design, what happens? Well, if asked to design a Japanese-style restaurant, for example, Iijima says, "I don't just let myself be taken in by the storyline 'Japanese restaurant,' and look instead to draw some sort of raw, fresh space out of this."

He has written about his environmental design for the first two floors of the Shinjuku Takashimaya department store (2007) in an essay entitled "Undōtai toshite no kioku" (Memory as a Moving Object), using motion pictures as a reference.[12] In undertaking this renovation, he says that he became aware of the spatial sequence in a manner similar to the way a series of separate cuts make up a temporal sequence in a film. The architect Bernard Tschumi had previously conceived of sequences of architectural space in terms of film theory and the works of Eisenstein, but Iijima's language—"durational time, motive space = film"—seems to be influenced more heavily by Deleuze and Bergson. In any case, Iijima sees a department store with its displays of products as a kind of motion picture—within the 10-meter space that humans are able to apprehend instantaneously as a basic unit or frame—and he edits his spatial sequence accordingly, making use of the hitherto unexploited and dynamic structural possibilities presented by the long horizontal lines and high ceilings of this renovation project, which focuses on the meta-interior connecting the shops rather than on the individual shops.

In the area near the ceilings, unlikely to be affected by any changes in merchandise displays, Iijima introduced a unified design. The space is divided using vertical louvers, transoms with a rose pattern, and eye-catching glass partitions extending like wing walls above the columns

Shinjuku Takashimaya, 2007.
(Photos by Kajiwara Toshihide,
above, and Satō Shin'ichi, below)

(the repetition of rectangles is reminiscent of the frames of a film). The span between columns is 7.5 meters, introducing a rhythmical punctuation to the range of vision at intervals slightly less than its normal 10-meter boundary. Illuminated wall panels soften the heavy columns. The mural on the first-floor ceiling, by the artist Hayashi Mariko, which has as its theme "Connections," is reflected in the mirrored faces of the columns on each side, in what appears to be a continuously repeating pattern. In this area both the walls and floor are clad in marble with a barcode-like pattern that deconstructs these huge planes into innumerable lines.

In the lobby between the escalators on the second floor, the large glass partitions are etched with a pattern of fine vertical lines, through which the up and down movement of the shoppers may be glimpsed intermittently like images on a screen.

Iijima was also responsible for the environmental design of the common areas of the commercial space occupying the first four floors of the Aoyama AO Building (2008). For an all-over effect, patterns of random dots, mosaics, and barcodes cover the floors, walls, and ceilings. These finely pixilated images not only unify the interior design, they also have been considered in terms of contextual relationship to their surroundings. Iijima says, "The exterior design of the building is cubic and edgy. It embodies the boisterous solidity of the Aoyama cityscape. So I thought the interior should also have a boisterous but solid feel. The solidity comes from a repetition of cubic forms and sharp-edged planes, integrated into a forest of illuminated columns. The boisterous part comes from materials that both optically and physically contrast strength and weakness (mosaics, veined marble, wet stone, rough wooden floors, copperplate, silky blacks, and scattered lighting)."[13] If urban planning is something that integrates relationships among a variety of different types of architecture, then this is interior design in the form of urban planning.

For the Nihonbashi branch of the Korean restaurant franchise Saikabou (2004), Iijima used a double skin of perforated metal that in places permitted peekaboo glimpses of what was on the other side, and in others places showed reflections of the interior from the mirrored walls behind, with the overlapping circular perforations creating an effect like the waxing and waning of the moon—all of this changing with the movement of the viewer, like scenes in a movie. While speaking of the constraints to which interior design is subject as a result of being enclosed within a work of architecture, Iijima also explained other possibilities in the following terms:

> You can create another autonomous space—another layer—inside, and then try to draw the two into a mutual relationship. Not by

dividing the interior into separate rooms, but by creating a sense of "here" and "there" within. You can create a single space in which separation and interpenetration occur simultaneously. In this restaurant, I tried to do this with walls that both enclosed light and let it shine through the circular perforations.[14]

The key here is not so much the specific design of a room but the way in which rooms can be made to relate to one another. It's what we might call interior design as architecture.

At the boundaries of interior design

For the common spaces of UDX Akibaichi (2006) in Akihabara, Iijima printed photographs of steel-framed electrical transmission towers on sheets of glass and used them to design a sequence of partitions connecting the shops. The repetition of these images of towers gives the space a rhythmical movement (the succession of photographic images resembles the frames in a movie), while mirrors behind the glass return complex reflections. The scale is smaller, but as in the Takashimaya renovation, the formalism of the design serves as a means of organizing the entire space. Slowly viewing each frame of a film in sequence does not make a movie. For a sequence of still images to become a motion picture, the frames must

UDX Akibaichi, 2006.
(Photo by Nacása & Partners)

149

be run continuously at a certain speed so that they are perceived as moving images. Iijima is approaching the design of interiors as a similar experience of sequence.

The architect Bernard Tschumi, while also referencing film, is less interested in continuity than in the fragmentary technique of montage. A motion picture is a repetition of individual frames that maintains an overall homogeneity while allowing radical changes in content. Montage is based on the sudden introduction of such heterogeneous elements. In the experience of space, this would probably translate into a collage sequence. Tschumi was deeply affected by his youthful encounter with the events of May 1968 in Paris. Iijima, only four years younger, is another member of the deconstructivist generation taking inspiration from the 1960s. Distrust existing structures. But do not simply destroy them. This was a new way of questioning the nature of interior design. Iijima has approached architecture, film, and the minimalism of contemporary art with deep interest, while at the same time keeping a certain calculated distance from them—redefining the boundaries of interior design, and generating new design by occupying that borderline.

PART

A LIGHT AND TRANSPARENT ARCHITECTURE

The Generation Born in the 1950s

SANAA

Design Reconfiguring Spatial Form

Architecture's top prize: The Pritzker

In 2010 the architectural firm SANAA (Sejima and Nishizawa and Associates) was selected for the Pritzker Architecture Prize. Created by the Pritzker family's Hyatt Foundation in 1979, this prize is awarded annually, usually to a single architect. Previous recipients include Jørn Utzon, designer of the Sydney Opera House; Frank Gehry; and Rem Koolhaas. The Pritzker Prize has avoided inflating the number of recipients and limited its selection to international architects operating at the very peak of their profession. It has thus come to be regarded as a kind of Nobel Prize for architecture. SANAA was the fourth Japanese recipient of the award, joining the ranks of Tange Kenzō (b. 1913), Maki Fumihiko (b. 1928), and Andō Tadao (b. 1941). Since Sejima Kazuyo was born in 1956 and Nishizawa Ryūe in 1966, they represent a later generation than Tange, Maki, and Andō, who led Japanese architecture from the modern into the postmodern era. Nishizawa, in his mid-forties, is the youngest architect to have received a Pritzker.

What sort of architects make up SANAA, to have achieved this level of international recognition?

Sejima began her career as a member of Itō Toyoo's staff, where she was dubbed *konbini shōjo* ("convenience-store girl") for her new lifestyle sensibility. She went independent in 1987, setting up her own studio and garnering attention with a series of innovative projects: Saishunkan Sei-yaku Women's Dormitory (1991), a pachinko parlor (1993), and the police box at the north exit of Chōfu Station (1994). Nishizawa worked with Sejima at Itō's office; he began designing with her in 1990. In 1995 they initiated SANAA as a partnership. Their light and transparent approach to design was a breath of fresh air for a Japanese architectural world brim-ming with the excessive decoration of postmodernism, and SANAA became the pacesetter for developments from the 1990s onward.

From quite early on SANAA attracted considerable interest from over-seas. The Spanish architectural journal El Croquis, known for introducing cutting-edge design, did a special issue in 1996 on Sejima—astonishingly early, since only one Japanese magazine had accorded her similar treat-ment prior to this. Later, in 2001, El Croquis devoted a special issue to SANAA. As the twenty-first century dawned, SANAA undertook a vari-ety of significant foreign commissions: the New Museum of Contemporary Art (2007) in New York; the Louvre-Lens Museum (2012), a branch of the Louvre; and others in Germany, the Netherlands, and elsewhere. Sejima was named the overall director of the Venice Biennale of Architecture in 2010—the first Japanese, and the first woman, to be so honored. Nishizawa also participated in the Biennale that year as a principal exhibitor in the Japan Pavilion.

Generally speaking, Sejima and Nishizawa work together on overseas projects and competitions and major domestic commissions, while also maintaining separate studios and practices at home in Japan. It's a unique setup, with three parallel streams of activity going on concurrently. I once asked them why they worked together, since it was obvious they both had more than enough talent to make it on their own. Their response was that the more people involved, the greater the possibility that good ideas would emerge. When they work together, each develops a proposal inde-pendently, then brings along staff, and they all work at building large-scale models in a large office space in a converted warehouse. In the process, they discuss what they are seeing, and refine their proposals.

Deconstructing spatial hierarchies

S ANAA designs are characterized by simplicity, transparency, and an airy feeling of lightness. The plans and the building program are simple but uncompromising in matters of architectural form, deconstructing existing hierarchies to invent new forms. Elevations also eschew the gaudy compositions of postmodernism, but meticulous attention is paid to everything from overall proportions to the width of window mullions. At first glance, everything is normal. Look again, and something seems odd. For example, in the Ogasawara Museum (1999) in the city of Iida in Nagano prefecture, the narrow, sashlike facade has a very subtle curve along its length. The aim is not drama or explicit novelty, yet this slight bend affects the entire structure. In this way, unanticipated compositions are born. It is as if the architects are in pursuit of the unrealized potential of modernist architecture. But a modernist architecture transformed into something different in nature as a result of slight manipulations.

The Pritzker committee gave high praise to one of SANAA's signature works, the 21st Century Museum of Contemporary Art (2004) in Kanazawa. More than 40,000 people visited this building within the first three days of its opening. That is a remarkable figure in a regional city with a total population of only 400,000. Just prior to the opening, SANAA had received the Golden Lion award at the 2004 Venice Biennale of Architecture for this museum and for a proposal for the enlargement of the Instituto Valenciano de Arte Moderno in Valencia, Spain, by enclosing the existing structure in a fabric of metal panels, creating an enormous indoor/outdoor space. In both cases it was SANAA's innovative approach to public space that impressed the judges.

The plan of the 21st Century Museum of Contemporary Art has the

Kanazawa's 21st Century Museum of Contemporary Art, 2004. (Courtesy of SANAA)

outline of a giant disc, inside of which have been inserted an array of different sized boxes—the galleries. Rather than creating a spatial hierarchy between a "front" where the main entrance is located and a "back" where offices, delivery, and service spaces are concentrated, the museum has numerous entrances and exits scattered around the perimeter of the circle. In an ordinary museum there is usually a well-defined traffic flow through a succession of long, narrow gallery spaces, but here rectangular exhibition spaces broken into numerous galleries intermingle on an equal basis with a square interior courtyard and broad connecting corridors, permitting visitors to wander freely among them. As you move deeper into the building, several atriums bring light into the interior, and the translucent facade makes the exterior landscape visible, so you do not feel trapped within. The perfect form of the circle can tend toward a closed monumentality, but here the circle has been redefined as a space easily accessed by anyone, like a convenience store. By giving new meaning to such a familiar form,

SANAA manages to simultaneously achieve both a sense of reassurance and of contemporaneity.

As it moved into the 2000s, SANAA began to produce new curves hitherto unseen in the history of architecture—curves undefined by circular or elliptical geometries or by structural engineering. The outlines of the Rolex Learning Center (2010) in Lausanne and the Serpentine Gallery Pavilion (2009) in London are described by unprecedented freehand curves, resembling topographical or biomorphic forms. The curves in Frank Gehry's work produce novel and eccentric forms, but those of SANAA bring about a fresh experience of space. For her university graduation thesis, Sejima Kazuyo chose to investigate the significance of curves in the work of Le Corbusier. Now, the curves of SANAA—in floor and desk lamps, greenhouses, a proposed observation tower and pathways for the palm groves of Elche in Spain, a factory in Germany for furniture manufacturer Vitra—from product design to major architectural projects, suggest unprecedented new spatial possibilities.

Sejima Kazuyo

Distorting Distance Through a Glass Landscape

Beyond the glass palace

Onishi-chō (now part of Fujioka City) is a small rural town with many traditional houses and no modernist buildings. Consequently, I assumed that Sejima Kazuyo's Onishi Multipurpose Hall (2005) would stand out as an alien presence. Surprisingly, however, the building does not announce itself until you are practically on its doorstep. The glass sheathing softens its intensity, and the overall height of the building has been restrained to fit in with the modest structures surrounding it. Clients for public buildings in Japan tend to request height as a way of proclaiming them symbols of the city or town. When I participated as a juror in a design competition for a regional municipal museum, I noticed that the local people involved in the selection process all chose height over design in casting their votes. I might also point out that Onishi Elementary School is located behind Onishi Multipurpose Hall, and is much more noticeable from a distance. By digging into the site and placing its largest volumes—a gym and an auditorium—below grade, the height of Onishi Multipurpose Hall was significantly reduced overall, beneath a flat roof. The result is that highly functional rectangular spaces are located partially underground, while the above-ground level has fewer functional restrictions and its outlines could be more freely drawn. The placement

Onishi Multipurpose Hall, 2005.
(Photo by the author)

of the gym and auditorium below grade also means that the difference in height with the ground level accommodates audience seating. With building functions concentrated below, the upper level has no elements that restrict the field of view, eliciting the greatest possible effect from the all-round glass sheathing, the building's most prominent feature. And because of this, one can also easily see the interior of the building from outside, aided by the hybrid construction, using local cedar and steel, which permits large open spans between the supporting columns. Everything is visible. The administrative offices are in a separate building from the gym and auditorium, but the transparency permits maintenance and management without extra personnel. Gropius applied similar ideas to the design of the original Bauhaus building in Dessau (1925–26). Sejima's design also recalls the severe glass palace of Mies van der Rohe's Neue Nationalgalerie in Berlin (1968). But in contrast to the modernist love of rectilinear form, the Onishi Multipurpose Hall is a landscape of flexible, curving glass.

Glass spaces for the twenty-first century

I n revisiting the glass spaces beloved of the modernists, Sejima is not simply pursuing transparency. Rather, she is engaged in a manipulation of transparency to produce a variety of phenomena. By subtly adjusting the degree of translucency and creating geometric patterns, she aims at Op Art–style effects. For example, at the Mutsukawa Day-Care Center (2000) in Yokohama, the glass facade is printed with different patterns inside and out, producing moiré effects. In SANAA's Christian Dior Omotesandō Building (2003), drape-like acrylic screens affixed to the inside of the glass summon flickering illusions with their translucent gradations. The irregular outline of Onishi Multipurpose Hall creates complexly layered interior and exterior views through overlapping glass, incorporating distorted refractions of

Christian Dior Omotesandō Building by SANAA, 2003. (Photo by the author)

the lush greenery of the surrounding environment. In many places, the visual effect created resembles that of the glass pavilions designed by the American artist Dan Graham. The spaces between the buildings in the Onishi complex form what might be called glass corridors—though outside and unroofed, their narrowness creates a sense of being enclosed in a corridor whose ceiling is the sky. SANAA's Glass Pavilion for the Toledo Museum of Art, completed in 2006, is also a glass-clad structure sited in a park, but it goes a step further, in that most of the interior walls are also glass. In other words, even the individual gallery spaces are not shut off from their surroundings; other rooms are visible through the transparent glass, and the surrounding greenery can also be enjoyed. While each space retains its independence, it is connected with the others visually. The convenience store, or *konbini*, has frequently been mentioned as a new model for Japanese architecture since the 1990s. One of its key features is an all-glass facade—but Onishi Multipurpose Hall takes this even further into the realm of openness and transparency, as its glass-sheathed structure allows one to see straight through to the landscape beyond.

Architecture as landscape

Japanese residences and public buildings are usually hidden from their surroundings by walls or fences. Fear of crime has also bred an excessive pursuit of security that has intensified this tendency to create closed spaces. Onishi Multipurpose Hall seems to resist this trend, as it has no walls or fences. Like SANAA's 21st Century Museum of Contemporary Art (2004) in Kanazawa, the entire facility is visible from outside, and from inside one can easily sense the surrounding environment. This is not only because the structures are entirely clad in glass but also because their sites contain no visual or physical obstructions. The mutual permeability of interior and exterior—the literal "openness" of these structures—is an innovative expression of their public nature. Children attending the neighboring elementary school quite naturally cross through the grounds of Onishi Multipurpose Hall on their way to and from school. The day I visited, the doors of three of the buildings were wide open—inviting the children to play there.

Here, the buildings and the gently sloping landscape are not separate from one another, and this spatial continuity produces a profound effect. The 21st Century Museum of Contemporary Art also works quite skillfully with the topography of its site, which is located on a slope rising toward the famous Kenrokuen garden in the center of Kanazawa. In order to keep the museum from towering over its surroundings, a modest artificial hill was created at the lowest end of the site, which gives one the impression that the museum as a whole is sinking into the earth. The low-slung, concave roofline of the Multimedia Workshop (1996) in Gifu prefecture also makes the building appear to sink deeply into the gently mounded surrounding landscape, and creates a new form of access to the interior of the building—from the roof.

In the design competition for Onishi Multipurpose Hall, the building was described as "Onishi Indoor Plaza"; this image of an "indoor plaza" prompted Sejima's proposal to blend and blur exterior and interior. The competition proposal and the completed building are somewhat different in form, but the basic concept—a linked archipelago of free-form structures—is the same. The plan resembles the malleable blobs formed by grilled *mochi* (rice cakes). As you stroll through the buildings and grounds, you can momentarily lose track of whether you are inside or out. There were a variety of opening events at the facility—traditional folk singing, a Tai Chi demonstration, a calligraphy exhibition, a concert, and classes for the elderly. It must have been quite enjoyable to see visitors wandering freely among the structures—since the human presence would provide a sense of scale and distance in this remarkable new space, and allow one to more keenly appreciate how unusual it is.

A distorted sense of space

In Onishi Multipurpose Hall, quite interesting distortions in perception of space arise: people appear quite close at hand, yet are separated by a glass wall; or they may seem quite far away but are in fact in an adjoining part of the same interior space. You know you are outdoors yet feel as if you are inside; or conversely, you are inside yet feel a strong connection to the external environment. A labyrinth of transparent glass. When I visited, an adult ballroom dance class had just begun, and I noticed an unusual acoustic phenomenon. Because of the twisting outlines of the buildings, I could be looking at the auditorium from the other side of the glass and hear no sound—yet at the entrance, where I could no longer see the auditorium, I could hear the music. Near and yet far. Or far and yet near. A glass landscape unfolds, in which distance is distorted. It seems to me that architecture of this kind reflects the changes in spatial perception that have accompanied our digitized society. And by a digitized society I do not

Umebayashi House, 2003.
(Photo by the author)

mean one in which everyone has a big flat-screen monitor on their wall, but one in which mobile phones and the Internet have become ubiquitous, one in which someone sitting beside you can be a world away, one in which people can feel connected, even over great distances.

Sejima Kazuyo's Umebayashi House (2003) uses thin steel plates (16 millimeters) to divide its tiny rooms. These are unusually thin walls for anything on the scale of normal architecture. Inside, there are no doors or windows that can be closed. There are only openings. As a result, there are a number of rooms, but they are all simultaneously part of a single connected space. As in Onishi Multipurpose Hall, you can hear what you cannot see. So it is in essence a one-room dwelling ramified into a multiplicity of uses. As a result, while the individual rooms are placed like drawers in a dresser, there is also a sense of spaciousness. And what you see through the openings is transformed by the thinness of the walls into something strangely removed from reality—even though it is literally the next room, it seems almost like a video image of something far away. Here, too, the sense of distance is altered into something quite different from reality.

Toyota Aizuma Hall, 2010.
(Photo by the author)

Taking the experiment of the Onishi Multipurpose Hall into the vertical dimension, Sejima's Toyota Aizuma Hall (2010) in Toyota City is completely sheathed in transparent glass. Aside from the toilets, garage, and elevators, almost every room in the building is transparent. All of the rooms—small, medium, and large meeting rooms; Japanese-style rooms; practice kitchens—are round and completely visible from outside, though when necessary curtains can be drawn to provide some privacy. The double-paned glass walls provide a see-through sonic barrier. Even in the heart of the building, one can see the exterior landscape.

Another noteworthy characteristic of the structure is its amoeba-like irregular outline. SANAA is known for using innovative curves, but in the Toyota Aizuma Hall they are stacked three stories high, with the curved outlines of each level slightly skewed from the one below. This produces an entirely different visual and spatial effect from structures with rectilinear walls. For example, cars passing in the street are reflected in the glass in ways that elongate or double their images.

This is not an architecture that aggressively asserts its form. It creates spaces that seem to merge with the surrounding landscape. And in fact, the Toyota Aizuma Hall is a building that permits one to directly experience nature, for behind it lies the landscape of the Aizumame River. It does not create the feeling of being inside a building, enclosed by walls. Even inside the structure, one has the liberating feeling of being outdoors. In addition, round skylights and an ovoid atrium allow the gaze to move freely in the vertical realm as well. The theme that Sejima is exploring is precisely how free architecture might become.

Nishizawa Ryūe

An Architecture Beyond Images and Words

The camera obscura as subject

The camera obscura is an optical device involving opening a small hole in the wall of a closed room or box and letting in light from outside, resulting in the projection of an inverted image of the exterior on the opposite wall. The basic principle has been known for more than two thousand years; by the mid-sixteenth century portable models had been developed for artists wanting to sketch outdoors, lenses were mounted over the aperture and other improvements made, resulting finally in the capacity to chemically fix the image projected into the interior—and the invention of photography in the nineteenth century.

According to the art historian Jonathan Crary, in early modern Europe the camera obscura was frequently used as a model for explaining human perception and subjectivity and as a symbolic expression of the relationship between the positioning of the human subject and the external world.[1] "First of all the camera obscura performs an operation of individuation; that is, it necessarily defines an observer as isolated, enclosed, and autonomous within its dark confines. . . . At the same time, another related and equally decisive function of the camera was to sunder the act of seeing from the physical body of the observer, to decorporealize vision."[2] The techniques of perspective drawing only determined the relationship between an observer and a two-dimensional representation; the camera obscura transcended mere technique, giving birth to a special subjectivity in the relationship between an interiorized observer and the exterior world. In *An Essay Concerning Human Understanding* (1690), John Locke writes, "External and internal sensation are the only passages that I can find of knowledge to the understanding. These alone, as far as I can discover, are the windows by which light is let into this dark room. For, methinks, the understanding is not much unlike a closet wholly shut from light, with only some little opening left, to let in external visible resemblances, or ideas of things without. . . . "

The camera obscura might be said to be an architecturally structured model. Four walls and a roof are needed to enclose the interior, so that it may be darkened. But it cannot be completely sealed off. A window must admit light (and for that matter, an entrance must permit access by the observer). So it is a box with holes punched into it. In a sense, perhaps the most basic architectural model. Certainly more than modern architecture, which can be sheathed entirely in glass, premodern architecture in the West, in which masonry construction allowed only a limited number of windows and also restricted their size, is closer to the model of the camera obscura. Someone once asked Frank Gehry what the difference was between architecture and art, and he replied, "Architecture has windows. Art doesn't." In architecture, there must be an interior space that communicates with the outside world.

The architect Kuma Kengo has said that in architecture "windows are holes for the subject to view the object."[3] In other words, the subject enters the interior of a structure, and observes what is outside as objects. Strictly speaking, in a camera obscura one is not looking directly at the outside world through a hole but viewing an image of the exterior projected onto a wall. This makes it slightly different from an ordinary building. But the art theorist Beatriz Colomina has pointed out the structural homology between modern architecture (as epitomized in the home) and the camera.[4] According to her, Le Corbusier was a visually oriented person who said, "I have lived only through what I see." In his residences, the windows functioned as cameras, capturing images of the landscape; living in one of his houses was to "live inside a camera."

The Weekend House as model

I would like to analyze the Weekend House (1998), which Nishizawa Ryūe designed as an individual, in the context of the foregoing observations—because I think in this project Nishizawa is attempting to shift and deconstruct the model of the camera obscura that has dominated architecture from modernism onward.

Weekend House, as the name suggests, is a weekend getaway nestled in the midst of a forest. The overall structure is a simple square, 13 meters on each side. It has a flat roof, giving it the appearance of a low-slung black box dropped into a natural setting. There are scarcely any windows in the exterior walls, which are clad in Galvalume steel sheeting, sealing it off from outside. The client asked for the windows to be kept to a minimum for security purposes, as the house is located in an area that is usually deserted at night, so large glass picture windows were ruled out. Instead, by introducing three differently shaped atriums into the structure, the homogenous interior is given unique spatiality, and there are essentially no hallways or corridors. Light and air are admitted from these atriums, which are topped by sets of louvers that cast lovely latticed shadows into the interior of the residence.

Nishizawa's houses reject the idea of knocking windows in the exterior walls to bring the landscape into the interior. If we define the camera obscura as something that—like ordinary architecture—opens a hole in a wall in order to admit a horizontally formatted image, then this is a completely different model. Nishizawa says that when the exterior landscape "is simply visible outside a window, it actually increases the closed quality of a building."⁵ Instead, the natural world is subtly introduced into the dwelling from above, through the atriums. The surrounding greenery is reflected in their glass and projected onto the plastic sheeting on the ceilings of the rooms, multiplying the external imagery. These images further harmonize with the structural members and the finishing materials inside. Indirect, reflected images blend and merge with actual objects. Thus, while physically confined, the interior of the residence is given a greater feeling of spaciousness than it actually possesses.

Exterior and interior of Weekend House, 1998.
(Photos by Hosoya Jin)

Nishizawa says that in the process of designing this residence he began to think it more interesting to actively avoid making openings in walls. SANAA's M House (1997) does not have any clearly defined windows facing the street, drawing its light instead from a sunken atrium garden. This, too, differs from a camera obscura in the sense of a room with an aperture in one wall. Rather than providing direct views of the exterior landscape through windows, however, Weekend House prioritizes an arrangement in which the residents of the house can enjoy images of the external world drawn, along with the sunlight, through the atriums. This method of projection actually makes Nishizawa's design, even more than ordinary architecture, closer in nature to the original camera obscura.

Aoki Jun, comparing Weekend House to a camera obscura, writes: "Precisely by being enclosed, it paradoxically invites the exterior to enter.

Yet while a camera obscura brings the exterior landscape itself into the room, Nishizawa's Weekend House feels more as if the green of the surrounding landscape has entered, rather than any distinct images of the outside world. You don't really know exactly what part of the surrounding greenery you are seeing. It is more a feeling that the external environment as a whole has been brought within."[6] This observation that Nishizawa's residential architecture does not project clear and accurate images of the outside into the interior rooms brings up an important point: this means that it does not inherit the role of the camera obscura as a device for making an accurate and objective record of the world.

Toward dataspace

In an earlier conversation with me, Nishizawa made the following critique of video installations.[7] He said that he used to make extensive use of such images in his exhibitions because he thought at first that such installations were highly autonomous, powerful, and useful in producing certain effects, but that he has come to question their utility. They place too many demands on the exhibition space, making them difficult to use well. They are shown to best advantage in a completely dark room, which means that exhibition spaces tend to all look the same. And film is still the acme of such visual images; it is virtually impossible for video to better it in quality.

This statement of Nishizawa's is quite interesting. Film, with a projector as a light source, is shown through a small aperture onto a screen on the wall of a dark room. But in both his residences and his exhibition spaces, Nishizawa creates bright, light-filled rooms (camera lucidas?).

The philosopher Azuma Hiroki, basing himself on the work of Jonathan Crary mentioned earlier, has discussed premodern consciousness using the model of the camera obscura, and modernity using the model of the movie camera.[8] A movie theater is like a camera obscura in that the observer sits in a dark room viewing an image, but it is not a simple image of the exterior world that is being projected. Modernity creates a grand narrative behind the visible world (the screen), and every incident is imbued with meaning. In other words, from the superficial worldview of premodern times, which presumed an identity between the interior and exterior of the subject, we have shifted to a modern worldview supported by the physiology of visual perception. According to his analysis, postmodern worldviews are modeled by the computer interface, and what lies behind the world is merely a mass of data of indeterminate meaning. A new depth has been created, requiring manipulation by the subject to impart meaning.

Nishizawa Ryūe's solo show at Gallery Ma, *Kūkan kara jōkyō e* (From Space to Situation, 2002), evinced a worldview close to the model of the database. In the exhibition space there were not only no visual images—there were no models or plans either. The room was an empty cave. At first it appeared that nothing at all was being exhibited. There was no attempt made to control the exhibition space by closing it off or darkening it. The architect's designs were not on display—the point of the show was to record the phenomena arising when the walls of the room were affected by changes in the external environment. Numerical readings of temperature, illumination, and airflow taken at various places on the wall, as well as verbal notations on tiny irregularities and imperfections of the surface, were pasted onto the white wall in various places. A multilayered data overlay had been superimposed on the reality of the exhibition space.

A massive accumulation of numerical data can hint at the weather outside, but it does not directly represent that world. The various bits of data do not possess any intrinsic meaning, and provide no sense of spectacle. The data waits for the viewer to elicit meaning from it. Or perhaps one could say that the contents of an underlying but invisible database had been brought to the surface as a visible interface by this exhibition. Like what happens in the last scene of the first version of *The Matrix* (1999), when the hero Neo becomes the One and is able to see through the data with which the computers are creating the illusion of the world. If the data in Nishizawa's show had been shown on digital counters that continuously displayed the subtle changes in the environment, this resemblance would have been even more powerful. In any case, Nishizawa's exhibition space was an effort to construct a room that transcended the camera obscura.

Stripping away concepts to see the richness of reality

Charles and Ray Eames's *Powers of Ten* (1977) is a short documentary film that takes the viewer on a journey from the familiar scene of a couple relaxing on a blanket in a city park outward to the margins of our galaxy and then inward once more to the nucleus of one of the atoms making up the man's hand—transforming our perspective by zooming out or zooming in by powers of ten every ten seconds of the film's running time. Nishizawa Ryūe's design similarly demonstrates how a subtle shift in magnification can radically alter our way of seeing the world. Rather than amazing people with unusual forms, rich effects can be created through the manipulation of modes of perception. In discussing Weekend House, Nishizawa made the following observation: "If you zoom in on an activity like 'dining,' a number of different actions suddenly come into view. People raise their arms, turn their heads, yawn. All sorts of odd little tics and repetitive movements appear, to the point that you begin to wonder exactly what we mean when we speak of the activity of 'dining.'"[9]

Initially, the dividing line between a meal and other aspects of socializing may seem clear, but a change in magnification reveals that the part of a gathering we call "dining" is packed with such a multitude of smaller actions that the boundaries begin to blur. We divide up the world with concepts such as "dining" and "socializing," but examined closely, our various actions and behaviors are seamlessly connected. Or take another example. We think of the rainbow as having seven colors. But the visible spectrum of light is a continuous band of wavelengths, within which are wavelengths we might call "red" or "blue," but some cultures see only three colors in the rainbow or as many as ten. We must question what seem to be obvious concepts.

Nishizawa's *Kūkan kara jōkyō e* exhibition, by recording data on illumination, temperature, airflow, and so on at various points on the walls of the room, and evidence of minor damage and imperfections, demonstrated anew that the supposedly homogenous environment of the typical "white cube" gallery space was actually brimming with innumerable differences.[10] His installation for INAX Housing Forum 1 (1997), a conference of 100 architects in their thirties, was an arrangement of chairs on a strict grid that gradually dissolved into randomness, with the limitless variations in this process being one of the main points of interest. In other words, "grid" and "random" were not set up as binary opposites—for if we adhere too strictly to such concepts, a diverse reality is concealed from us. Looked at from a broader perspective, they are included among the limitless possibilities for the arrangement of objects. However, we have not really developed the vocabulary to name each of the individual states within this realm of possibility. Here, Nishizawa explains why he makes so many preliminary models:

> Form has by no means been adequately verbalized. It's a terribly primitive realm, and we don't have the language to accurately express its subtle nuances. So we make models, so we can look at these differences—make distinctions by comparing them—and decide which ones are better. . . . You might start out with two curves that don't seem particularly different, but as you make a bunch of different iterations you begin to understand the difference. . . . And through a gradual process of repeatedly altering the forms, what was once Model A vs. Model B becomes Model B-1 vs. Model B-2, and then B-2.1 vs. B-2.2, and so on, as the work becomes more detailed.[11]

Architecture that changes the way we articulate the world

This type of architectural design is not guided by previously established concepts but instead creates innovative spaces through the production of models and the feedback gained from the realities encountered in their manipulation. Nishizawa's plan for the Ichikawa Apartments (2001) is a simple rectangle in outline, but the interior spaces are articulated with a series of complex curves. The plan for his House in Kamakura (2001) abandons the common rectangle for a parallelogram with slightly skewed ends. Both of these designs seem to be the result of seeking something unnameable. Introducing a competition proposal for the new Tomihiro Art Museum in 2002 that featured a conglomeration of rectangular units joined at their corners in a complex pattern, Nishizawa commented, "There are a lot of spaces here for which the world doesn't really have names."[12]

In a large project for a private residence in Tianjin, Nishizawa accepted the standard functional divisions such as living room, dining room, and so on. Yet looked at from a macro perspective, the relationships among the individual parts are innovative. For example, although this is a luxury house, rather than creating grand spaces within it, the interior is finely divided into a large number of small spaces—a 40 LDK in Japanese real estate parlance, where a normal apartment might be described as a 2 LDK (two rooms plus living/dining/kitchen). Here, Nishizawa is not rejecting the LDK system so much as deconstructing it from within to reduce it to its essence.

In a Tokyo site surrounded by typical single-family houses and apartment buildings, the Moriyama House (2005), a collection of ten white boxes of various sizes, does not look particularly unusual. There is no surrounding wall, and the boxes are skillfully separated from one another by the breadth of a typical alleyway—creating a new landscape that simultaneously blends with the urban fabric. It is a very modern design, but one whose layout almost nostalgically recalls the back alleys and neighborhood ties of an earlier time. It is also possible to interpret it as an experiment in applying

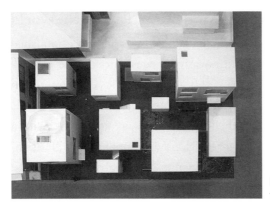

Moriyama House, 2005. (Courtesy of the Office of Nishizawa Ryūe)

the same formal system as the 21st Century Museum of Contemporary Art in Kanazawa—minus the enclosing ring and on a smaller scale—to residential housing. The project consists of the owner's private home plus five rental units, an arrangement that would normally be achieved with a single building, internally subdivided. Here, however, the units are not brought together into a unity, but seemingly dispersed at random. The result is a variety of different sized cubes, from a three-story house to a large-sized one-room apartment with access to the roof, and even a small box serving solely as a bathhouse. By ingenious placement of windows, a varied relationality is achieved: in some cases, residents may see one another; in others, privacy is carefully maintained.

Nowadays it is becoming common for a home renovation to retain part of the residence as the owner's home and convert the remainder into a rental unit or units. This is a kind of intermediate step between the single-family home and the housing complex, and in many cases the transformation is not readily discernible from the exterior of the building. One might say that Moriyama House is a clever adaptation of architectural form to these real estate conditions. At present the owner occupies three of the "boxes" on the property, but in the future he intends to gradually take over some of the rental units for personal use. The buildings are structured in such a way that they can be adapted to such changes. Another example of this type of evolutionary design is the Towada Art Center (2008), where white boxes of varying sizes are strewn across the site, each housing a particular artwork, and all of them connected by corridors of glass. This design might be seen as what would happen if the enclosing circle of the 21st Century Museum of Contemporary Art suddenly dissolved, freeing the boxes packed within it.

At Teshima Art Museum (2010), on the island of Teshima in the Seto Inland Sea, architecture and art are indivisible. Instead of a museum exhibiting works of art, it is space born of a collaboration on the theme of water by Nishizawa and the artist Naitō Rei. The outline of the structure is a free-form curve, like a water droplet, and its roof also describes a gentle curve. The form is quite unlike anything in ordinary geometry; it does not even seem architectural. Yet at the same time, it is not a sculptural object that asserts itself in the landscape. Rather, the volumes of the museum seem to have been conceived as part of the surrounding topography on the hilly island. The approach to the museum is impressive. A footpath winds around the lower slopes of Myōjinyama, affording visitors a breathtaking view of the natural beauty of the Inland Sea before entering the grounds. In the interior of the building, which the roof covers like a seashell, there are no supporting columns. Some 60 meters in its longest dimension, the

Teshima Art Museum, 2010. (Courtesy of the Office of Nishizawa Ryūe)

space is the size of a gymnasium, but because the ceiling is set low, there are no walls. The water installation is on the floor at one's feet. The roof was made by a special process: earth was mounded up to create a form for casting the concrete; after it was poured and set, the earth was dug away again. There is no door at the entrance, and the large oculi in the roof are not covered with glass. Rain and wind are allowed to enter; the environment is essentially the same as outdoors.

Naitō's artwork allows water to percolate up through the floor, forming droplets and rivulets that move about like living things—because the floor slopes almost imperceptibly. In other words, the water is reacting to the incredibly subtle interior topography that has been created. Meanwhile, the exterior of the structure forms an architectural landscape that resonates with the topography of the island as a whole. The water droplets on the floor join other drops and continue to transform. Look closely at them for a while and you can see in their form the model for the Teshima Art Museum. This is an architecture in which micro and macro resonate with one another. With no dependence on words, simply by altering the breadth of one's vision, the world reveals itself to us in richer guise.

(Nishizawa Ryūe was born in 1966 but has been included in this chapter because of his association with SANAA.)

Kuma Kengo

High-Speed Gamer

Bubble architecture and postmodernism

They were called the Towers of Bubble, in ironic homage to the Tower of Babel. When the concatenation of economic phenomena associated with the surge in land prices that swept Japan in the late 1980s had finally blown over, this was how local people mocked the high-rises and apartment buildings standing empty here and there all over Tokyo. Tenantless, they could only assert their empty magnificence; without ever being occupied, they became the ruins of the bubble economy. Kuma Kengo debuted as an architect in the midst of these social conditions. Taking a cue from the title of Vitruvius's *De architectura* (published in English as *Ten Books on Architecture*), Kuma published *10-taku ron* (Ten Discourses on Houses, 1990), in which he discussed patterns of client lifestyles and residential design, and then boldly laid out a classic postmodern argument for design, quoting from architectural styles of the past. Born in 1954, Kuma is a theoretically oriented architect who studied with Hara Hiroshi at the University of Tokyo; after completing his master's degree in 1979, he studied at Columbia University in New York.

Kuma played with the semiotics of Western architectural styles in a series of early works: Kenchikushi Saikō (Reconsidering Architectural History, 1989); Rustic (1991); and Doric (1991), which features a gigantic

Doric column at one corner of a building designed for a tight triangular site in the Aoyama district of Tokyo. With projects like A Small Bathhouse in Izu (1988), he also participated in the deconstructivist movement popular in the United States in the 1980s. M2 (1991), a building collaged out of bits of architectural vocabulary from classical to modernist, was designed at the peak of his interest in deconstruction. In the 1980s, Isozaki Arata's Tsukuba Center Building (1983) and Ishii Kazuhiro's radical sampling of world architecture of all eras attracted

M2, 1991. (Photo by the author)

attention, but M2 startled the architectural community with what is likely the most immense Ionian capital in the world. With a random collage of elements, Kuma created a chaotic spectacle that proposed the elimination of the subject in architecture. M2 also came to be seen as a work of architecture that symbolized Tokyo in the era of the bubble economy.

M2 is a building that consciously embodies a meaningless, empty monumentality, and thus serves as the perfect emblem of an era. The extraordinarily swollen Ionic capital, already devoid of any cultural context, floats nihilistically in midair, as if laughing hysterically at its own absence of meaning. This prodigious emptiness, like the hulks of untenanted buildings all over the city, is indisputably a product of the Babel of the bubble. According to the biblical story of the Tower of Babel, after the Flood there were still people who did not fear God and attempted to build a tower that would reach Heaven—which angered God so much that he confounded their language and made them unable to understand one another. This gives M2 an interesting double meaning, for it is both an empty tower and a manifestation of confused vocabulary.

Ionian orders, cornices, pediments, arches, aircraft boarding ramps, Leonidov's proposal for the Soviet House of Industry, a high-tech atrium, a blank rear facade, an Escher-esque endless staircase—all of the architectural elements used in M2 can be verbalized, making the chaos of this architectural montage all the more apparent. Yet at the same time this is not Lautréamont's "As beautiful as the chance encounter of a sewing machine and an umbrella on an operating table." Rather than an assemblage that should not exist on the same plane, this is an autonomous play of architectural language, a critique of architecture through architecture. Kuma was aiming to create a paradoxical space for discourse liberated from all of the constraints of architecture—meaning, function, scale, and so on.

In certain respects this type of architecture resembles the house music that became popular in the 1980s; with its sampling, cut-ups, and remixes, it announced the end of the age of symbols and deconstructed even the myth of originality. In M2 Kuma set out to destroy classical symbols with changes in materials and scale, rearrangement, shifts in aspect—a gigantic device that demanded a change in consciousness on the part of the viewer. A conceptual monster. M2 rejected symbolism but has been unable to avoid historicization, and ironically enough has come to symbolize the bubble economy era.

Kuma has written that architects, with their ability to pick up on subtle changes in their surroundings, are in the process of morphing into highly conscious designers of game software. The questions repeatedly raised in Tokyo projects such as Kenchikushi Saikō and Rustic paralleled simulation art and the economic bubble. M2 was of course the culmination of this, and at the same time can be understood as a turning point for Kuma— never one to be bound to a personal style—as he prepared to make the leap from playing with the language of architecture to the next game he would take up. The high-speed game player, Kengo Kuma, was aiming for a high score that would clear his way to the next level.

Erasing the subject

From the 1990s onward, Kuma bid farewell to postmodernist style and began to pursue the exact opposite—minimalist design. But what remained unchanged in his approach was the weakening of the subject. Kuma was now critical of object-oriented architecture, which stood out against the environment, and said that neither modernism nor postmodernism had been able to escape from that particular pattern. Taking a cue from classic Japanese architecture such as the Katsura Detached Palace as well as from Bruno Taut's Hyūga Villa, he proclaimed the concept of the "anti-object." In his book *Anti-Object* (2000), he identified a number of key words for design, including "connection," "emanation," "erasure," "line," "minimal," "reversal," "electronic," and "particle." This was followed by a series of proposals: to connect consciousness and materiality through the rejection of form; to fill the rupture between the individual subject and the world with emanation; to erase the pedestal of architecture; to minimize as a critique of materialism; to eliminate mass by dissolving it along the line of a route; to escape from dependence on the visual via digitization; and to deconstruct form by reduction to particles.

For example, the Kirosan Observatory (1994) cuts a sequence of staircases into a mountainside, while the Kitakami Canal Museum (1999) aims at a nearly invisible architecture, also buried in the topography, that does not assert its formal properties. Water/Glass (1995), built on a site adjacent to Taut's Hyūga Villa, features a broad shallow reflecting pool that connects visually with the ocean beyond, creating a space in which the viewer, surrounded by transparent glass, feels about to merge with the water. Kuma also noted the potential of the computer for erasing architecture. Project for a Memorial Park (1998) experimented with connecting

Kitakami Canal Museum, 1999.
(Photo by the author)

real and virtual environments by creating a sunken garden in which visitors could walk to access memories of the dead. And in a project for the Aichi Expo, he proposed providing visitors with interpretive virtual reality headsets for their walks through a forest, thereby transforming it into an outdoor natural history museum. Kuma has an acute sense for media: the November 1997 special issue of the magazine *SD* devoted to his work was accompanied by a CD-ROM of visual images, revolutionary for the time.

In his book *Makeru kenchiku* (Defeatist Architecture, 2004) Kuma proposed a softer, more passive model for architecture than the "victorious architecture" characteristic of the twentieth century, with its tendency to overwhelm and dominate the environment. Perhaps this was a strategy for survival for an architecture that had become alienated from society. In the twentieth century, public investment and policies geared to individual homeownership combined with democracy and Keynesian economics to respond to the global explosion of human activity with skyscrapers and high-rises and monumental architecture, but this model had already lost its relevance. Kuma was searching for an architecture that was not about enclosing space but which would instead throw itself open to the urban environment.

In Kuma's renovation of the facade of the Hachikō entrance to JR Shibuya Station (2003), he was highly cognizant of the jumbo digital displays on the QFront building and the 109 department store on the other side of the famous pedestrian crossing (known as the Shibuya Scramble). He replaced the nondescript wall of the station building with a facade of chaotically reflective transparent glass printed with ambiguous images of clouds. The architect himself took photos of clouds over Shibuya, digitally processed them into a dot matrix, and had them ceramic printed on specially layered tempered glass. The glass was a sandwich of three sheets: one sheet printed with cloud images in gray, one sheet with images printed in white, and a third, transparent layer between the two that separated the two printed layers by 6 millimeters, giving this apparently flat composition a subtle sense of depth. Clouds printed on glass; images of clouds reflected in glass; real clouds seen through transparent glass—real and imaginary images overlap and interact in complex ways. The glass walls are deployed as if cutting through the building wall, the remainder of which is used for advertising, and this juxtaposition is intriguing. From the exterior, one sees white clouds; but when you stand on the railway platforms inside, you glimpse the scenery of the plaza through the dotted patterns on the glass. From the 1990s onward, more and more commercial buildings in Shibuya have featured the transparency of glass, but it was not until the station itself incorporated it in this way that one became aware of how close the platform of the Yamanote line is to the plaza in front of the station. A little ingenuity can greatly alter our impression of the city.

Minimal design with louvers

In the years after the turn of the millennium, Kuma's extensive use of louvers and experimental use of materials became especially noteworthy, beginning with his "Nasu trilogy"—Nakagawa-machi Bato Hiroshige Museum of Art (2000), the Stone Museum (2000), and Nasu History

Nakagawa-machi Bato
Hiroshige Museum of Art,
2000. (Photo by the author)

Stone Museum, 2000.
(Photo by the author)

Museum (2000)—in Tochigi prefecture. At the Hiroshige Museum, the outermost layer of the roof and walls is formed by louvers made of thin planks of local cedar. The Stone Museum treats stone—which tends to be a heavy material—with surprising lightness by slicing it thin and by using porous stone for making the walls. Both of these buildings bring a digital sensibility to repurposing historical local materials for innovative design. And the Great (Bamboo) Wall (2002), a villa on the outskirts of Beijing, makes deliberate and extensive use of a flexible material in an architecture based on louvers of unfinished bamboo.

As he wrote in *Shizen na kenchiku* (Natural Architecture, 2008), Kuma came to harbor doubts about an architecture fixated on strength and power, and began producing a series of experimental works that replaced steel and concrete with a variety of materials—wood, bamboo, stone, and so on—used in innovative ways. Plastic House (2002) is a critique of the closed box of the twentieth-century urban dwelling, using thin FRP (fiber-reinforced plastic) louvers and translucent FRP walls to create an environment somewhere between the natural and the artificial. The clients were the photographer Rowland Kirishima and his mother, the writer Kirishima Yōko, and incorporated a studio and gallery. The ground-floor living room is all glass at front and back, a free and open space that connects the park across the street with the garden in back.

Plastic House is made of plastic, but not like a plastic model. The structure makes extensive use of FRP. The FRP, which is translucent and a very light green in hue, has an unusual texture, in between natural and artificial. The delicately thin FRP louvers in the garden are a work of minimal art, casting lovely shadows. FRP is a composite material developed during World War II. It is lighter than metal and does not rust. And while it offers the malleability of plastic, the fiberglass reinforcement gives it considerable additional strength for applications such as aircraft or bathtubs. In the postwar era, FRP was used by Charles and Ray Eames in chairs, but Kuma is perhaps the first to use it so extensively in architecture.

The FRP wall panels allow a muted light to pass through, blurring the boundaries between interior and exterior rather than completely separating them. A new method for backing the panels with trim of pressure-mounted butyl rubber enhances the sense of translucence and somehow suggests a warm atmosphere. FRP panels used vertically in the garden give the appearance of a bamboo fence. The staircases and projecting terrace are also made of thin slats of FRP that allow one to see the ground below, creating a slight sense of danger that makes one freshly aware of bodily sensations. However, while FRP may appear light and fragile, it is actually quite strong. Here, Kuma created an architecture that anticipated the developments of the twenty-first century, using plastic to create a new sense of space.

In 2009 the Nezu Art Museum in Tokyo, known for its outstanding collection of Asian art, reopened after renovation. The museum expanded its display area 1.6 times, but Kuma's skillful design avoided both an oppressive sense of increased scale and the incongruity of expanding the existing traditional Japanese structures. A refined architectural vision for the new construction was relentlessly pursued, with careful attention to the cross-section, making the eaves as low as possible and giving them a crisp and well-defined edge, as well as carefully articulating large planes into more finely divided units. One does not approach the museum directly from the front; instead, you follow a pathway leading along the side of the structure between a grove of bamboo and a bamboo fence, which serves to detach you from the surrounding noise and bustle of the city as you walk along—a unique approach, reminiscent of the garden path leading to a traditional teahouse.

A louvered design presenting a graceful accumulation of slender lines—as seen in Nakagawa-machi Bato Hiroshige Museum of Art and the Suntory Museum of Art (2007) in Roppongi—became a kind of golden formula for success for Kuma. If cedar or bamboo were used as the cladding, then a Japanese atmosphere would be produced; if he was working on an overseas project, use of local stone would give it a regional flavor. It proved to be a convenient, multipurpose system. The Nezu Art Museum can be seen as an extension of this series of works, and in fact, as a culmination based on his past experience. Guided not simply by feel, but logically determining each detail, Kuma developed methods that could be effectively applied to all aspects of the design, from fixtures and equipment to lighting, umbrella stands, concealment of beams and joists, and so on.

The Nezu Café, located in the museum garden, is also lovely, but what is even more impressive is the extent to which the architect involved himself in the design of the galleries. In many cases, gallery design is sub-contracted to specialists in exhibition design, but at the Nezu Art Museum the display cases and lighting are part of the overall architectural vision. In the permanent collection on the second floor, there are galleries for Chinese art, crafts, and tea ceremony utensils, each of which has been made into an individually appropriate space in close consultation with the curators. The subtleties of contemporary Japanese architecture have evolved to a very high level, yet this may make it more difficult to be understood abroad. Kuma's designs, however, reject being pent up in the hermeticism of our island nation, and instead develop in tandem with globalism.

ADAPTING TO CHANGING CONDITIONS

The Generation Born in the 1960s

Atelier Bow-Wow

Post-Bubble Japanese Realism

Pop fieldwork

When members of Atelier Bow-Wow compared, at the same scale, the plan of one of their tiny houses to the plan of a house designed by a European architect, they discovered their entire house would fit into a single room of the European house. Even though they had deliberately set their hand to the design of tiny houses, this was surprising, even to them. Atelier Bow-Wow's work is inextricably linked to the Japanese socio-historical environment, so let's start with a quick review of the general currents in postwar Japanese architecture.

The American air raids and atomic bombings of World War II reduced Japan's major cities to smoking rubble. After the war Japan was virtually starting from zero. But as Japan entered its high-growth era in the 1960s, urban development proceeded at a breathtaking pace. In preparation for the 1964 Tokyo Olympics, the gargantuan concrete structures of the Shuto Expressway were erected throughout the city, and as if timed to coincide with Expo '70 in Osaka, Japan's first truly modern planned city, Senri New Town, was completed. These developments irreversibly changed the face of urban life in Japan. It was during this period that the members of Atelier Bow-Wow were born, and as a result they have virtually no traditional landscape to look back on with nostalgia. Dreams of the good old days had already been lost to war and urban development. Tsukamoto Yoshiharu was born in 1965, the year after the Tokyo Olympics; Kaijima Momoyo was born in 1969, the year before Expo '70.

When they were studying architecture in the 1980s, a Tokyo made delirious by the overheated bubble economy was awash in a promiscuous profusion of postmodern architecture. Starchitects were producing buildings with bizarre forms, gaudy decoration, and lurid colors. Many foreign architects designed buildings in Japan—even the theoretician Peter Eisenman, whose realized structures are so few. Young architects found that without much effort, large projects with ample budgets were falling into their hands one after another. It was a dreamlike era for architects. And then, at the beginning of the 1990s, the bubble burst. By the time Tsukamoto and Kaijima formed Atelier Bow-Wow in 1992 and were embarking on their practice, the ladder to success had been removed. So they developed a different strategy from the previous generation of architects. And that was to take a close look at Tokyo, just as it is. In concert with their university research work they began to investigate the city, and published their observations, not as an academic monograph, but as a pop guidebook.

Their *Made in Tokyo* project, started in 1996, documents existing structures that might seem bizarre at first but are in fact functional multipurpose facilities making effective use of limited sites—for instance Namakon Apāto (Raw Concrete Apartment), which integrates a cement mixing plant with a corporate dormitory; or Super Car School, which situates a driver's training school on the roof of a giant supermarket.[1] Such architectural oddities were a product of the exploding costs of land in the Tokyo area. This research is often compared to Robert Venturi's *Learning from Las Vegas* (1972), but it probably makes more sense to think of it in the lineage of the more programmatic approach of Rem Koolhaas and others. The radical advocacy of the program advanced by Bernard Tschumi was already being achieved in Tokyo. Atelier Bow-Wow, as if in protest at the way famous architects had been elevated to the status of superstars during the bubble era, conducted a serious re-evaluation of anonymous, B-class architecture. Their elevated multipurpose sports complex in Miyashita Park (2011), situated along the railway tracks in Shibuya, might be called a practical application of the lessons of *Made in Tokyo*.

In *Shuto Expressway Guidebook*, they pointed out that the expressway system in metropolitan area is the largest structure in Tokyo, and examined this feat of civil engineering from various perspectives.[2] In contrast, *Pet Architecture Guidebook* surveyed the microstructures—somewhere between architecture and furniture—that have sprung up in the interstices of the city, such as a real estate office with a frontage of only 0.8 meters and a depth of 10 meters.[3] Buildings like this, mocked as "bedrooms for eels" (*unagi no nedoko*), are a direct reflection of the land situation in Tokyo. Through the process of such research, Atelier Bow-Wow discovered a number of remarkable relationships between the functions and composition of a variety of spaces. Later, they would expand this urban fieldwork to include cities such as Paris, Hiroshima, and Kanazawa.

This research also spawned exhibitions, which traveled abroad and drew quite a bit of attention. This made sense, since they responded faithfully to the desire of Westerners to see in Tokyo a symbol of chaos and postmodernity. This was the diametrical opposite of Bruno Taut's vision of Japan when he arrived there in the 1930s and "discovered" in the simple beauties of Ise Grand Shrine and Katsura Detached Palace a sensibility resembling modernism. Sixty years had elapsed since then and Orientalism had reversed itself. It is also worth noting that Tsukamoto studied abroad at the École nationale supérieure d'architecture de Paris-Belleville (ENSAPB) in the late 1980s and Kaijima at the Swiss Federal Institute of Technology (ETH Zurich) in the late 1990s, and it is likely that this overseas experience contributed to their observations of the Japanese cityscape.

Residential interventions in the city

After 2000, the architectural world in Tokyo became extremely polarized. On the one hand, there was a rush of major development projects encouraged by deregulation; on the other, the general magazines were alive with stories of a boom in tiny house construction stemming from a trend toward repopulation of the urban core. In postwar Japan, a policy of aggressively promoting single-family homeownership had been favored over the creation of urban housing complexes. High inheritance taxes encouraged an ongoing subdivision of land into smaller parcels. These were the conditions that led to the tiny house developing into a specific genre in Japan. Big development projects became the province of major general contracting firms and foreign starchitects, while young Japanese architects set their sights on tiny houses—and the twain would never meet. Atelier Bow-Wow was in the latter camp. If the major realtors looked down upon the city from the penthouses of their skyscrapers, Atelier Bow-Wow observed it from the perspective of a dog prowling the back streets. "Bow-Wow" thus seems an appropriate name for the studio.

Tsukamoto Yoshiharu studied at the School of Engineering at Tokyo Institute of Technology, while Kaijima Momoyo studied in the department of Housing and Architecture at Japan Women's University before she also enrolled at Tokyo Institute of Technology—where both of them learned the meticulous approach to residential design of their mentor Sakamoto

Mini House, 1999. (Photo by Hiraga Shigeru)

Kazunari. Their observations of how space was being used in the city also influenced their designs. Although Atelier Bow-Bow got their start designing tiny houses, their perspective has never been limited to that—they have always been acutely aware of the urban environment. And they have continually looked for ways to take what are generally seen as poor conditions—such as a cramped and narrow building site—and reinterpret them in a positive manner. For example, Moca House (2000) actively utilizes an extremely confined space between existing structures. Their research method of looking dispassionately at the various elements making up the city has been put to advantageous use in their design work.

Ani House (1998) and Mini House (1999) paid careful attention to the placing of the structures within their sites to create generous spaces around them.[4] And by conceiving them as a stack of single large rooms placed one atop the next, they were unconfined by a floor plan, making each story an open and inviting space with windows on all four sides. Ani House calls into question the fixed idea that a garden should be created on the south side of a house and exterior space on any of the other sides is wasted. This is typical practice in Japanese housing construction—sites open to the south, the other directions are closed off in one way or another, and the house itself is subdivided into a number of small rooms. Instead, Atelier Bow-Wow conceived of the interiors as one-room, loft-like spaces punctuated with openings here and there that connected with the city outside. Taking into consideration the urban context in Tokyo, where development can instantly alter the surrounding environment, Mini House does not privilege any side of the house and makes it equally accessible from each direction. In a densely packed urban environment, this also does not give rise to a formulaic distinction between front and back.

Gae House (2003) is a tiny house in Tokyo designed to suit the lifestyle of the book reviewer Nagae Akira. The client felt no need to lead his entire life within the house; for meetings he could go to a local coffee shop; for research, there was the nearby public library. The house has three stories: the study on the ground floor, partially below grade and filled with built-in bookcases of brown plywood, connects gracefully via a white central atrium to the kitchen on the top floor, whose exterior is clad with sheets of silver Galvalume. Architecturally, the skewed offset of the large roof over the smaller box upon which it sits is quite interesting. Glass windows are set horizontally into the underside of the overhanging eaves, letting in soft light and a sense of the surrounding environment; they

Gae House, 2003.
(Courtesy of Atelier Bow-Wow)

might also be interpreted as a transparent portion of the floor. And conscious of the surrounding neighborhood, where hedges once enclosed the majority of the houses, the space beneath the eaves is apportioned to a parking space and area in which to plant a hedge.

Izu House (2004) is not in an urban area; it stands on a perfect cliffside site with an ocean view. Atelier Bow-Wow designed the house to encourage positive interactions with the surrounding environment rather than passive viewing of nature. The terrace projects out over the ocean, the bedrooms are configured in a stepped arrangement down the face of the slope, while a pair of artist's studio spaces hug the contours of the cliff. Atelier Bow-Wow's sensitivity to reading the urban environment carried over into this project as well.

Architecture with character

The 2004 solo show I organized for Atelier Bow-Wow, *How to Use the City: From Design of Tiny Houses to Big City Observation*, featured their first decade of work. Several full-scale models of Atelier Bow-Wow's signature works gave visitors the opportunity to experience first-hand the interior volumes of residential structures they would not otherwise be able to enter. The show was mounted in a housing exhibition space that had been created within the KPO Kirin Plaza Building in Osaka. Mini House was represented mainly by its first floor, with its upper and lower portions cut away to fit into the space, but House Asama (2000), the villa in Karuizawa, was included in its entirety. In short, Atelier Bow-Wow's houses are small enough that several could fit into the exhibition space. The material used for these models was mosquito netting—light enough to be delivered by parcel post. Although they are tiny as houses, they are actually quite large as mosquito nets.

One of the characteristics of Atelier Bow-Wow's works is their porousness, their openness in all directions. In the exhibition, video screens and interpretive panels were installed on the walls and the windows of the recreated houses, introducing selections from their urban field research and interventions in public space. In other words, the centerpiece of the exhibit consisted of houses with many windows, through which visitors could gaze upon Atelier Bow-Wow's mandala of urban life. Another part of the installation featured a revolving display of 1/100th-scale models of all of their buildings, set on a revolving turntable. This was intended to encourage visitors to see the work as 360-degree design, viewable from any angle, and without a predetermined "front" or "back." Atelier Bow-Wow's architecture brings a breath of fresh air to the proliferation of closed spaces seemingly inspired by the excessive concern with security issues in contemporary society.

Like Mikan Gumi, Atelier Bow-Wow is an architectural practice that enlivens the art gallery scene. Atelier Bow-Wow contributed to the design of the exhibition space for the Yokohama Triennale in 2005; for the Echigo-Tsumari Art Triennale in 2003, they designed the White Limousine Yatai—a white-painted food cart of unusually long and thin proportions,

White Limousine Yatai, 2003.
(Courtesy of Atelier Bow-Wow)

Furnicycles at the Shanghai Biennale, 2002.
(Courtesy of Atelier Bow-Wow)

which can be seen as a small work of rolling architecture; and for the
BankART Life exhibition, also in 2003, they contributed a pavilion—for
which visitors could make reservations to spend the night—outfitted with
a linked series of *kotatsu* (the low heated tables traditionally used in the
winter in Japanese homes). These art projects might also be described as
small, humorous architectural works. Thus, Atelier Bow-Wow has participated in a variety of art events, developing an extensive network of contacts with artists of their generation. They have designed a house for an
editor of art publications, and are good friends with Honma Takashi, who
has photographed much of their residential architecture.

Atelier Bow-Wow is acutely sensitive to the urban landscape. For the
Shanghai Biennale in 2002, they made a set of Furnicycles—hybrids of
bicycles and furniture—inspired by the vibrant street life they observed
in Shanghai, where the streets are often the place for sharing meals and
other social encounters. And for an installation at Spiral in Aoyama in
2005 they constructed a bizarre globe covered with relief renderings of
neighborhoods in Tokyo and in Spain, highlighting the difference in their
streetscapes. In their designs, Atelier Bow-Wow has never aimed at the
beautiful refinement of modernist residential architecture divorced from
its surroundings. Their architecture is always conscious of the city. Yet
at the same time it is not like that of Kikutake Kiyonori or Andō Tadao,

bravely battling with the urban environment. But neither does it attempt, like the architecture of the romantic Hara Hiroshi, to embed an urban cosmology in the interior of a residence. Instead, it deciphers the surrounding environment, and contemplating its structuring of space, embraces the city and opens itself to it. Their tiny houses—like Mini House, designed in part for a Mini Cooper to be parked there, or Gae House, designed to meet the needs of a professional writer—are examples of architecture with a lot of character. Perhaps you could say that rather than being an unapproachable, elegant beauty, they seem more like the cute girl next door.

Atelier Bow-Wow's other buildings, like their houses, have a lot of character. MB-1 (Mado Building, 2006), conscious of the many windows of other buildings surrounding the site, has been provided with a plethora of windows of its own—hence its name (*mado* = window). The building is a polyhedron, and the windows and walls form a checkerboard pattern over all of its faces. This design gives the building such a strong character that even tipped over on its side it would still work as an architectural form. It is shoehorned tightly into the front portion of a triangular lot, reminiscent of a number of the buildings that Atelier Bow-Wow documented in their *Pet Architecture Guidebook*. The increased scale does not diminish the character present in such structures. It is sort of like the monsters in a TV show that are of human scale on first appearance but in the latter half of the program morph into giants.

Strategies for a generation born too late

It has been said that large public plazas are more difficult to create in Japanese cities than in the West. Because of this, Atelier Bow-Wow has proposed small-scale public spaces as part of the environment surrounding street-corner food carts and tiny houses. The first full-scale public facility they had a hand in designing was the Hanamidori Cultural Center (2005) in Shōwa Memorial Park in Tachikawa. Up to this point their

Hanamidori Cultural Center, 2005. Principal Concept: Suzuki Masakazu and Kaijima Momoyo; Architects: Hanamidori Cultural Center Architectural Design Team; Cooperation: Atelier Bow-Wow. (Photo courtesy of Atelier Bow-Wow)

efforts at public spaces had been something like guerrilla operations, but the Tachikawa project involved the creation of a major public structure and landscaping. The center building itself is of generous proportions. The space is defined by a scattered grouping of fifteen large cylinders of different heights and widths, each one just large enough to contain an office, a kitchen, or a room for some other function. The space between the cylinders then becomes a multipurpose space that can house galleries, cafes, and so forth. Modernism introduced the idea of spatial flexible achieved by introducing movable dividers into a large homogenous space; here, the squat, immovable cylinders create a space around which all sorts of things can happen.

Here as well is a kind of aerial garden reminiscent of Miyazaki Hayao's animated film *Laputa: Castle in the Sky* (1986). The upper parts of the cylinders also serve as planters, making it possible to accommodate fairly sizable trees on the roof. The structural dynamics of the forest of cylinders supporting it directly determines the rolling topology of the roofline. Since the area in front of it is a swath of flat parkland, this undulating rooftop landscape is all the more apparent. When you stand in this green and floating rooftop stroll garden and gaze toward the city, the towers and buildings of the Tokyo suburbs appear on the other side of the park, providing a strangely blended landscape. Overall supervision of this project was by Itō Toyoo, whose Sendai Mediatheque inserted a contrasting New Age forest of undulating tubes into the classic glass box of modernism. But the overall outline of Hanamidori Cultural Center is also wavy and deeply indented, the influence of which assists the cylinders in giving rise to an effective artificial landscape on the rooftop. A hybrid of a roof garden and a public park. Atelier Bow-Wow's sensibility is instrumental in creating a new type of common space, neither public square nor street.

Tange Kenzō, hitting his stride in the postwar recovery, designed ideal modernist buildings and public plazas intended to provide a new face for a nation whose cities had been reduced to ashes. The principals of Atelier Bow-Wow, born more than half a century after him, belong to a generation with no direct experience of the war. For this generation, the necessary public facilities and infrastructure were already in place, the land had already been divided and subdivided, and housing developments sprawled endlessly into the remote Tokyo suburbs, where it was almost impossible to tell where the boundaries of the megalopolis lay. Precisely because of this, they hit upon a methodology that involved learning how to decipher, adapt, and customize the built environment they had been handed. In the late 1990s, the critics Alexander Tzonis and Liane Lefaivre coined the term "Dirty Realism" to refer to methods of effectively designing architecture to adapt to the attributes of less than ideal sites.[5] One could easily speak of Atelier Bow-Wow as the Japanese version of this approach.

Of course, this approach is not immune to criticism. Older architects and critics take Atelier Bow-Wow's architecture to task for merely affirming the status quo, or losing track of larger concepts while getting bogged down in playing with minor details. I must admit that when *Made in Tokyo* was first published, I was struck by the lack of overt social criticism and irritated by the relentlessly cheery pop tone of it all.[6] But as I listened to later statements of theirs, I began to see their body of research as laying the groundwork for a future consideration of the city in its totality.

So I do not think that Atelier Bow-Wow is indulging in a total affirmation of urban life. But at the same time, they are skeptical that a utopia can suddenly and miraculously be created on some repurposed site. They have grasped the reality of the Japanese city, and have built a critical perspective on that understanding. First, thoroughly investigate the environment. Use whatever is there that can be used. Seek out any overlooked slivers of space. And then introduce Atelier Bow-Wow's architecture to upgrade the potential of the environment. This is how they are trying, a little bit at a time, to change the cities we live in.

Abe Hitoshi

Architecture as Media Suit

Between form and environment

Abe Hitoshi is an architect of such talent that even if he confined himself solely to formal pursuits he would be successful. When examined in terms of form, materials, texture, and color, his various projects evince a strong and consistent authorial voice. Yet it is not only the "hard" side of his profession that interests him—in his home base of Sendai he has engaged in events and workshops with local residents and collaborations with the architectural planner Onoda Yasuaki intended to draw people into considerations of the "soft" issue of how we should utilize space. Asked in an interview if an architect was a person who makes a box to contain space, he replied, "We are the people who discover the possibilities of that box."[1] And it was Abe who proposed, in the days after the completion of the glorious box of the Sendai Mediatheque, the Sendai Design League competition that has become a rite of spring for students of architecture across the country. He has renovated an empty warehouse in the Oroshi-machi district of the city as the headquarters for his activities. It does not merely function as the office for his architectural practice—the generous light-filled space with its large atrium is also used for lectures, parties, and other events, bringing a lively feeling of human activity to a warehouse district otherwise deserted at night. Abe is an architect making a practice of moving from building boxes to making things happen.

Even with regard to the sculptural aspects of architecture, he does not fall into a manipulation of form for form's sake; he values a process in which the design is informed by a careful reading of the various conditions and factors presented by the surrounding environment. The result might perhaps be described as geometries that blend formalism with contextualism. His designs for Yomiuri Media Miyagi Guesthouse (1997) and the Japanese restaurant Setsugetsuka (1999) were grounded in this type of thinking. Abe sees form as a way to mediate between interior and exterior. In other words, architecture is a medium between human beings and their environment. Its form should be mutable and even mobile, in response to its situation. A box does not have to be merely hardware—we can perhaps conceive of it as having the potential to be software as well.

Miyagi Stadium (2000), designed by Abe in collaboration with the architect Haryū Shōichi and his office, was a facility built to host the 2002 FIFA World Cup cosponsored by Japan and Korea, which readers may remember as the venue for Turkey's dramatically narrow loss in the semifinals. After graduating from Tōhoku University, Abe studied at Southern California Institute of Architecture (SCI-Arc) and began working in the Los Angeles offices of Coop Himmelblau. He used his success in winning the competition for Miyagi Stadium as an opportunity to return to Japan and make Sendai his base of operations. So his debut as an architect

Miyagi Stadium, 2000.
(Photo by Atsumi Shun'ichi)

in Japan was a sudden leap to a major stadium project after a few smaller commercial projects in the late 1990s. It was a rather different launch of a career than is common in Japan, where architects tend to slowly step up into the big leagues after a series of small residential projects, including their own homes.

The outstanding design feature of Miyagi Stadium is its utilization of the surrounding topography. Here, too, the form of the structure is defined as a mediation between disparate elements. The typical stadium is built as an almost violently immense bowl completely closed to the exterior. It exists as an alien presence confronting the surrounding neighborhood. But Abe took the gentle hill existing on the site and proposed it as the centerpiece of open parkland into which the stadium would be embedded. This allowed the slope of the hillside itself to be used for rear bleacher seating, topped by a roofline that also appears to be a continuation of the hill itself. In contrast, the main stands describe a large and elegant arc, with dynamically sculpted concrete supporting piers where it meets the ground. In other words, the stadium combines elements that are open to the exterior with elements that enclose the interior. And the way the two differently shaped roofs of the two sections come together has been favorably interpreted as resembling the iconic helmet of the feudal lord Date Masamune, a symbol of the city of Sendai.

Miyagi Stadium skillfully integrates a natural hillside with a manmade structure. The Romans built theaters and stadiums as completely artificial structures set on flat land, while the Greeks used the slope of natural hillsides as backdrops for their amphitheaters. Miyagi Stadium fuses both traditions. Abe carefully read the topography of the site, but also labored attentively with the geometries of construction. Projects such as this tend to fall into timid designs that bow too readily to the environment, or else radical experiments in form that ignore their surroundings almost completely. But in Miyagi Stadium, Abe succeeds in harmonizing these conflicting tendencies.

Architecture as a medium

A wareness of architecture as a medium is something that can be seen even in Abe's earliest projects. For example, in an installation piece called *Blob* (1988), made during his time at SCI-Arc in California, the body is wrapped in a thin, transparent plastic membrane, expanding the personal domain by fusing it with a second, artificial skin. *B-Mask* (1988) involved walking the streets of the city while wearing a black spherical apparatus on the head—another piece that questions the relationship between the body and the environment. The *Blob* experiment is reminiscent of Mori Mariko's performance pieces in Shibuya and Shanghai using transparent body capsules (1995–97); like them, Abe's projects are probably closer to contemporary art than architecture.

Abe's early projects also show the influence of Coop Himmelblau, the architectural firm where he worked at the time. In its early years Coop Himmelblau engaged in a variety of radical projects resembling contemporary performance art. Their *Villa Rosa* (1968) had spherical rooms in which one could immerse oneself in a spiritual realm. Taking inspiration from Leonardo da Vinci's drawing of *Vitruvian Man*, with its overlay of classical architectural geometries on the human body, they proposed something called *Pneumatic Man*—in which an air-filled membrane expanded the spatial dimensions of the human body.

Archigram, a British design firm that attracted considerable attention in the 1960s, also conceived of projects that involved mobile architecture or clothing that could expand into housing. Abe has inherited the experimental design ethos of this

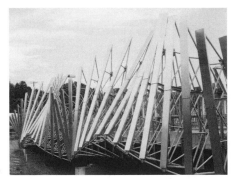

Shirasagi Bridge, 1994.
(Photo by Atsumi Shun'ichi)

earlier social activist generation. His installation *FA-1* (1995) deconstructs a set of cubes of identical size—2 square meters on each face—to create a structure in which each unit could be altered to transform the whole. XXBOX (1993–95) is a proposal for a system of hypothetical spatial units that can be reassembled like a set of Lego blocks. Shirasagi Bridge (1994), with its waveform railings, and Land Pack (1997) are also designs that capture a movable or malleable form at a single moment of rest.

Abe has this to say: "When internal and external forces press against one another, something like 'wrinkles' appear in both interior and exterior space, forming designs that human activity then overlays and alters—this is the image of architecture I always have in mind."[2] That is, he thinks of architecture as forms that act as interfaces between human beings and their environment. If we consider the subculture to which someone born in 1962 belongs, in addition to radical architecture, we should also think of the mobile suits appearing in the popular *Gundam* anime franchise, or the exoskeletal work suit worn by Ripley in *Aliens 2* (1986). And in fact Abe is known to be fond of anime and science-fiction films featuring robots and the like.

The critic Ueno Toshiya describes as "media suits" the mechanical devices used in science fiction to expand and enhance the human body. There would seem to be considerable overlap between this and Abe's architectural vision. For the *Virtual Architecture* exhibition at the University of Tokyo Museum in 1997, rather than presenting unrealized projects or renderings shown on a computer monitor, Abe submitted a product design prospectus for something called COMCO, a Hypernetwork Communications Tool. This was conceived as a portable device with both communications and game-playing features, featuring evolving characters and a compass for moving about the community. This was not architecture in the conventional sense, though it had forerunners in Archigram projects such as Manzak (1969) and Electronic Tomato (1969) that prophesied the transformation of architecture into media. Portable devices and games similar to COMCO have since been realized. Abe's architecture as media suit has activated new circuits for conceiving of the possibilities of the human body in an age of information technology.

Rainbow space, an interplay of light and architecture

The Kanno Museum of Art (2006) in Shiogama is an architectural realization of the interaction of forces. After passing through a residential neighborhood near the station you come upon a large cuboid structure of rust-red Corten steel on a sloping hillside, measuring 10 meters by 12 meters by 10 meters. The exterior is simple in appearance, but when you enter, a complex space unfolds before you. There is no sense of a first or second floor; instead, you descend into the building in a helical pattern through a series of white polyhedral rooms. This is not your normal architecture, with predictably configured floors and walls. Abe says that the image he had in mind when designing it was a box crammed full of soap bubbles. It is a private museum, designed for the display of eight pieces of sculpture owned by the client, and the concept was that each sculpture would serve as the center point of its own space, which would interact with the spaces surrounding the other sculptures to form a variety of different-shaped rooms.

The result is a set of floating polyhedrons in which you can occasionally lose your sense of direction, or even spatial orientation—you might call it a zero gravity environment. Particularly when you look at photos of the interior without any artwork on display, the sense of scale disappears as well, and it

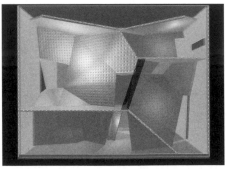

Rendering of Kanno Museum of Art, 2006.
(Courtesy of Atelier Hitoshi Abe)

is like looking at a scale model. In fact, the outstanding characteristic of this museum is the beautiful match between the forms and structure of the space. There is no back or front. In architecture, bold forms sometimes result in fragile structures, but in this case everything is assembled out of welded steel plates—as if the building were a life-size steel model of itself. Because of this, it has been purged of impure elements, presented as a new spatial model without losing any of its intensity. The Kanno Museum represents an important achievement in Abe's career—his arrival at a conception of architecture not as an assemblage of columns and beams, but as a space enfolding the body.

When the Kanno Museum opened in 2006, it featured an exhibition entitled *RAINBOW* designed by Abe. Despite being a show by an architect, it displayed neither drawings nor models, nor were there any 3D installations. Rather than monopolizing the walls and interior spaces with drawings or models, the space itself was configured to be shown to best advantage—by using light. The interior of the museum was transformed into a space in which seven colors interacted with one another. Seven special sources of illumination were installed, in addition to which color filters were applied to the spotlights normally illuminating sculptures and lighting the entryway. The illuminations reached beyond the boundaries of the rooms in which they were placed, sometimes infiltrating the areas behind the sculptures, creating colorful but illusory volumes. Where fields of different colored light overlapped, they gave rise to subtle blends and gradations. One might call this an abstract sculpture rendered in particles of light.

RAINBOW was not a static display. Three of the illumination sources were equipped with automatic controls, altering the direction and intensity of the light from moment to moment in tandem with the movement of the sun. In short, an entirely different space of shifting light overlapped with the actual architectural environment. This was an exhibition that had to be experienced in situ; it was irreproducible in any other medium. Techniques of using strong sunlight as a means to emphasize the formal characteristics of architecture, such as those used by Le Corbusier, are well known, but Abe aimed at something more like a colorful "In Praise of Shadows" achieved through the mutual interplay of differently hued light. One can sense affinities with the stained glass of Gothic cathedrals, the architecture of Luis Barragán, or perhaps the lineage of contemporary artists such as James Turrell, but it seems that the effective manipulation of light as an intervention in space has potential for development as a new theme in Abe's architectural design. In that sense, this exhibition was not only an attempt to create a new experience for visitors in a space he had designed—it was also a step in the direction of his next work.

Having a solo show in a museum one has designed is a once in a lifetime chance for an architect. Abe Hitoshi's *RAINBOW* was not a display of movable models but a skillful realization of the inherent nature of the building he designed. For example, the white walls. Precisely because they are a blank canvas, his palette of light could shine. Then there were the embossed surfaces of the interior. Lit from different sides by different colors, the embossed depressions in the surface held both colors, side by side. It looked like a 3D image seen without 3D glasses. Using light as a medium, the spaces could be expanded, and made to jostle with one another—resonating with the basic design concept of the Kanno Museum, the box crammed full of soap bubbles. In other words, as expanding spaces pressed up against one another, their interaction gave rise to a variety of polyhedral rooms. The light also expanded outward from each of the illumination sources in all directions, with interference patterns arising where different lights met one another. These seven streams of colored light created another Kanno Museum within the Kanno Museum.

Enfolding space

Jōzenji-dōri, one of the main avenues in downtown Sendai, attracted a great deal of attention when Itō Toyoo's Sendai Mediatheque opened

Rendering of Aobatei, 2005.
(Courtesy of Atelier Hitoshi Abe)

there in 2000. The buzz was renewed in 2005 when it was joined across the way by Aobatei, a French restaurant designed by Abe Hitoshi. This was an interior remodel of an existing building; the exterior remained unaltered. Into a space occupying the first and second floors, he introduced an interior design featuring enormous thin steel plates bent so that the walls and ceilings were connected in a wavelike landscape. The steel plates were perforated with hundreds of thousands of tiny holes, allowing light to leak through from behind, and preventing one's body from feeling completely entrapped within an impenetrable surface.

If you look closely at the steel plates, an evanescent image emerges. This is an effect achieved by determining the pattern of the holes through computer rendering of a photograph of one of the zelkova trees lining the avenue outside. Depending on where you stand, you can see through to what is beyond the steel plate, and the overlapping of plates and shadows of people give a sense of movement and depth, an interesting visual effect. Although there are many trees, they are all based on the same photo image, which has been subtly replicated and shifted to create a diverse interior landscape. The tubular structures of the Sendai Mediatheque also harmonize with the trees along the avenue, but in Aobatei the zelkovas are transformed into a video screen enfolding the body.

At Abe's *BODY* exhibition at Gallery Ma in 2005, I heard a comment during a discussion session that was very revealing of his sense of space. In a conversation with the architect Fujimori Terunobu, who insisted that the origins of architecture can be traced to when people first erected columns, Abe countered that he thought the space created when people wrapped themselves in skins was also important. And in fact, Abe's graduation project was called *Urban Cave*, and conceived in a way that prioritized an interior space cut off from the outside.[3] Certainly, Aobatei was an interior renovation project with no columns and no exterior aspect—but precisely because of this it might be considered the beginning of a new type of architecture.

Abe Hitoshi has made an important contribution to the revitalization of the city of Sendai as a professor at Tōhoku University. He has had a very active career in Japan, including winning the Architectural Institute of Japan Award in 2003 for his Reihoku Community Hall. He has also received international recognition, and in 2007 Abe was appointed professor and chairman of the UCLA Department of Architecture and Urban Design—the first time a Japanese architect has occupied such a prestigious position at an American university. Once again Abe is shifting his base of operations overseas, while at the same time continuing to serve as an important bridge to the architectural community in Japan.

Reihoku Community Hall, 2003.
(Photo by Ano Daici)

Tezuka Architects

Straight Modern, or the Strength of Architecture

The communicative power of the hand-drawn

I receive many invitations from architectural offices to weekend open houses for newly completed projects, but the faxes I get from Tezuka Architects are unique. In addition to the usual address and map, a simple sketch in bold pen is always attached—something increasingly rare for architects these days. No fancy photos or computer graphics, but the sketch holds up well to the rather low resolution of the fax machine, conveying at a glance what they are about. Of course, their work has from the beginning been marked by strong concepts. But they are also good at conveying them simply and clearly.

The power of the hand can convey information without relying on the computer. Tezuka Takaharu had already mastered powerful pencil drawing skills in his student days at Musashino Institute of Technology (now Tokyo City University). Later, when he was working in the offices of Richard Rogers, a leading British high-tech architect, he was treasured as the "cartoonist" who could quickly work up a perspective drawing.[1] At a Tezuka Architects solo exhibition at Gallery Ma in 2006, the first room was occupied by a giant scale model of Fuji Kindergarten, set squarely in the middle of an otherwise empty space. This was not so much to give visitors room to peer down at the model as it was to make them feel the sort of space in which children might freely play and romp about. For a Gallery Ma exhibition, this was an unusually direct approach.

Tezuka Takaharu was born in 1964, Tezuka Yui in 1969. They are another husband and wife architectural team of the same generation as Tsukamoto Yoshiharu and Kaijima Momoyo of Atelier Bow-Wow. Atelier Bow-Wow debuted during a period in which major contracts were drying up, and so they began to articulate a post-bubble strategy for architecture. In contrast, the Tezukas were pursuing something more timeless, and do not evoke such a strong sense of their temporal context. And while Atelier Bow-Wow leverages the idiosyncrasies of Tokyo in their work, the Tezukas, though cognizant of locale, strive for a more universal architecture rooted in modernism. They create spaces with punch—modernism, straight up.

That the Tezukas would be different from the other architects of their generation seemed destined from the beginning. Tezuka Takaharu is the son of a man who worked in the design division of the giant general contractor Kajima Corporation, and from childhood he was surrounded by books on architecture. He lived in a house his father designed, and used architectural models as sets for playing with his toy cars. When he was still in elementary school he came across a special issue of an architectural magazine featuring Peter Chermayeff and pored over it until it fell apart. And remarkably enough, while still a child he made tracings of the plans of the imperial palace, related to a project his father was working on, and even had the number of columns committed to memory.[2] Tezuka Yui's father was a staff member at Dai-Ichi Kobo, a major architectural firm. So they are a dyed-in-the-wool family of architects.

Tezuka Takaharu always wears a blue shirt; Tezuka Yui's trademark is wearing red. They stand out at parties. Their two kids wear yellow and green. Like their architecture, their fashion sense is clearly defined. The couple has appeared on popular TV shows introducing young talent from a variety of fields, such as *Jōnetsu tairiku* (aired November 30, 2003) and *Toppurannā* (aired May 14, 2006), making them known to the general public beyond the world of architecture. And in fact, compared to others of their generation, they seem to be constantly at work on numerous residential commissions.

Rooms with a view

Here, I would like to discuss the work of Tezuka Architects in terms of buildings I have been able to visit in person. Soejima Hospital (1996) was the project that occasioned Tezuka's return to Japan from his work with Rogers in London, and its colorful street facade shows Rogers's influence, but the patient's rooms are designed to give them the best view of the streets below. Wood Deck House (1999) in the Kamakura hills faces and opens expansively to the surrounding forest. After this house was featured in the magazines, there was a steady stream of commissions for houses with mountain or ocean views. Clients intuitively understood the Tezukas' approach to design. For example, Megaphone House (2000) in Koshigoe looks out over the Pacific, while Roof House (2001) is designed so the scenery of the nearby mountains may be viewed from its roof. Canopy House (2002), a home for a food writer, has eaves and a deck that extend as much as 4 meters out from the sides of the house, with private rooms arrayed on the ground floor and the second floor dedicated to a view that immediately pulls the gaze outward. The sharp angle of the deck some-how reminded me of the *Titanic* in the popular film of the same name. By cutting off the upper part of one's field of vision, the overhang frames the landscape.

Wood Deck House, 1999, in the Kamakura hills.
(Photo by Kida Katsuhisa / FOTOTECA)

Megaphone House, 2000, in Koshigoe.
(Photo by Kida Katsuhisa / FOTOTECA)

Roof House, 2001.
(Photo by Kida Katsuhisa / FOTOTECA)

If you then turn around and look behind you, the irregular parallelogram of the floor plan creates a strange perspectival phenomenon.

The rooftop of Roof House is equipped not only with table and chairs but also with a kitchen and shower, making it usable for a wide range of activities. All of the rooms on the first floor have skylights through which ladders give access to the roof. The design of the entire house was premised on the clients' desire to be able to dine on the roof. Nor is the rooftop perfectly flat—its broad expanse slopes ever so slightly, a constant reminder that it is, in fact, a roof. Megaphone House in Koshigoe, located on a clifftop, has a trapezoidal plan. At its larger end, the opening (9 by 6 meters) gives the living room a panoramic view of the ocean. This sends a straight message that you do not have to be an expert on architecture to understand. It is a lovely space that feels as if you were aboard a boat. The seascape is reflected in the windows, where you can enjoy the play of light. One strong concept provides the rules, which determine the structure, permeating everything from the overall design to the smallest details. When I visited the actual site, I was freshly persuaded that this is in fact the correct way to do architecture.

House to Catch the Sky II (2002) and My Own Sky House (2006) are situated on sites that have no potential for landscape views, and therefore take a form that focuses one's attention on the sky, through a skylight or atrium. Like the artwork of James Turrell, the interior of these white-framed spaces changes dramatically with the passing of the time. The headquarters of Toyota L&F Hiroshima (2003) is an office and factory, but like an enlarged version of the Tezuka's residential projects, it has massive sliding doors and is open on all sides.

Serpents and rings

Tezuka Architects are not dangerously avant-garde. They have said, "All we want is simply to continue to do our work in a straightforward way."[3] For Temple to Catch the Forest (2007), the Kannon Hall of the Shingon temple Kanjōin, they were unintimidated by the religious character of the commission, and expanded methods they had pioneered in their residential architecture to the larger scale demanded by this project, without distorting them. I have had occasion to see work by students of the Tezukas in graduation shows, and they largely seem to have inherited from their teachers a craftsmanlike and straightforward approach to design.

Tezuka Architects was launched with a hospital project, and then for some time focused on residential architecture, before once again setting their hand to large-scale public facilities and breaking new ground in their practice. Their design for the Echigo-Matsunoyama Museum of Natural Science (2003) came about as the result of an open design competition

Echigo-Matsunoyama Museum of
Natural Science, 2003.
(Photo by Kida Katsuhisa / FOTOTECA)

that made news by having no requirements for previous experience in the design of public facilities. The jury for the competition included no local big shots, just a team of established architects (Aoki Jun, Kojima Kazuhiro, Sejima Kazuyo). In recent years, qualifications for entry into competitions have become increasingly rigorous, and it has become more difficult for promising young architects to make the step up from residential work to larger public buildings. Projects such as this one, which discover and nurture new talent, are rare.

The Echigo-Matsunoyama Museum of Natural Science, which the Tezukas designed in collaboration with the structural engineer Ikeda Masahiro, might appear to be a somewhat more complex form than their previous residential projects. The museum is 160 meters long, rising abruptly at one end to a tower 34 meters high. Yet the design, resembling a writhing gigantic serpent, could also be interpreted as a series of units like Megaphone House, strung together like beads, while tracing the footpaths that used to thread their way through the paddy fields in the surrounding Niigata countryside.

The museum rises like a mythical beast out of the surrounding forest, clad in Corten steel rather than scales. There are no projecting eaves, and the entrance, carved into the belly of the creature, gives one the feeling of entering a great serpent's womb. The steel cladding is patinated with deep rust-red patterns that harmonize with the greenery of the landscape. The museum has a dignified atmosphere, as if it had stood on that site from antiquity. When I visited it in the heavy snows of winter, both sides of the road were lined with towering walls of snow that seemed like layers of the earth had suddenly been thrust upward. The body of the serpent had disappeared, transformed into a tunnel burrowing beneath the snow. Through huge acrylic windows one could observe the layers of the snow in cross-section, a stunning scene reminiscent of a Romantic landscape painting. Here as well, one sensed an atmosphere that seemed to transcend time.

Fuji Kindergarten (2007), about fifteen minutes by car from Tachikawa Station in western Tokyo, was a project that came to the Tezukas through the well-known designer Satō Kashiwa. This was a project for a unique educational institution whose building was in need of renovation; Satō had proposed a concept for reimagining the building as an immense playground and handled the design of the logo and identity. The Tezukas' design for Fuji Kindergarten won Japan's most prestigious architectural prize, the Architectural Institute of Japan Award, in 2008. What immediately draws the eye is its immense ovoid form. And what is unique about it is that the entire surface of the roof is usable space. In fine weather the

Fuji Kindergarten, 2007.
(Photo by Kida Katsuhisa / FOTOTECA)

children can have class outside, and run about and play during breaks. Expanding on concepts originally developed for Roof House, this structure transforms the roof concept into a vast, ringlike play area—a roof deck for five hundred children rather than a small family. Moreover, the building encircles an inner garden, almost like a village around a plaza. From the number of children enrolled, I had envisioned a large facility, but when I actually visited, I found that an intimate sense of scale had been maintained. Children are, after all, smaller than adults, and the space was designed for them.

The interior of Fuji Kindergarten is very nearly a single room, with columns kept to an absolute minimum. There are no walls closing it off from the outside; everything is transparent, completely visible. When all the glass doors are open, the structure has the open, airy feel of a traditional Japanese house. While there is a strong formality to the space, the architecture does not force itself on you. It is like a ring floating in the air. When I visited, I was fortunate enough to experience the cheerful prelunch bustle. When classes were over, groups of children appeared out of nowhere and began to play here and there in the courtyard garden. I was invited to sit in the principal's chair, from which I had a panoramic view of the garden and could hear the voices of children on either side. From the ceiling, I heard the patter and felt the vibration of little feet scampering across the rooftop. This dynamic experience of the space, through all my senses, gave me an intense sense of the life that can be breathed into architecture.

Endō Shūhei

Geometries for Measuring the Earth

Architecture mingling interior and exterior

In the spring of 2006, I visited Osaka Castle Park when the cherry trees were in bloom. Amid the bustle of the blossom-viewing crowds, the three Halftecture pavilions designed by Endō Shūhei blended quite naturally into the scenery. Although they were newly constructed, their patinated surfaces gave the impression that they had stood there for much longer. The gently curving rooflines of one of the pavilions looked like a huge steel hammock suspended from the surrounding trees. The white cubic volumes of the structures provided a brilliant contrast to the reddish brown metal, while at the same time resonating with the white walls of Osaka Castle, visible through the trees. There were long lines of visitors at the public toilets and cafe. The pavilions had few functional constraints on their design, resulting in a clear connection between concept and form. This is because, like Endō's Cyclestation Yonehara (1994), a parking shed for bicycles at a rail station, and Transtation Ōzeki (1996), an unmanned rail station, these structures boldly address the most fundamental challenge for architecture: how to enclose a space.

By this point in his career, Endō Shūhei had already opened new horizons in architecture with a series of projects employing corrugated steel. Born in 1960, he graduated from Fukui University of Technology,

Springtecture Harima, 1998. (Courtesy of Endo Shuhei Architect Institute)

Springtecture Biwa, 2002. (Courtesy of Endo Shuhei Architect Institute)

completed a graduate degree at Kyoto City University of Arts, and worked in the office of architect Ishii Osamu before establishing his own practice. Although this was not the standard trajectory through either the University of Tokyo or Tokyo Institute of Technology followed by so many prominent architects, the powerful sculptural forms he achieved using corrugated steel won him international attention. In fact, Springtecture Harima (1998), which took the form of a coiled ribbon, was featured in a variety of media, and Endō himself has said it may be "the most famous toilet in the world."

Corrugated steel is a material more commonly used in civil engineering and public works, but Endō was not the first to introduce it into residential construction. Kawai Kenji (1913–1996) used it to build his personal

Kawai Residence, 1966. (Photo by the author)　Gen-an, 1975, designed by Ishiyama Osamu. (Photo by the author)

residence in 1966 and Ishiyama Osamu, born in 1944, used it for Gen-an (Fantasy Villa, 1975). A comparison of these self-built structures with Endō's own home, Springtecture Biwa (2002), confirms the unique characteristics of Endō's work. All three of these structures are wrapped in corrugated steel, forming a continuity between roof, walls, and floors. One way to think about these three well-known pieces of contemporary Japanese architecture is to associate them with different periods in traditional European architecture; if we see the Kawai Residence as Renaissance and Gen-an as Mannerist, then Endō's architecture is Baroque.

What does this mean? As an engineer, Kawai, like Buckminster Fuller, was less interested in aesthetics than in technology—and in imagining what industrial materials could do to create new forms. His is a closed and self-sufficient form. It is reminiscent of the type of architectural innovation through technology achieved by Brunelleschi. What struck me when I visited the Kawai Residence was that it was surrounded by a scattering of old cars with their engines removed. I heard that Kawai liked taking apart engines to study the mechanics of how they worked—but had no particular interest in driving. On the other hand, Endō liked building things from the time he was small, and collected car catalogues and sketched them.[1] He was first introduced to the use of corrugated steel as an architectural material when he read of Ishiyama and Kawai's experiments in architectural journals while a student at university.

Unlike the Kawai Residence, Ishiyama's Gen-an, while taking a similar form, has created an abundant space with a surprisingly dense accumulation of decorative detail. While somehow recalling traditional *sukiya* architecture, it is also enveloped in a kind of post-apocalyptic bomb-shelter ambience. In Endō's Springtecture, the closed ring of corrugated steel is sliced open to allow its drastic undulations to enfold both interior and exterior spaces. This interpenetration of inside and outside in a series of extreme convexities and concavities is a hallmark of the Baroque. But in Baroque architecture, this effect was largely limited to the plan; in Endō's work it is developed into elevation and section, merging environment and architecture in a startling way. Endō has invented a new spatial form and expresses it clearly, without concealment. Once seen, such forms are impossible to forget.

The subtle curves of the Information Age

Roof design is a key feature of Endō's work. In traditional Japanese architecture, roof design has often been seen as a hallmark of regional character. And this is reasonable, for in fact climatic conditions such as sunlight and rainfall have exerted significant influence on the forms taken by roofs in different parts of the country. In Asia, where the majority of structures have traditionally been built with wood, the form and shape of the roof has probably been the most prominent feature in the exterior appearance of most architecture. Precisely because of this, modernism, which sought to become an international style, rejected the roof as an iconic form. Japanese modernist architecture also eliminated the characteristic silhouettes of traditional rooflines, aiming instead for flat roofs. In effect, this allowed them to replace a pitched roof with a flat one, sitting atop the building like another floor. In contrast, Endō has revived the roof, but unlike postmodernist architects such as Philip Johnson and Ishii Kazuhiro (1944–2015), he does not directly quote traditional roof designs as symbols. Instead, using the roof as his axis, he has reconfigured its relationship to the walls and other elements of the structure.

Halftecture Ōsakajō Ōtemae (2005), Halftecture Ōsakajō Jōnan (2005), and Halftecture Ōsakajō Resthouse (2006) continue the attention to roof design characteristic of Endō's work, but they initiate a new trajectory for him.

In the eighteenth century, the English artist William Hogarth classified lines into a variety of types: straight lines, distinguished only by length; curved lines, determined by a combination of length and degree of curvature; waving lines, which like the stems of plants, have points at which the curve runs in the opposite direction; and serpentine (S-shaped) lines, which he judged to be of the highest order and the most beautiful. While this was not a discourse on architecture, when we apply these same principles to Endō's work, we can see he make comprehensive use of all three

Halftecture Ōsakajō Ōtemae, 2005.
(Courtesy of Endo Shuhei Architect Institute)

types of line. Healtecture Komori (1996) combines curves of different radiuses with ogee, or reflexive curves. In *Terimukuri* (2000), Tateiwa Jirō writes that the ogee curves of *terimukuri* roofs, with their smooth continuity of convexities and concavities, are a distinctive feature of Japanese architecture that are intended to embrace and calm disorder, invigorate their surroundings, and unite disparate elements in a continuous cycle. Springtecture Harima unfolds in a spiral pattern. But in the project for Osaka Castle Park, the subtle curves are achieved according to a different logic. Their lines are influenced by gravity.

The architectural critic Reyner Banham wrote in 1960 that the First Machine Age of the early twentieth century responded to the advent of the automobile and motion pictures with the belief that only geometrically simple designs could be mass produced at low cost.[2] For example, the Italian Futurist F.T. Marinetti argued that the new age would be dominated by simple geometries—rectangular offices filled with rectangular desks with rectangular objects on them. And Le Corbusier recommended cubes, cones, spheres, cylinders, and pyramids as primary forms that enhance the effects of light and shadow. The Kawai Residence mentioned earlier was a radical pursuit of the geometries of this era. According to Banham, the Second Machine Age of the second half of the twentieth century was symbolized by small household electrical appliances (the television, the vacuum cleaner) and by synthetic chemical products. In architecture, decorative and regional elements were given greater attention than strong geometry. It was the era of postmodernism. If this is the case now, at the beginning of the twenty-first century, we have already entered the Third Machine Age. Or perhaps, since the term "machine" no longer seems appropriate, we should call it the Information Age—one that will be characterized by computers and genetic manipulation. The nature of geometry is changing as well.

Endō's Bubbletecture M (2003) is a series of wooden domes, but all of the 284 joints used in it have a different configuration. Computer-controlled fabrication made this building possible. The Machine Age demanded repeated use of standardized parts. And once upon a time, geometry gave a clearly defined order to architecture. But now highly sophisticated computers enable complex structural computations and are also transforming production. Endō's previous work mainly focused on combinations of circles and straight lines, but the Osaka Castle Park project involves forms that are defined geometrically but then sag and bend under their own weight. These are not curves arrived at by connecting segments of circles with different radiuses. In other words, this is a decisively different geometry than that of the classical era, with its ideal circles and squares, or the functionalist geometries of the gears and cylinders of the Machine Age. Endō is seeking an architecture based in new geometries.

Geometries working with materials and gravity

The original meaning of *geometry* is earth (*geo*) measurement (*-metry*). Thought of in this way, Endō's Osaka Castle Park project can certainly be said to embody a geometry that measures the earth. Gravity is the force of attraction between the earth and other objects. This is especially noticeable with Halftecture Ōsakajō Ōtemae, whose roofline curves in a way that is not achieved by the application of any artificial force. It is a form that reflects the gravitational pull on an enormous steel plate. (Etienne-Louis Boullée's famous proposal for a cenotaph honoring Isaac Newton, who formulated the law of universal gravitation, took the form of an immense globe, representing the earth). Halftecture Ōsakajō Resthouse (2006) also does not resist gravity, but receives it naturally, as one accepts the opponent's force in judo, affirming it with a slight bend and creating a sloping surface that aids in the disposal of rainwater.

Halftecture Ōsakajō Ōtemae, while taking seriously the tendency of roofs to express a regional character, is not tied to any particular locale—because the condition determining its form is simply that it exists on the surface of this planet (although, strictly speaking, the centrifugal force of the earth's rotation would create subtle variations depending on latitude). Or, to put it another way, different curves would emerge if the structure were built on another planet.

The idea of gravitational deformation was also applied by Ishigami Jun'ya in his Tables for a Restaurant (2003), though in this case structural calculations have been made to allow the tables to be constructed with a slight initial warp that is corrected to a flat plane by the force of gravity. Ishigami also created *Table* (2005) for an exhibition I organized: when you touched its surface, it quivered like a large, thin plane floating weightlessly in space. In other words, while using the force of gravity, it created a space that seemed to deny its existence. In this sense, one could see this as an extension of the modernist drive toward lightweight architecture. Le Corbusier's Villa Savoye, supported by pilotis, appears to be floating in midair. Gothic cathedrals are massive piles of stonework yet achieve a kind of dematerialized space. The ultimate dream of architecture has been to eliminate the sense of weight. Conversely, Endō's works express the pull of the earth.

A well-known form derived from the natural force of gravity is the catenary, the curve formed by a string hanging between two fixed points. As early as the seventeenth century, mathematicians argued that its inversion would form a structurally stable arch, and Antoni Gaudí is known for having incorporated this concept into his structural designs. The catenary curve existed as an alternative line of development for modern architecture. But Endō's projects do not employ such inversions to stress resistance to the power of gravity.

Rather, they are closer in spirit to *Cut-Off No. 2* (1969), a work by the Mono-ha artist Yoshida Katsurō. A long thick piece of lumber with a square profile rests lengthwise on the floor; over it are laid four steel sheets of varying thickness—the thinner sheets sag, while the thicker ones remain taut and virtually flat. The shapes are determined by the weight of the steel material itself. Yet they also resemble the melting clocks depicted by Salvador Dalí, and are accompanied by a certain impetus toward dematerialization. Ishigami's tables also make use of the characteristics of their materials, but this materiality is diminished by the application of veneer. In Endō's Osaka Castle Park project, steel is steel, and it is deformed by the force of its gravitational attraction to the earth. It is the acceptance of both of these aspects that makes these works so distinctive.

A ferry between modernism and paramodernism

Endō Shūhei has produced at least one project directly related to Le Corbusier.[3] In the late 1920s a battered old barge, the *Louise Catherine*, built in 1915 and originally used to transport coal, was permanently anchored in the Seine in Paris. It was purchased by the Salvation Army, which commissioned Le Corbusier in 1929 to repurpose it as a homeless shelter called Asile Flottant (Floating Refuge). It became a virtually unknown work in the center of Paris by the great twentieth-century modernist master. After renovations in the 1950s and again in the 1980s, it continued to be used as an emergency shelter, but it was shuttered in 1994 out of safety concerns. In the twenty-first century, however, a movement began to breathe life back into this vessel. Although ultimately unrealized,

Springtecture Asile Flottant Project, 2008. (Courtesy of Endo Shuhei Architect Institute)

this was a project to restore and strengthen this historic vessel so that it could accommodate a gallery and a cafe. Moreover, during the period of the proposed construction, the Asile Flottant would have been encased in a temporary shelter, also to be designed by Endō Shūhei.

The original Asile Flottant renovated the flat-bottomed barge, approximately 70 meters in length and 8 meters wide, into a shelter accommodating 150 single beds, a dining room, kitchen, bath, private rooms for crew and staff, and a rooftop terrace. From contemporary photographs we know that double-tiered bunks were arrayed like church pews along a line of columns running down either side, lit by long horizontal windows set high into the side walls. In fact, this project was intended to provide emergency shelter to the homeless of Paris during the cold winter months, and provide poor children with a place to play during the summer. What is interesting is that Le Corbusier saw the ocean liner as a model of modern architecture. Such a vessel was configured with residential and recreational spaces, a dining hall, athletic facilities, and so on. And the passenger cabins were functional, minimalist living spaces. A floating hotel. The first edition of Le Corbusier's *Vers une architecture* (1923) features a picture of the deck of a passenger ship on the front cover. Modernist architecture sometimes imitated the round portholes of such ships. Conversely, boat construction looked on land-based architecture as an ideal, and worked in the direction of larger, rectangular windows rather than round portholes. In other words, boats and buildings longed for one another, and when they got together, the result was Asile Flottant.

Endō Shūhei, born seventy-three years after Le Corbusier, proposed a project for wrapping the Asile Flottant in aluminum sheeting. Le Corbusier had a deep relationship with Japan, and was the architect of the National Museum of Western Art in Tokyo. Moreover, his office produced a stream of Japanese disciples, including Yoshizaka Takamasa, designer of the Japan Pavilion at the Venice Biennale, Maekawa Kunio, and others. Yet surprisingly, there have been no previous projects in Paris involving

Japanese architects connecting directly with Le Corbusier and his legacy. Perhaps Endō's project can be seen as a manifestation of a globalism transcending national boundaries. In response to Le Corbusier, who transformed the interior of a vessel, Endō proposed to alter its exterior, moving to a new geometry of curves. Rejecting imitation or copying, as Le Corbusier once did when challenging the conventions of the Beaux Arts tradition, Endō is proposing principles for a twenty-first-century architecture.

Le Corbusier's famous "Five Points of a New Architecture" included roof gardens on a flat roof. But Endō is an architect of roofs who seeks not a revival of the past but a redefinition of other constituent elements such as walls and floors. This might be called an attempt to disassemble Le Corbusier's model for modern architecture, such as in Maison Dom-Ino, structured around the pillar (piloti) and slab, and explore its alternative. Endō calls his approach "paramodern." In contrast to the postmodern critique of modernism, which sought to reintroduce into architecture the decorative manipulation of form, a proclivity for semiotics, and regionalism and historicism, Endō seeks to return to the level of geometry that modernism once worked with, and reconfigure architectural forms at their root. This is why he calls it "paramodernism"—a liberation of the diversity of suppressed possibilities contained within the modernist project. In the works of his final years, epitomized by the Ronchamp chapel Notre Dame du Haut (1955), even Le Corbusier began to make use of bold curves, suggesting that he, too, was perhaps in search of an alternative modernism. If this is the case, then Endō's project may be a kind of acrobatic inheritance of Le Corbusier's interrupted trajectory. A battered barge. France and Japan. A plan to build a ferry to connect past and future, or modernism and the paramodern.

Alternative modern architecture

Endō thus proposes the "paramodern" as a concept for exploring the possibilities of an alternative modernism. When I organized a series of symposiums for TN Probe in 2004, and invited Itō Toyoo, Aoki Jun, Nishizawa Ryūe, and Fujimoto Sōsuke to discuss "alternative modern" as an important trend in contemporary architecture, the discussion that resulted overlapped in many ways with Endō's thinking. In addition to proposing a reconfiguration of architectural form, Endō's designs also redefine such basic elements as walls and roofs. In particular, the attitude of returning to the level of geometry is something "alternative modern" shares with "paramodern" thinking. It is an attempt to escape from conceptual geometry and configure new geometries. This was why I organized the exhibition *New Geometries in Architecture: Toward an Alternative Modernism* at the KPO Kirin Plaza Osaka in 2006, focusing on the work of Endō Shūhei and Fujimoto Sōsuke, who will be discussed in the following chapter.

Architecture is the art of ordering space through geometric form. Twentieth-century modernism, while based in abstract formalism, employed as its major methods the straight line and right angle, the grid and symmetrical arrangement—and ended up trapping itself in boxlike buildings. However, in the Information Age, the introduction of computers has produced structures based on new geometries. The blobby, free-form designs arising with the virtual architecture of the 1990s had been tried before by offshoots of modernist architecture such as Expressionism, but were repressed by the dominant International Style. Because of this, Alternative Modernism seeks to reintroduce these ideas sidelined by the standardized modernist narrative. Modern formalism certainly did not realize all of its potential. In that sense, a modernism that might have been is finally breaking out of its shell. Endō is one of the architects who is making this happen.

GLOBALISM OR GALAPAGOS

The Generation Born in the 1970s

Fujimoto Sou

Toward a New Geometry

The last architect

In August 2003 *Kenchiku bunka* devoted a special issue to "The Potential of U-35," the rising generation of architects under the age of thirty-five. At the symposium held in conjunction with its publication, Fujimoto Sou (also known as Fujimoto Sōsuke) referred to himself as "the last architect."

On a panel that included three young computer scientists in the field of information environment, two structural engineers, and an organizational design specialist, Fujimoto offered the final comments. Was the architecture of the next generation about to plunge into a realm completely different from that of traditional design? Such was the atmosphere of the symposium, when Fujimoto began to speak, calling himself "the last architect." He spoke as someone trained in architecture, who in a time in which attention was shifting to things outside of architecture, nevertheless remained committed to the profession. A new century was dawning, and everyone and everything seemed to be rushing breathlessly toward the future, but in the midst of this Fujimoto looked back to the origins of architecture, one of the world's oldest professions, stretching back to antiquity. But his interest wasn't simply revivalism.

Looking at the well-known "Fujimoto mandala," which mixes examples of his own work with that of the anonymous designers of the Colosseum in

Rome and Hōryūji temple in Nara and the plan of Mies van der Rohe's Neue Nationalgalerie in Berlin, one senses that Fujimoto possesses an awareness of history transcending space and time. But this is not a postmodernist quotation of signs and symbols of the past. It is a parallel arrangement of past and present at the level of abstract form. In fact, because Fujimoto's buildings are not excessively dependent upon the latest technology, they could have been built in the past. In his proposal for the Annaka Environmental Art Forum competition (2003) the free-form outline of the structure was radical, but the design centered on the construction of the walls was suffused with the image of archaic masonry. Putting a roof on it probably would have required contemporary technology, but the walls look as if they could have been constructed two thousand years ago. T House (2005) is a one-story structure comprising thin wooden walls extending outward in a radial pattern, but I'd like to think that if someone simply had the idea, this was a design that could have been conceived in any premodern culture with a tradition of wood construction.

The late 1990s saw the emergence of a generation of architects—such as the members of Atelier Bow-Wow and Mikan Gumi—that were forming multimember teams of architects. Born in the 1960s, they were keen observers of the city, and working from the various situations and external constraints it imposed, developed an architecture imbued with a sense of everyday life. This attitude was inspired in part by their rejection of the overly self-conscious excesses of postmodernism that had been popular in the era of the bubble economy. This generation dislikes the heroic pretensions of big-name architects and their fantastic formal manipulations. Yet Fujimoto has a straightforward regard for the work of masters such as Louis Kahn and Le Corbusier.

Fujimoto and other architects of the generation born in the 1970s, such as Ishigami Jun'ya and Hirata Akihisa, are conspicuous for working independently. In terms of their general approach, rather than prefacing their architectural work with an explication of the surrounding site, they are engaged in a more direct attempt to grasp the principles of a new architecture. They are immensely interested in the experience of phenomena arising in a specific place—the way light is experienced, and the interaction among people. Fujimoto is the architect leading this next generation of architects. Born in 1971, he did not apprentice himself to any specific architectural office after graduating from the University of Tokyo, choosing the rather unusual path of immediately establishing an independent practice. Initially he returned to his home base of Hokkaido. In 2000 he took second place in the design competition for the Aomori Museum of Art, propelling himself into the spotlight.

Primitive huts for the present

In 2008, Fujimoto presented two designs as archetypes of residences for a new era. The first was for the Kumamoto Artpolis competition, the other was created for the Sumika project of Tokyo Gas. In addition, his design for the Children's Center for Psychiatric Rehabilitation (2006), which won the Japan Institute of Architects Grand Prix in 2007, proposed new forms for communal living. It might be noted in passing that winning this prestigious prize while still in his mid-thirties—when it is not at all unusual for architects to be winning "new faces" awards—was an impressive achievement for Fujimoto.

Kumamoto Artpolis, inaugurated in 1988, is a project that has received global attention for its role in realizing a number of outstanding works of contemporary architecture in Kumamoto prefecture. In 2005 and 2007, Artpolis sponsored design competitions entitled "Next Generation Wooden Houses" (*Jisedai mokuban*) that made valuable contributions to the discovery and nurturing of young architects. The concept was for the young architects to design vacation bungalows for a holiday village established by the local Kuma Village Forestry Cooperative; materials and building sites were to be provided by the cooperative and construction carried out by a local contractor. Fujimoto was the winner of the first of these two competitions. He says his Final Wooden House (2008) was an attempt to make the ultimate wooden architecture. It is a space achieved simply by stacking 191 massive lengths of cedar lumber, measuring 35 centimeters square in cross section. Wooden construction is usually done with very clearly defined post-and-beam framing. But in this case, the wood is piled up like stone or brick masonry. Log-cabin style construction similarly stacks timber to form exterior

Final Wooden House, 2008.
(Photo by the author)

walls, but Final Wooden House creates the interior spaces using the same method. The overall result is a small cubic structure measuring 4 meters on each side, but it is a tremendous volume of wood—even the door pull is a block of wood 35 centimeters square.

It gives the impression that the interior spaces were actually carved out of a single massive block. Across the river, which bisects the site, there is a cave called Kyūsendō. Final Wooden House is itself like a wooden cave, or perhaps a wooden landscape. It rejects the concept of the traditional interior, divided by vertical walls and horizontal floors. Inside, 35-centimeter changes in level create seats and tables. Previously, for his N-House project—a concept first developed in 2001 in response to Le Corbusier's Dom-Ino system—he had proposed a new architectural model that also did away with columns and walls, basing construction on the stacking of 35-centimeter-thick planes. Final Wooden House inherited this concept, but to even more massive effect. Inside, you climb up it, and crawl over it. This wild space returns human beings to some sense of their animal bodies.

Itō Toyoo was commissioned by Tokyo Gas to direct the Sumika project in Utsunomiya; he called upon trusted associates such as Fujimori Teru-nobu, Nishizawa Taira, and Fujimoto Sou to design the residences. Itō proposed "primitive living" as the keyword, and sought new designs for dwellings that would not be sunk in urban conformity but instead arouse people's animal instincts and reconnect them with nature. Itō's own Sumika Pavilion was an open structure blending into the natural environment but based on a complex geometric structure that elaborated itself from four pillars like the branches of trees. A computer-aided design system was used to give a contemporary interpretation to a space under a grove of trees. Fujimori's Coal House (2008) has a unique exterior like something out of a fairy tale, and also somehow manages to evoke a gaping entrance to a cave and nights spent huddled about a fire.

Fujimoto's House Before House (2008), the most visually stunning, is a house that looks like a set of white boxes scattered on the site. The individual rooms, stacked like a child's set of blocks, are accessed by external stairways or ladders. Tiny rooftop gardens planted with single trees extend from the second or third floor. At first glance this does not even look like a residence—more like a set of playground equipment mated with an ordinary home. And in fact, when it was being shown, the visitors could not help but smile at the experience of such an unusual space. When you

House Before House, 2008.
(Photo by the author)

Children's Center for Psychiatric
Rehabilitation, 2006.
(Photo by the author)

reach the top of the site, you feel as if you have scaled a small mountain. It seems possible that we once lived this sort of primitive, sensual lifestyle before the human race began residing in cities and before housing became so thoroughly standardized and institutionalized.

Next let's look at communal housing. The Children's Center for Psychiatric Rehabilitation in the city of Date in Hokkaido is a facility where children dealing with trauma live communally as they move toward recovery. What is unique about it is the spatial plan, which appears to have been arrived at by scattering twenty-four dice onto a table. At first glance it looks like a totally random assemblage of cubes, but in fact the positioning of each one of them has been carefully determined. They form loose clusters of six to seven cubes each, with a commons at the center of each cluster. The result is a village-like atmosphere. It is neither a large nor a small facility in traditional terms, but combines the merits of both in a space designed to support the communal life of about fifty children divided into three groups. One box facing a number of the others serves as the administrative office; not for surveillance but for discreet oversight by the staff.

Fujimoto has invented a new form of geometry, which appears to be random yet is meticulous in formulating interrelationships and creating diverse spaces. Perhaps it could be called a polycentric architecture.

Rather than an overall plan in which everything is determined from a central point, each box measures and defines its own relationship with the others around it—like birds flying in a flock. This facility is situated on a hill with splendid views of both mountains and ocean. Several other facilities have been designed by Fujimoto on this site: a family therapy center, a gym, and a dormitory—creating a kind of utopian commune in the wide open spaces of Hokkaido.

Hyper-houses and Columbus's egg

I will never forget the shock of seeing the model of Tokyo Apartment (2010) for the first time. I was dumbfounded by this unbelievable jumble of house-shaped boxes, large and small, stacked willy-nilly. This was in 2006, when I was visiting Orléans, France, to attend Archilab and saw the wooden model in an exhibition of Japanese architecture entitled *Japan: Nested in the City*. It stood out among the other works on display, with a form that was, at a glance, instantly unforgettable. Herzog & de Meuron's VitraHaus also stacks house-shaped volumes, and so does Igarashi Jun's competition design for the Aizuma Lifelong Learning Center in Toyota City. But compared to these Fujimoto had a better fastball—cutting

Tokyo Apartment, 2010.
(Photo by the author)

straight to the idea of stacking up houses into an apartment building. (Maybe others had thought of this before but rejected the idea.) This is architecture that works to transcend the concept of the house by piling it on. I must admit that standing in the exhibition hall, I thought to myself: *He'll never get this built.* It was architecture that made me want to ask, "Are you serious?" And I recall that in about the same period, when he and I were jurying a conceptual competition, he was prone to choose plans that made him laugh. Tokyo Apartment is rare architecture that both amazes and invites a smile.

There is no need, as with postmodern architecture, to reference deconstructionist philosophy or avant-garde art. Through a frighteningly simple manipulation, the familiar form of the house rises up as alien presence. But after being confronted with this new discovery—what is this?!—we can share in its obviousness. The feeling of surprise that Fujimoto elicits is like the story of Columbus's egg—a brilliant idea that seems simple after the fact—a variant version of which has the Renaissance architect Brunelleschi as its protagonist. It seems like anyone could have done it, but no one did it before—and the first to do it had a flash of genius.

After this, there were various obstacles to the project's realization, but thanks to an enthusiastic client, Tokyo Apartment was finally completed in 2010. That it did not end as a bright idea, but was actually built, is an event in itself. Not surprisingly, a comparison of the final building plans with the initial design at Archilab reveals a more compact building, occupying a site about half the size. This was due to the state of the real estate market and budgetary constraints, but the result was that the number of house units was reduced by about half. Tokyo Apartment is a Metabolist type of architecture based on these units, a design system that permits them to be added or subtracted as necessary. The scale was reduced, but there were still a sufficient number of units to clearly express the conceptual essence of the project—stacking houses—without the slightest loss of its integrity. It stirs the imagination. The external staircases and stairs to the rooftops have been realized. After you gaze at it for a while, you feel as if it is waiting for a host of similar units to proliferate throughout the city.

After emerging from the Kotake-Mukaihara subway station and experiencing the surrounding residential environment, it is still somewhat startling when you come upon Tokyo Apartment standing on its corner lot, but to a surprising degree it does not really feel out of place. When first encountered as a model, its formal properties as a discrete architectural object are striking. But surrounded by a landscape of nondescript residences and rooftops, with an old wood-framed apartment building and a small park across the way, it possesses a strange familiarity. Perhaps this is because the scale of the individual "house" units is appropriate to the general sense of volume in this residential neighborhood. Nishizawa Ryūe's Moriyama House (2005) experimented with ordering an apparently random distribution of cuboid forms on a horizontal plane, but it seems that only a design based on iconic house-like forms (boxes with peaked roofs) can really achieve this effect when stacked in the vertical dimension. In any case, what impressed me when visiting the actual site was that this was a type of architecture well suited to the clutter of the Tokyo streets, with their telephone poles and tangles of electrical wires. Contemporary architecture—at least that designed by prominent architects—normally abhors such elements. But Fujimoto's architecture is more tolerant, and accepts them with a grin.

The spatial composition is not rigorous or tight; in fact, it seems at first glance to be more or less random. That's Tokyo. When you enter one of the units, there are a variety of small apertures in almost every direction, including skylights, which are occasionally interrupted by columns or braces that obscure the view. Ordinarily architects like to show you some nice scenery through a large expanse of window, but Fujimoto is aiming for something different. These deliberate interruptions by structural members in front of what seem almost randomly cut openings overlap with the clutter of the streets outside and the walls of the neighboring houses,

Musashino Art University Library, 2010.
(Photo by the author)

creating a Tokyo-style picturesque landscape. Glimpsing the outside world from the interstices of this cluster of house-shaped units is rather fun. In the Musashino Art University Library (2010) as well, views and overlaps from apertures in the building were a principle theme of the design.

Using glass walls to partition off the kitchen and bath areas within each unit is another unique feature of Tokyo Apartment. This was suggested by the client, and it functions to prevent the "house-shaped" design from being broken up, even in the interior. Fujimoto's House Before House drops this house shape but resembles Tokyo Apartment in its compositional style, which is an apparently random jumble of white cubes. Where it is located in Utsunomiya, the relationship with the surrounding landscape is not very important. Both of these buildings excite some form of animal response in people, but there is something about the house-like appearance of the Tokyo Apartment units that offers some of the psychological thrill of clambering over rooftops.

Unlike a simple cube, house-shaped units have gable ends and a ridgeline that emphasize the different directions in which each unit faces. Modernism rejected this form of the traditional house. But postmodern architects, beginning with Venturi, rediscovered this form, and in the early 2000s, the shape of the traditional house underwent a second revival.

The postmodern period treated this "house shape" as a symbol and a product of history; in the 2000s it came to be utilized not just as a typology but also as a form for creating unique spaces and phenomena. Prior to this, Fujimoto himself has used it in different ways. For example, in Hokkaido his Dormitory for the Mentally Disabled (2003) in Date combines a series of peaked and shed roofs to create a rich variation in silhouette, the Vocational Center (2003) alters the pitch of the roofs at different levels, while his Family Therapy Ward (2006) plays with skewing a series of house-shaped roofs in relation to the walls that divide up the interior plan. Tokyo Apartment uses the arrangement of house shapes to manipulate one's sense of distance, aiming at an architecture suggesting contemporary, Tokyo-style communication. Regardless of the pitch of the roof or the materials used to build it, the form itself is interesting in the abstract. Yet even so, the arrangement of the house-shaped units and the compositional rules determining it give expression to the regional character of the surroundings, and furthermore present a spatial interpretation of the environment we call Tokyo. The house is a form that is both old and new, and this type of design opens up its possibilities.

A geometry without right angles

Fujimoto had begun to attract attention both at home and overseas before he built anything in Tokyo. The year of Fujimoto finally arrived in 2010: he completed both Tokyo Apartment and Musashino Art University Library, and had a solo show at the Watari Museum of Contemporary Art. The all-glass facade of the library, reflecting the surrounding trees and melding with the landscape, may recall the highly transparent architecture of the French architects Dominique Perrault and Jean Nouvel. But its most impressive structural feature are the walls of immense wooden bookshelves that stretch from floor to ceiling and curve slightly as they connect into a spiral pattern that eventually breaks the outer perimeter of the building. He has aimed at what might be called a forest of books, perhaps also inspired by the image of the intricate geometries described in Jorge Luis Borges's short story "The Library of Babel."

The immense walls of bookshelves do not feel at all confining, because a series of rectangular openings have been made at periodic intervals, which overlap to allow the gaze to move freely in a variety of directions, interior and exterior. This is a trademark design element for Fujimoto, a realization on larger scale of the technique he used in House N (2008) in Ōita, whose composition was essentially three nested boxes punctuated with a number of different openings, or in his entry in the competition for the Towada Art Center, with its series of gate-like frames. At the second-floor level, branching catwalks intersect with the openings in the walls of bookshelves, providing a joyful experience of the space. At the heart of the spiral is a counter, from which shelves containing books of every genre radiate in all directions. Interestingly, the architect collaborated with the graphic designer Satō Taku to develop user-friendly signage specifically for this project. Because of this, even though the space is labyrinthian, navigational assistance is always provided to the reader with a purpose. For example, the signage for the higher shelves and lower shelves is different, to increase legibility and ease of use.

I once had a discussion with an artist about how humanity might have first discovered the right angle. We imagined a number of possible scenarios, and came up with a hypothesis that when you are building something piecemeal, right angles are not so essential. However, when you are building or imagining a whole, then dividing it into units, neatly assembling the units, and arriving at your final configuration, right angles have to be part of the picture. Sure, in the earliest spaces—caves or primitive dwellings—they probably didn't use many right angles. You might say that spaces without strict right angles predate "architecture."

I think that this issue of right angles is connected to the idea of "an architecture of parts" that Fujimoto often speaks about. His proposal for the Annaka Environmental Art Forum envisioned a space whose outline was molded by pushing and pulling it into an irregular, free-form contour. The plan for T House, which appears to have been formed by swelling from the inside out, positions its interior walls in a broken radial pattern, rejecting any right angles. The Dormitory for the Mentally Disabled and the Children's Center for Psychiatric Rehabilitation in Date, as well as his proposal for the competition for the Aomori Museum of Art, while using right angles in individual units of their structures, all use non-right-angle systems to connect them into a whole. It is this technique that gives Fujimoto's architecture an aura of great antiquity, even though it has never been seen before.

Fujimoto's aim is to shake up the frames of reference established by geometry. This is why I invited him to participate in the exhibition I curated at Kirin Plaza Osaka in 2006, entitled *New Geometry Architecture: Toward an Alternative Modernism*. Fujimoto's contribution was a full-scale model built for the exhibition, called K House, which in plan consisted of a single large wall that followed a continuous line to form two interconnected concentric rings. Obviously there were no right angles here. Where the wall intersected itself, large apertures were cut in either the upper or lower portion, avoiding any sense of confinement. The result was a kind of tubular space in which exterior and interior penetrated one another. There were no divisions between rooms; everything was connected in the form of a kind of winding corridor. If ordinary geometry gives a clear order to architecture with right angles and parallel lines, this new geometry, while simple, gives birth to complex and diverse spaces. By introducing a sensibility preceding the right angle, Fujimoto elicits a contemporary perception of space.

Ishigami Jun'ya
Weightless Landscapes, Spaces of Relativity

The fastest path to the highest award in architecture

In 2009, Ishigami Jun'ya's design for the KAIT Workshop at Kanagawa Institute of Technology won the 61st Architectural Institute of Japan Prize, the most prestigious architectural prize in Japan. So when it was awarded to a young architect born in 1974, it was a major event. Of course, there have been other young recipients of this award. Maki Fumihiko (b. 1928) won it in 1962 for the Toyoda Memorial Hall at the University of Nagoya; Kikutake Kiyonori (b. 1928) in 1963 for the Izumo Grand Shrine Administration Building; and Isozaki Arata (b. 1931) in 1966 for the Ōita Prefectural Library. These three internationally acclaimed architects were all in their mid-thirties at the time they won. But that was more than fifty years ago. In more recent years, Nishizawa Ryūe (b. 1966) shared it in 1998 in partnership with Sejima Kazuyo as SANAA, but as a solo recipient Ishigami was still unusually young.

Ishigami had already participated in the 11th International Architecture Exhibition at the Venice Biennale and in the Milano Salone, winning international acclaim in the worlds of art and architecture, but his contributions were temporary exhibition pieces, not permanent works of architecture. The shop he created for designer Yamamoto Yohji on Gansevoort Street in New York City in 2008 was a renovation. He had only completed

one other substantial new building in Japan. It is impossible to
imagine anyone winning Japan's
highest architectural prize more
speedily than he did. He had
left Kazuyo Sejima and Associates in 2004 to establish his own
firm. When you consider that in
2008 he had already represented
Japan as the main architect for
the Japan Pavilion at the Venice
Biennale, you might say that by
his mid-thirties he had already
won the highest honors that his
country had to offer. And he
belongs to a thoroughbred lineage of teacher-student relations
in contemporary Japanese avant-

KAIT Workshop, Kanagawa Institute of Technology,
2009. (Courtesy of Jun'ya Ishigami + Associates)

garde architecture, running from the Metabolist Kikutake Kiyonori to Itō
Toyoo to Sejima Kazuyo to Ishigami.

The design for KAIT Workshop was certainly epochal: a forest of
almost randomly distributed slender columns with varying cross-sectional
forms. The text of the AIJ Prize gave the following reason for its selection:
"What we have here is a perfect unification of the nature of the structure
with the essential characteristics of the space; an astonishing attempt to
conceive and to actualize for the first time an architectural space premised solely upon density." In fact, when Ishigami submitted his application
for the award, I wrote a letter of recommendation describing the KAIT
Workshop as "an event in the history of pavilion architecture" and "the
birth of a truly awe-inspiring structure" (claims that one of the judges later
informed me were unusual in such recommendations). Winning the AIJ

Prize has come to require a certain level of past achievement, so I thought the odds were against him.

In the past, a number of promising works have been passed over by the judges because the architect was too young, or the project was for a private residence rather than a public institution. As a result, there are cases in which truly important works have failed to win the AIJ Prize, and then, much later, the architect has been awarded the prize for completely different work. For example, Azuma Takamitsu did not win for Tower House (1966), a masterpiece of residential architecture in a confined space that is now part of architectural history; almost forty years later he was finally given the prize in 1995 for what the judges termed "his series of urban residences." In this sense as well, Ishigami's first-shot win was major news. Apparently there was quite intense debate among the jurors. Unfortunately, the AIJ Prize in architecture does not garner the same amount of media attention as the Akutagawa Prize in literature or the Kimura Ihei Award in photography, but his achievement in winning this award at such a young age still had significant impact.

An event in the history of pavilion architecture

When I first learned of the KAIT Workshop project, the plans for it were quite different. In the initial studies, the columns were not scattered randomly, but distributed along a strictly defined grid within the rectangular plan. But the columns did not simply replicate one another without variation: they were flat bars with a specific orientation, placed at different angles, and they helped provide an overall structural balance. In other words, a uniformity of distribution coexisted with a range of orientations. This alone read as fairly ambitious architecture, but it goes without saying that the KAIT Workshop project later evolved far beyond this. In its present form it is freed from the grid, the columns have been given an irregular distribution one would not associate with an architectural plan, and they are no longer limited to the original flat bars. Even the plan morphed into an irregular parallelogram.

In September 2006 I served as interviewer for an interview Ishigami gave at TN Probe. When I heard how the KAIT Workshop project had developed into something like its present form, I was stunned by the magnitude of this transformation. A new world had been opened up, a new direction articulated, and I was certain that if it were to be realized, it would be inscribed in the history of architecture. As I listened to Ishigami's presentation, my thoughts were this: There are not many architects who have the capacity to so swiftly and radically execute what is in a sense the standard process leading from intuition to reasoning to implementation and realization. As I looked at the progression in his series of works, I began to understand that he had been consistently pursuing the question of how the meaning of a particular place can be radically altered by the position of the observer. The fact that there were more than five hundred people attending this lecture by an architect who as yet had no realized works of his own was testimony to the magnitude of the hopes that had been placed in him.

It's a competitive field in which to battle, but there is always something miraculous you are not likely to see anywhere else in the world happening at the offices of Junya Ishigami + Associates. When I visited in August 2006 the firm had outgrown its previous location and moved to a new studio in Iidabashi, where they were in the process of building several large models of the KAIT Workshop. Looking back over my *Twisted Column* journal, I find an entry that reads: "As always, Ishigami has a genius for sensing how to create realities we have not experienced before."[1] For a time the office had also been crammed with rows of mockups of the columns, but now the landing of the high-ceilinged stairwell was also home to a forest of actual-size columns of varying types, like monstrously enlarged models. For a plan with identical columns arrayed along a regular grid, it is fairly easy to imagine how the actual space will look and feel, but being able to read a standard blueprint is insufficient when you are trying to create an almost unimaginably unprecedented space, so this sort of real-world check is invaluable.

Meanwhile, Ishigami had called on Tokuyama Tomonaga to undertake the CAD programming for the studies of the KAIT Workshop project. This is because changing the position or orientation of a single column could impact the balance of the entire structure and affect all of the other columns and parts. Using custom-designed software, it was possible to position viewers at any point and give them a 360° view of their surroundings; a change in settings could then be immediately checked in terms of how it affected the whole. Thus, for the KAIT Workshop project, Ishigami continued SANAA's practice of building numerous large-scale physical models, while at the same time reaping the benefits of the information revolution brought into design studios with the introduction of the computer.

In November 2007, I visited the site of the KAIT Workshop just before the project's completion. Ordinarily, the repetition of columns tends to produce a sense of monumentality, like that of the massive multi-pillared rooms of Egyptian temples, the Hall of a Hundred Columns in ancient Persepolis, and Isozaki Arata's Toyonokuni Libraries for Cultural Resources (1995). But here the columns created a space unlike anything I had experienced before, in which my normal sense of distance was completely lost. If the columns had been arranged on a grid, distant columns would look smaller and thinner, nearby ones larger and thicker. In short, the columns would serve as a perceptual cue for depth and distance. But in the KAIT Workshop the columns are distributed randomly and also vary in profile and orientation, challenging one's senses. A column that looks thick and nearby might have its flat side facing you, and actually be much farther away. Or you might be looking at a nearby column edge-on, and thinking it is farther away because it seems so thin.

Also, as you walk in this forest of columns, it is clear that if it were arranged on a regular grid, the experience would be fairly predictable. But

Plan of KAIT Workshop, Kanagawa Institute of Technology. Scale = 1/500.
(Courtesy of Jun'ya Ishigami + Associates)

in the KAIT Workshop, the relationship of viewers to the columns surrounding them is unstable and the perception of distance is continually
and confusingly shifting. Things you thought were close are suddenly far
away, and vice versa. It feels as if space is expanding and contracting. But
even this experience is not uniform or predictable overall; it operates differently depending on the direction in which you are facing. In fact, if you
look at the plan you see what looks like a random scatter of numberless
groups of tiny dots crawling about. It is such an unfamiliar image that it

does not even look like an architectural plan. You might imagine such an arrangement of columns for a roofless outdoor installation, or perhaps a non-structural interior design project. But KAIT Workshop is a major piece of architecture, with a full-fledged structure.

Discovering how to pose the right questions

I first met Ishigami in 2004, at an opening in Tsukishima for *Hi-Energy Field*, an exhibition that I had a hand in planning and that originated at KPO Kirin Plaza Osaka. It must have been right after he established his own office, and I had learned of him through a mutual friend. Later, as a juror for Kirin Art Project 2005, I chose the proposal he submitted. Among the prodigious number of entries in that competition, his caught my eye: a simple drawing of a 10-meter-long single-line table laid with large still-life objects. He had already made restaurant tables measuring 2 meters by 2 meters by 4 millimeters, and I was quite intrigued by this challenging notion of removing the dining function in order to achieve an extreme extension in the length. The great French architect Jean Nouvel had already designed an extremely thin table called *LESS*, but it was equipped with a reinforcing rib running lengthwise along the underside of the table-top, where it was concealed from view. Ishigami's table, which is perfectly flat, surpasses Nouvel's.

In January 2005, I visited Ishigami's office, then a small place in Nakameguro, for the first time. We were meeting to prepare for an exhibition, and he showed me examples of his previous work. I recorded my impressions in my journal: "I learn that he has a talent sharp as a knife—or rather, like an innocent piece of paper that will slice your fingers if you are not careful." He had not completed many projects at that point, but the one he did for his master's degree left an especially strong impression on me. It was titled *Black: A Study in Light* (2000).[2] When I heard the concept behind it, I knew he was a genius.

When you get right down to it, since the beginning of recorded history, architecture has developed only a handful of techniques for the effective use of light: beautiful designs for the openings that admit light; manipulation of shadows to emphasize three-dimensionality of form; and the creation of walls that emit light, such as stained-glass windows. Ordinarily, the game has been to produce the greatest refinement of design within these basic parameters. For example, Le Corbusier used bright light to emphasize volume, a technique not fundamentally different from that of the temples of ancient Greece. His Ronchamp Chapel, where light passes beautifully through apertures in the thick walls, can be interpreted in terms of the precedents set by Romanesque churches. But Ishigami's *Black* takes a completely different approach to the relationship between architecture and light. It is like a scientific invention. Or perhaps a sensibility similar to that of artists such as James Turrell and Olafur Eliasson.

Let's explore this further, following Ishigami's own description of the project. Our ability to see things is made possible by the ceaseless reflection and refraction of light off surrounding objects and into our eyes, from every direction. Now imagine a kind of science-fiction scenario: what if there was a tunnel-like space in which light flowed in only one direction, and without reflection. And what if you walked through it, in the same direction as the light. The light from behind would of course overtake and pass you, but with nothing to reflect it back into your eyes, the view ahead would be totally black. If you turned around, however, the light would enter your eyes, and you would see that the tunnel was filled with light. It would be the same if you took a few steps forward, changing your position: what lay ahead would always be completely dark; what lay behind, completely illuminated. In other words, the position of the observer becomes the dividing line between light and darkness. It is a light-filled space, but one that can be plunged into total darkness, depending upon the position and orientation of the observer. That is, the same space could be sensed as either dark or bright.

Ishigami's *Black* project was an attempt to expand this linear hypothetical model—as much as possible—into the realm of three-dimensional architectural design. Obviously, in ordinary architecture the areas where light falls are illuminated. But in Ishigami's hypothetical space, which is filled with light, the perception of light or darkness is determined by the relative position of the observer. This is not a matter of the quality of the design of the apertures admitting the light. The genius of it is in the completely unprecedented way in which he has defined the problem. The KAIT Workshop was not designed with this problem of light in mind, but it is similar in its pursuit of the issue of spatial relativity.

Powerful works that can hold their own with art

Architectural exhibitions can be difficult to understand. This is because they are usually displays of models and drawings, and a certain kind of literacy is required for reading floor plans, cross-sections, and exterior elevations and being able to see how they describe an actual structure. Moreover, architectural language is rather specialized. Of course, the majority of architectural exhibitions in Tokyo take place at Gallery Ma or other specialist venues, where most of the visitors will be involved in architecture and there is not much need to worry about those outside the profession. If I had not had the opportunity to serve from 2002 to 2006 on the planning committee for KPO Kirin Plaza Osaka, I don't think I would have become aware of this issue myself. But as I participated in organizing art shows and at least one architectural exhibition a year for this venue, I stopped being able to think of the two as completely different, and began to be able to see them comparatively.

This is what led me to plan *Uses of the Streets* (2004) at KPO, the first solo show by Atelier Bow-Wow, who were already quite well known in the art world, and to invite Endō Shūhei and Fujimoto Sou to create full-scale models for the *New Geometry Architecture* (2006) exhibit. I wanted to see

Ishigami Jun'ya, *Table*, 2005, mixed media, 260 x 950 x 110 cm.
(© Jun'ya Ishigami / Courtesy of Gallery Koyanagi)

exhibitions that were not mere installations but possessed architectural properties in their own right. In other words, I wanted to see exhibition pieces that were not representations of something else, but objects that could stand on their own and compete as works of art. And I was awaiting the appearance of architects who could deliver such work.

It was from this orientation that I selected Ishigami Jun'ya for the Kirin Art Project in 2005. I recommended him because I was confident that he was an architect who was making powerful work that could compete on equal ground with the guest artist Tabaimo, and with the three groups of artists selected through a public competition.

The work he created was *Table*, whose top was extraordinary in its dimensions—9.5 meters long and only 3 millimeters thick. Because this was only achievable through the use of computer-aided structural computations, as far as I was concerned, this was no mere installation—it was a full-fledged work of architecture.

What I found fascinating, however, was that the architect did not choose to display the piece in a way that overtly emphasized its structure. An architect fond of the Metabolist and structural expressionist design of 1960s figures such as Tange Kenzō and Kikutake Kiyonori would no doubt have found ways of drawing attention to its almost acrobatic length and thinness. But Ishigami applied a thin-grained veneer to the tabletop, deliberately erasing the feel of the material. The 3-millimeter-thick top was not displayed at eye level, but at ordinary table height, so that people looked down at it rather than seeing that edge. In other words, at first glance it might seem quite ordinary.

As a result, as I can testify from having been present, there were more than a few visitors who went home from the show without ever realizing what it was that was so extraordinary about this table. It was a group exhibition, and only some of those attending came specifically to see Ishigami's work. Moreover, since the tabletop was laid with fruit, tableware, and other objects, and since many of the visitors were from the art world, it would appear that some of them thought this still-life composition was the work on display. (In fact, the group of objects on the table were not mere decoration: their weight and position had been carefully calculated in order to achieve the final leveling of the long tabletop.) In that case, the table was perceived as nothing more than a countertop.

On the other hand, visitors who thought they were looking at an ordinary table but happened to notice its extraordinary length suddenly felt the space in which they found themselves completely transformed. Then, if they leaned down for a better look from the side, they discovered that the tabletop had virtually no thickness. There were no hidden reinforcements, no tricks. This table, with proportions that one's ordinary senses indicated were impossible, was supporting a large number of objects. When they realized how odd this was, visitors must have felt as if they had wandered into a space where gravity was off-kilter. Or in which the weightless designs possible inside a computer had somehow sprung to life in the real world. If they touched the table, it trembled slightly, like an animal breathing. Ishigami had used steel for his restaurant tables but had shifted to aluminum for the KPO project, and the vibration it produced was truly otherworldly. By the way, the total weight of the tabletop and still-life objects was about 370 kilograms. Yet it was like a single gigantic plane, floating weightlessly in space.

An architecture evoking weightless space

Ishigami Jun'ya is probably the first architect to have made the cover of the art magazine *Bijutsu techō* before being featured in the architectural trade journal *Shin kenchiku*. The latter, in the March 2008 issue, caused something of a sensation by running photos using Ishigami himself as a model in a piece on the KAIT Workshop, while the cover of the December 2007 issue of *Bijutsu techō* displayed Ishigami's piece *Balloon*. It was the featured work in the *Space for Your Future* exhibit, curated by Hasegawa Yūko at the Museum of Contemporary Art, Tokyo—another indicator of how much attention it was being given by the art world. In fact, after the Kirin Art Project 2005 exhibition, Ishigami was picked up as an artist by Gallery Koyanagi, and *Table* was exhibited in 2006 at Art Basel and purchased by an art museum in Israel. A polystyrene chair he made for the Milano Salone then became part of the collection of the Pompidou Center.

A 14-meter-high silver balloon floats in the gigantic atrium of the Museum of Contemporary Art, Tokyo. Andy Warhol once did an installation in which several much smaller silver balloons floated about a gallery, but Ishigami's balloon has the volume of a four-story building. When filled with helium gas, it floats—even though the balloon itself, along with its aluminum frame, literally weighs a ton. Insofar as it exists on earth, architecture must obey the law of gravity, but eliminating the sense of weight is the ultimate dream. For example, Gothic cathedrals, though built of massive blocks of stone, were somehow able to achieve dematerialized, radiant interior spaces that seemed to have completely lost the feeling of the material from which they were constructed. Modernism, liberated from

Ishigami Jun'ya, *Balloon*, 2007,
mixed media, 1,400 x 730 x 1,280 cm.
(Photo by Yasushi Ichikawa © Jun'ya Ishigami
/ Courtesy of Gallery Koyanagi)

using walls as a structural element, aspired to lightness—working with the transparency of glass, abstract structural compositions that could work even if inverted, raising buildings up on pilotis, and so on.

But *Balloon* does not merely look light. It is, quite literally, floating architecture. Like Miyazaki Hayao's *Laputa: Castle in the Sky*. During the exhibition, I received permission to touch the gigantic balloon and move it with my hands—a completely new and magical experience. Normally, an object with a volume nearly ten times that of one's own body would be too heavy to move. But I could control it with one hand. This, too, was an experience of a weightless realm. Of course, twentieth-century architects also dreamed of floating buildings and cities. In Russia, Georgy Krutikov envisioned a ring-shaped *Flying City* (1928), while in America, Buckminster Fuller conceived *Cloud 9* (1962), reasoning that if one of his geodesic domes was expanded to sufficient size, its structure would become lighter than the air it contained, making possible a floating sphere 1.5 miles in diameter that could house a thousand people.

Ishigami often uses metaphors involving the clouds or weather. People respond to phenomenon such as rain or thunder without thinking much about the mechanisms that produce them. He says he'd like the same to be true of his architecture. The environment and phenomena produced by the architecture are more important than the technical mechanics of its production. The silvery surface of *Balloon*, a slightly distorted square, reflects the surrounding environment in complex ways as it moves slowly about. There were moments when it would rise all the way to the ceiling; at others, it might brush the floor. Changes in the weather would influence the temperature and air currents in the atrium, which would cause *Balloon* to behave differently. It was, indeed, like a cloud. With enough visitors, I imagine their combined body temperature would also affect its movement. In this sense, it might be called a work of relativistic architecture.

Initially, the curator Hasegawa had invited Ishigami to design the layout of the exhibition space. In the end, he decisively affected the atmosphere of the exhibition by creating *Balloon*. In a way, this might be considered a form of exhibition design. *Tables for a Restaurant* also began as a commission to do the interior design of a business. But Ishigami counterintuitively thought that he could create this interior by making tables with a unique feel of materiality. A table as interior design—creating an object and creating an environment as a single, unified proposition.

The new sensibility of "cute"

Of all the exhibitions I have been involved in managing, Kirin Art Project 2005 was the most challenging. The schedule was so tight that I was actually afraid we might not meet the deadline. Even so, in May 2007, when I was first approached about entering the competition for commissioner of the Japan Pavilion at the 11th International Architecture Exhibition at the Venice Biennale, I knew that I wanted to call on Ishigami Jun'ya to join me in the challenge.[3] This was because his completed *Table*, which opened up such vast possibilities in terms of structure and materials, was such a marvelous piece. Of course, at that point I had no idea whether or not we could win the competition, but with a sense of embarking upon a dangerous and thrilling adventure, I submitted a plan at the beginning of August naming Ishigami as the exhibiting artist.

Looking back on it now, the selection of Ishigami as the representative of the Japan Pavilion may seem like an obvious choice. But at the time of the competition, KAIT Workshop and *Balloon* were still in the future. He had no completed architectural projects. The jury was unable to reach a first-round decision, and called for supplementary presentations and submission of additional documentation, and I am told that even at the end there was considerable disagreement—perhaps inevitably. This was because, as later became clear, there were a number of other thoroughbreds in this race—submissions to the competition from curators whose proposals spotlighted architects with much longer track records than Ishigami, including Isozaki Arata, Kurokawa Kishō, Mikan Gumi, and even Tange Kenzō's firm.

To be honest, if *Balloon*, the standout piece of the *Space for Your Future* exhibition, had already been completed when the competition was held, victory probably would have been more certain—since the jury was made up entirely of people from the art world. We were aware that Ishigami had art-world appeal, but compared to figures like Isozaki, he had no name recognition. In any case, we had confidence in the content of our proposal and did our utmost to persuade the jurors with Ishigami's striking images of a cluster of small greenhouses and my own explanation of the concept, but it still seems remarkable that we were selected, despite *Table* being the only actualized piece we had to show. Nevertheless, at the end of September, we learned that we had won the competition.

In January 2008, we traveled to Venice for an on-site inspection of the Japan Pavilion in Giardini Park, the venue for the Venice Biennale. Overhearing some of the conversations among Ishigami Jun'ya and his staff,

I was a bit taken aback. They were going over design studies, and saying things like, "Morita-san, which one do you think is cuter?" In other words, "cute" seemed to be the basis for value judgment. While this might be used in the fashion industry, which of course must be conscious of feminine preferences, it is an adjective you don't hear used very often in the world of architecture. We tend to use other terms—beautiful, stylish, well proportioned, functional, rational, and so forth. From the classic texts of Vitruvius onward, the keywords in architecture have been *firmitas, utilitas,* and *venustas* (solidity, utility, and beauty).

But a design symposium titled "The Cute Paradigm," organized by project planner Makabe Tomoharu at the end of 2007, occasioned discussion on the theme of "cute" even within the architectural community. Thus I was aware of it, and thought of it as relating to completed work, and as a word only students would use. I now found that "cute" was being used in Ishigami's office in the process of creating new work. He told me that when he worked in Sejima Kazuyo's office, it was a word she frequently used.

Come to think of it, in addition to an extreme avant-garde edge, Ishigami's design also definitely has a sensibility one might describe as cute. For example, consider the small chairs he produced in 2005 for the Lexus exhibition at Milano Salone. Fashioned from polystyrene, they gave the impression of mockup models rather than a finished product. But special fabrication methods had made the polystyrene durable enough to actually sit on. Their delicate ephemerality made them cute. Also, their surfaces were covered with a pattern of white flowers that had nothing to do with structure or functionality but gave them a decorative, feminine finish.

Small things tend toward cuteness, and Ishigami uses this. For example, there is the palm-of-the-hand miniature book he designed, *Plants & Architecture* (2008). The white chairs installed in the KAIT Workshop are just slightly smaller than usual. And then there is *Little Garden* (2007), a work consisting of 370 silver containers arranged atop a round table. All were no bigger than a fingertip, but of different shapes and sizes, and tweezers were used to insert dried flower petals into each of them. When examined closely, the scale is forgotten, and it feels as if you have entered a space in which a variety of artworks are on display in a number of different galleries.

The model *Small Row-House Garden* Ishigami showed at SD Review in 2005 was also remarkable. (SD Review is an annual exhibition sponsored by the journal *SD*.) Normally architectural models are intended to demonstrate layout and spatial composition, and are not made to be altered or moved. Even detailed models usually have no furnishings other than perhaps a table and a couple of chairs to give a sense of scale. However, for *Small Row-House Garden* miniatures were built of everything: the landscaping, laundry on a line, the plates on the table, and even the food on the plates. This attention to detail made it feel more like a dollhouse than an architectural model. But the goal was not to create a realistic depiction of everyday life. Rather, this was an expression of Ishigami's worldview, which does not privilege architecture over all the countless details of the world surrounding it. It is likely that it is Ishigami who started the recent fad among architecture students of including laundry in their models.

The interior of the Japan Pavilion at the Venice Biennale, which opened in September 2008, also left a lasting impression. With the exception of some white chairs, there was nothing three-dimensional in the space, which was otherwise quite empty. Under Ishigami's direction, stunning miniature drawings of plants and architecture were executed directly on the walls by teams of young women from Tokyo University of the Arts, Shōwa Women's University, and Tōhoku University. For three weeks they meticulously worked with pencils, filling in the fine details of every leaf. From a distance, it looked simply like a series of drawings on a white wall, presenting some utopian vision. But if you approached the wall and looked more closely, the prodigious amount of artisanal labor required to realize this vision became apparent. This had a power that transcended "cute." In the art world there are examples, such as some Outsider Art or the works of Deki Yayoi, that exhibit a similarly obsessive replication of tiny elements, but I have never seen anything like it in an architectural presentation. Visitors were clearly impressed by the work, and I was asked many times for the name of the artist.

Toward spaces of relativity

The winning proposal for the Japan Pavilion in 2008 was *Extreme Nature: Landscape of Ambiguous Spaces,* a project that involved surrounding the pavilion with a cluster of small, specially designed greenhouses. Much as we had done at Kirin Plaza Osaka, the aim was to present this as a work of architecture. If we consider the Crystal Palace (1851) of the Great Exhibition in London, or Mies van der Rohe's Barcelona Pavilion (1929), international exhibitions have frequently given birth to great works of experimental architecture and opened the way to future possibilities. They are not museums displaying the works of the past. Ishigami's greenhouses, while responding to "Out There: Architecture Beyond Building," the overall theme articulated by the Biennale architecture exhibition's general director Aaron Betsky, were an experiment in creating a space that delivered a premonition of new beginnings.

Precise structural engineering enabled the construction of delicate greenhouses just this side of immaterial. Incredibly slender 16-millimeter-square columns, girders, and curtains of ultrathin 8-millimeter glass were special-ordered—materials that could not be sourced locally and had to be shipped from Japan, along with technicians trained to assemble them. The construction process took more than a month. The latticework girders were so delicate that they could not be welded and had to be cut from sheet steel. In order to conceal the above-ground foundation and irrigation systems, a large volume of earth had to be mounded, leveled, and landscaped, which took another two weeks. Few visitors would have noticed, but the level of the ground surrounding the Japan Pavilion had been raised by as much as a meter in some areas. The finished product was so unaffectedly natural that it did not look like it required much effort. In fact, we were frequently asked by staff of the neighboring pavilions of other countries if the greenhouses were intended to be a permanent installation.

It was not our initial aim, but the resulting Japan Pavilion was in fact very Japanese. This might be seen in the carefully calculated, ikebana-like precision of the plantings, and in landscaping that skillfully assimilated the surrounding trees, an example of the traditional Japanese garden design technique called *shakei*, or "borrowed scenery." Seen through the transpar-

Greenhouses at the Japanese Pavilion, Venice Biennale of Architecture, 2008. (Courtesy of Jun'ya Ishigami + Associates and Gallery Koyanagi)

ent glass, the Korean Pavilion in back, the Russian Pavilion next door, and the greenery surrounding the site all resonated with the plants inside and outside the greenhouses, and were integrated into the Japan Pavilion exhibition. At the private opening I was surprised to be asked by several members of the international press whether this interpenetration of exterior and interior space was related to the traditional wood-framed architecture of Japan. The precise construction, meticulous drawings, organized teamwork, and overall cost of the exhibition might also be mentioned as Japanese elements. So, too, the elegant restraint of expending such an enormous amount of labor moving such large quantities of earth, and then saying nothing about it. In contrast, there were pavilions of other countries that had produced "making of" videos boasting of the advanced technology employed in exhibits that scarcely needed any explanation at all. This manner of presentation would have never worked at the Japan Pavilion.

The area around the greenhouses became a pleasant garden, enhanced with outdoor furniture and new plantings around the existing trees. There was no need for visitors to understand any sophisticated techniques. It was satisfying just to see them simply sitting on the benches, looking at the plants, relaxing and enjoying themselves. One of the things I found fascinating during the installation was the number of times I saw Ishigami giving precise instructions for changes in the placement of plants and the positioning of furniture and pottery inside and outside the greenhouses. It goes without saying that architecture alone does not complete a space. Ishigami thinks of plants, furniture, and pots in equivalent terms, and if one element is moved, others must shift in response. He seems to have an awareness of space that sees everything—plants, furniture, architecture, topography, environment—as simultaneously coexisting and mutually interrelated.

The Japan Pavilion was a great success during the *vernissage* (the three-day private showing of pavilions) of the 11th International Architecture Exhibition at Venice Biennale 2008—winning high marks for its consistency with the overall theme of the Biennale, its overwhelming beauty, and the atmosphere of its garden. Other countries introducing the work of Ishigami's generation did so in the form of group shows; the Japan Pavilion was alone in the way it focused on acknowledging and spotlighting the creativity of a single young artist. A bilingual collection of his work that we had prepared as an official catalogue[4] and a smaller book of illustrations sold out before the event was over. The response of the press was also positive, and we immediately received favorable reviews. One night at dinner our waiter said he'd heard how nice the Japan Pavilion was supposed to be—so word had certainly got around, even at the local level.

Unfortunately, the Japan Pavilion did not win the Golden Lion that year, but the 2008 Biennale will no doubt be remembered as the stage upon which Ishigami Jun'ya, standing at the forefront of contemporary Japanese architecture, made his world debut. Fujimori Terunobu's exhibit at the Japan Pavilion for the 10th Biennale had been cited by the international jury for "outstanding merit," and it was rumored at the award ceremony that Japan would not be named again. Yet on the day of the opening, one newspaper headline was "From Warsaw to Tokyo" (the previous winner of the Golden Lion was Poland), and newspaper reviews were giving the Japan Pavilion high marks.

One thing that struck me while I was in Venice was that Ishigami scarcely visited any of the other national pavilions. Of course, during the installation he had been focused on his own work, but the other pavilions were all close at hand in the same park, and it would have taken only a matter of minutes to check them out. After his work was completed, he was busy with press interviews and the like, but even when he finally found some free time, he did not seem particularly interested in visiting the national pavilions or the exhibits at the Arsenale. Ishigami is not the type to develop his own architectural strategies after a careful survey of what architects in other countries are doing. It confirmed for me that he has an absolute standard of value, unrelated to global trends, and creates new work as a solitary architect.

Architecture, creating and expanding the future

The architects of the generation born in the 1960s and rising to prominence in the 1990s, such as Atelier Bow-Wow and Mikan Gumi, began to involve themselves in art-world events such as the Yokohama International Triennale of Contemporary Art and the Echigo-Tsumari Art Triennale. In the early 2000s, such crossovers between architecture and art increased in number. Sugimoto Hiroshi, Olafur Eliasson, Arakawa Shūsaku, Nakamura Masato, and other artists moved along the vector from art to architecture, while Ishigami Jun'ya was a representative example of someone moving in the opposite direction. Whether his work was located at an actual building site or in a gallery, he was always designing that space as architecture.

Why is it that Ishigami has drawn closer to the domain of art? One factor has been the dearth of executable projects, as young Japanese architects have continued to have difficulty finding work since the collapse of the bubble economy in the early 1990s. But this probably is not the only reason. Ishigami's consistent efforts to break through the limitations of architecture are probably part of the picture as well. The process of realizing a work of architecture requires clearing a number of hurdles: social constraints, legal restrictions, budget, and so on. Art venues, with their limited periods of display, liberate the creators from some of these conditions, enabling them to pursue pure possibilities.

As a result, with works such as *Table* at KPO Kirin Plaza Osaka, *Balloon* at the Museum of Contemporary Art, Tokyo, and the greenhouses at the International Architecture Exhibition at the Venice Biennale, Ishigami has been working at the cutting edge of what is possible in real-world architecture. One might say his work is pure—a utopian architecture. If Japan's circumstances permitted more experimental efforts, it is likely that Ishigami would be engaged in more built projects. But in the risk-averse present, society has become conservative and has lost the capacity to accept the bold proposals of people like Ishigami. It looks for design that does not break the existing mold. So it seems inevitable that it should be in the realm of art where Ishigami finds acceptance.

Ishigami has been preparing a number of projects for inclusion in a collection of his work scheduled to be published by Thames & Hudson. He's exploring several ideas: If you built a skyscraper tall enough to pierce the earth's atmosphere, how would the spaces change from floor to floor? Would it be possible to create and maintain an aquarium in outer space held together purely by the surface tension of the water? How would we experience the topography of a cuboid planet? Could the earth be encircled in a series of arch-like structures? Some of these were presented in a show at the Shiseidō Gallery in 2010 entitled *How Small? How Vast? How Architecture Grows,* and are among his many projects that break out of the framework usually inhabited by architects. In this solo show, utopian proposals were arrayed on tables in the form of nearly sixty small models, giving the appearance of a career retrospective in miniature. The variety of his ideas was rivaled by the variety of ways in which they were expressed.

This may be reminiscent of Archigram and Superstudio, recognized in the 1960s for their fantastic architectural visions and drawings of cities, but Ishigami is not presenting mere notions or doodles. Insofar as possible, he is conceiving spaces no one has yet experienced, but only after doing a careful check of the physical conditions involved. While he may not be terribly interested in social factors, his is not a dream world in which anything is possible. He explores the utmost limits of a given set of rules. This is his architectural process. In the breadth of his imaginative range he is like Buckminster Fuller, though compared to Fuller's geometric focus, Ishigami has a more fantastic bent. And in another sense, Ishigami goes beyond Fuller. Given the greater freedom permitted in a book compared to gallery exhibitions, he is expanding the possibilities of architecture to include the environment in its broadest sense—planets, topography, weather—within the purview of design. It is as if Ishigami were to become a god, and his project, to recreate the world.

Architecture as Air crowned with the Golden Lion

Sejima Kazuyo served as the general director of the 12th International Architecture Exhibition at the Venice Biennale in 2010, and Ishigami Jun'ya was given the opportunity to exhibit again, at the Arsenale. His entry, *Architecture as Air,* as its title suggests, was an insubstantial construction, built with a forest of unbelievably slender columns only 0.9 millimeters in diameter and 4 meters high—like leads from a mechanical pencil standing more than twice the height of a human being. When photographed, the columns look like scratches on the display monitor. The work exists at the outer limits of what can be represented in other media. Each of these incredibly slender columns was held erect by 52 strands of filament that were only 0.02 millimeters thick—13 strands of filament running in each of the four directions—attaching them to the floor. These filaments were almost invisible to the naked eye. When I examined them closely, on site, I found that you could only see them when certain portions caught and briefly reflected the light. Because of this, I am told that when the installation was being set up it looked like the crew was engaged in some sort of pantomime.

The artist Yves Klein once proclaimed an "air architecture," but Ishigami has actually realized an architecture that pursues the limits of things to the point where they virtually melt into air. The long history of architecture, originating in massive works of stone such as neolithic monoliths and the temples of ancient Greece, has finally brought us to this. However, because of the remarkable delicacy of Ishigami's structure, an unfortunate incident occurred: during the private showings, it began to collapse. Repair was attempted, but an old man who strayed past the barriers and a child who ran into the space collided with the installation and did further damage. When I arrived at the venue on the last day of the *vernissage*, the piece had lost its original form, retaining only a few of its columns. In fact, it had become more like a work of conceptual art, inviting the visitor to trace the image of what had been by viewing the wreckage of the piece and the elevation drawings displayed on the wall. Perhaps you could call it "architecture as incident." But permanence alone does not make a work of architecture. There are, after all, temporary pavilions. This was indeed a transient, ephemeral existence.

According to the artist Tezuka Aiko, who assisted with the installation, when the original version of 44 columns in four groups of 11 was completed late on the night preceding the previews, it was an otherworldly sight, like a computer wireframe drawing come to life. And this makes sense, since the expression of weightless space has been a consistent theme of Ishigami's, manifested previously in *Table* and *Balloon*. Like them, *Architecture as Air* transformed the nature of the space in which the viewers found themselves. Yet the installation staff was exhausted, and everyone was so taken with the beauty of the completed piece, that no one managed to take a photo of it before its first collapse. But there is no question that at the 2010 Biennale, no other architect advanced the ball as far as Ishigami. His work may have collapsed in the end, but it was like a broad jumper falling after a 300-foot leap. Even so, it seemed his chances for a prize were slim. After all, he had not won in 2008, despite the extraordinary quality of his work.

So when Ishigami's name was read at the awards ceremony on August 28, I was truly astonished. He had been crowned with the Golden Lion for Best Project of the 12th International Architecture Exhibition. The jury acknowledged Ishigami's vision, grounded in unique and powerful convictions, and praised his piece for having pushed the boundaries of materiality, visibility, structure, thinness, and architecture itself. Since I honestly felt he could have won the Golden Lion two years previously for essentially the same reasons, I felt as if his true value was finally being recognized (though he is still quite young for such recognition). And it was certainly unprecedented for an entry that collapsed to be awarded the highest honor. Ishigami had simply and sincerely explored possibilities to their ultimate conclusion. (It might be noted that this same installation was exhibited in a solo show at the Toyota Municipal Museum of Art in autumn 2010, and though it was completed a bit late for the opening, survived in its completed state for the duration of the exhibit; in 2011 it was featured as a complete and stable work in an exhibition at the Barbican Center in London.) That his winning of the prize developed into an incident, and his work came to be seen as "problematic" was a combination of the jury's decision and the Biennale as a venue, not any intention on the part of Ishigami himself. It stirred up a vigorous debate on issues such as whether a broken piece should be awarded a prize, and whether it was a work of architecture or of art. But even this turmoil arose precisely because this was "architecture" that ignored borders and transcended boundaries.

Principles and Phenomena

Looking to the Future

From situation to principle

As the pop sensibility of the generation born in the 1960s faded, a cooler sensibility dominated by solo architects came to the fore. Yet they, too, eschewed any overt, heavy-handed approach to design. And the number of young architects whose careers were boosted by overseas work and study under famous architects increased—such as Matsubara Hironori (b. 1970), who worked with Itō Toyoo, and Sako Keiichirō (b. 1970), who worked with Yamamoto Riken, both of whom are based in Beijing. This generation also uses computers much more extensively in the design process.

A number of other tendencies might be enumerated as well. The two top figures in terms of international name recognition, Fujimoto Sou and Ishigami Jun'ya, are resetting architectural history by defining new principles. Hirata Akihisa (b. 1971), with his fascination for natural forms, is also exploring new architectures involving pleated compositions and twisted topologies. While the previous generation had avoided an emphasis on individual personalities, these architects were charismatic-genius characters. Atelier Bow-Wow and Mikan Gumi had based their architecture in detailed urban observation and fieldwork; these younger architects were less interested in explaining the environment and external constraints than they were in articulating their architectural principles. In 2001 there

was an exhibition at Gallery Ma on the generation born in the 1970s entitled *From Space to Situation*. If a similar show were to be done today, it
should probably be called *From Situation to Principles*.[1]

From the 1990s onward, postmodernist stylistics fell out of favor, and
there was a return to modernism. It was recognized that, methodologi-
cally, a simple and clear formal language could be used to construct quite
complex spaces. A kind of gentle formalism—neither rigorously functional
nor given to fantasy—ruled architecture. On the other hand, the Unit-ha
disliked overly clear and direct expressions of concept, and in some cases
was intentionally obscure. While Fujimura Ryūji (b. 1976) shares this to
some extent, in all his designs he emphasizes logical visualization of the
process. In the early 2000s, several established architectural journals—
including *Kenchiku bunka, SD,* and *10+1*—were forced to suspend publication. Fujimura responded by starting up media enterprises of his own,
sparking cross-disciplinary debate with other fields such as sociology,
strengthening the solidarity of his generation while simultaneously developing a theoretical discourse around such keywords as "suburbanization"
and "information society."

With the collapse of the bubble economy in the early 1990s, funding
in Japan for construction of public facilities contracted. Large-scale rede-
velopment in Tokyo was monopolized by big general contractors and
foreign starchitects, and young Japanese architects turned to residential
projects. Interior and renovation work came to be thought of as worthy of
consideration as "architecture." Crossovers into the art world were another
indicator that the social context surrounding the new generation was too
severe to permit adequate scope for their activities if confined to the terms
of architecture as previously defined. However, global brands with a large
share of their market in Japan were willing to provide Japanese architects
with a chance to actualize experimental work. Architects who worked at
Aoki Jun & Associates, such as Inui Kumiko (b. 1969), Nakamura Ryūji
(b. 1972), and Nagayama Yūko (b. 1975), as well as Nakamura Hiroshi

(b. 1974), who worked for Kuma Kengo's office, have tried their hand at commercial spaces, crafting meticulous designs marked by a contemporary decorative sense. They create phenomenal spaces that must be experienced first-hand. Conversely, one might say that the gritty street sense of Atelier Bow-Wow or Mikan Gumi are not particularly suited to brand-name shops.

Hirata Akihisa: Form creates landscape

Hirata Akihisa, who went independent in 2005 after working in the offices of Itō Toyoo, employs a strong formal sensibility to create unique phenomena and landscapes. For example, he has used the fundamental form of the pleat (alternately projecting and folding in), extended fractally, to structure both chairs and buildings. Or, by offsetting them from one another, developed diagonally interactive spatial relations. In both plan and section, House H (2004) joins two contiguous rectangular volumes at their corners. By drastically restricting the area where they join and overlap, an odd and ambiguous sense of both proximity and distance is created. Incidentally, the idea for the offset volumes in Itō Toyoo's National Taichung Theater was originally conceived by Hirata when he was working in Itō's office.

The type of space Hirata is aiming for is almost impossible to convey in photographs alone. The beauty might come across, but without actually setting foot in them, you cannot experience the thrilling transformation of space achieved through the distribution and relation of various elements in projects such as the equilateral triangle walls inserted into the Masuya Honten Building (2007) or the grove of mirrored columns in the beauty shop Hair OORDER (2006). Inventive formal experimentation initiates unprecedented phenomena, giving birth to new landscapes. Hirata, who while at Itō's office was involved in the work on Sendai Mediatheque, is continuing the exploration of architectural principles opened up by that pathbreaking project.

Sarugaku (2006) in Daikan-yama is a commercial facility that emphasizes the outdoor landscape rather than simply cozily enclosing the interiors of the shops. The site has been divided among six structures situated to create both a common central plaza and intriguing gaps between the buildings. The individual units are of mod-

Sarugaku, 2006. (Photo by Nacása & Partners)

est size, and some are sunk partially below grade, so they look rather like a row of houses with balconies and external staircases. In fact, Sarugaku bears a greater resemblance to Labyrinth (1989), a communal housing project by Hayakawa Kunihiko (b. 1941), than it does to an ordinary set of shops. They both have a dramatic outdoor common space. But Sarugaku avoids the fictionality of postmodern architecture like Labyrinth. It aims at being a real landscape, one with shops and people in them, aware of one another—a place that cannot be experienced except by being there. This commercial establishment is an extension of the streets, and thus one that uses the division into separate units to create the ambience of an alleyway, not unlike Nishizawa Ryūe's Moriyama House. Hirata's R-Minamiaoyama (2006) is also a commercial building with a rich exterior, quite effectively wrapped with external staircases.

In a project I supervised in conjunction with the 2008 Yokohama Triennale, Hirata Akihisa designed and constructed Ienoie (House of Houses, 2008), a new concept for a residence based on the traditional shape of a house—that is, one with the triangular pitched roof that almost anyone imagines when they hear the word "house." Modernist architecture developed an antipathy toward the peaked roof, preferring a flat and horizontal profile. But in the heyday of postmodernism in the late twentieth century, there were several attempts to reintroduce this motif as a semiotic statement. And in the early twenty-first century, an increasing number of architects also began to make use of this traditional form, inaugurating what amounted to a second rediscovery of the "house shape"—focusing not on the semiotics of this motif, but upon its formal architectural properties and the experience of space it conveys. Ienoie is a representative example of this latter tendency.

Ienoie gives us the astonishing experience of encountering a roof

Ienoie, 2008. (Photo by Nacása & Partners)

for the first time. This is not your ordinary triangular pitched roof, but a concatenation of many smaller roofs. And because the valleys between the roofs cut deep into the volume, there are no walls on the second floor, which becomes a single continuous space with rooms only minimally demarcated from one another. As a result, sound carries from one room to the next, but there are no direct lines of sight. On the other hand, you can look out over the roof and see in the window of the house across the way. Giving birth to such phenomena, Ienoie seems to give spatial expression to the quality of contemporary communication, where people find themselves somehow connected, and at the same time distanced from one another. What is interesting is that this phenomenon was created not by fiddling with the layout, but by the decision to create separate roofs. The form of a typical house emphasizes its role as a gathering place for a family, but the individual little roofs of Ienoie embody both sharing and distance. Hirata's apartment complex Alp (2010) in Akabane is a further evolution of the design of Ienoie, responding to variations in the surrounding topography.

Nakamura Hiroshi: Decoration as phenomenon

In the early twenty-first century, architects sought to unify structure and decoration, rather than adding decoration to structure. Increasingly sophisticated computer-aided design (CAD) has enabled complex designs in which structure itself can achieve decorative effects. For example, Itō Toyoo's Tod's Omotesandō Building (2004), a concrete structure whose design is based on the concept of overlapping patterns created by the zelkova trees lining the avenue outside, with glass inserted into the interstices of the concrete to complete the outer shell of the building. This type of design, blurring the dichotomies between structure and decoration, framework and skin, abstract and concrete, can also be seen in Itō's Mikimoto Ginza 2 (2005).

Nakamura Hiroshi engages in even more subtle modes of expression. Born in 1974, he worked in Kuma Kengo's offices, where he was responsible for projects such as Plastic House before going independent. For the Lanvin Boutique Ginza (2004) he covered much of the facade with steel plate perforated with myriad circular holes of different sizes. This perforated plane formed a third element in the facade that was neither an opaque wall nor a transparent window. By day, the perforations cast enchanting circles of light like droplets of water in the interior; in the evening, lit from within, the facade looks like a night sky glittering with stars. During construction each of the 3,000 holes in the facade had to be filled with clear acrylic plugs of the same diameter, and as Nakamura did not want to use seals or adhesives, a special fabrication process was devised. The small acrylic cylinders were frozen, slightly reducing their size, and inserted in the holes. When they reached ambient temperature again, they fit snugly and perfectly. Thus a perfectly flat steel and acrylic plane was achieved with a minimum of elements.

For Lotus Beauty Salon (2006), approximately 50,000 perforations were drilled in the steel plate forming the ceiling. The areas of the ceiling where the perforations are not concentrated form images of lotus leaves,

Lotus Beauty Salon, 2006.
(© Nakamura Hiroshi and NAP)

and because the holes are small (9–13 millimeters in diameter), as you move away from them, they fade out, and as you approach them, they define the outlines of the leaves. This is different from standard decorative motifs of plants or animals, or even geometric patterns. For one thing, the representational image is formed by a massing of perforations. For another, it is not merely a graphic but also functions as a kind of skylight through which light enters from above. When you look up at the ceiling, the images of the lotus leaves appear, not as a figure drawing, but as the ground—arising in the areas where the perforations are not concentrated.

Itō Toyoo executes a fusion of structure and decoration with a clarity anyone can understand; in contrast, Nakamura experiments with decoration as a phenomenon—neither three-dimensional sculpture nor flat images. The almost magical light filtering through the countless holes into the interior creates a variety of expressions that stimulate the perceptions as the sun moves through the day, creating an experience of space. In Lotus Beauty Salon, edges are blurred, and colors are manipulated through subtle gradations. While these are conceived as a surface treatment, they are at the same time decoration as phenomena, and give birth to rich transformations that cannot be read from an architectural plan.

In House SH (2005), one white wall has a gigantic, round hollow scooped into it, disturbing one's sense of perspective and creating a space that gives the visitor a unique experience of color, intensified by natural light from the light well above. In Gallery Sakuranoki (2007), 3-centimeter-thick wooden walls divide the space into a series of narrow rooms, which are then connected by openings in the shape of an element once decisively rejected by modernism: the arch. Architects usually favor rectangular openings, but Nakamura was aiming at a more feminine atmosphere. And even though he is using the arch, it is not as a postmodernist exercise in semiotics—the emphasis is on the phenomenon of how people might perceive a series of arches as they moved through them.

Fujimura Ryūji: Designing a space for discourse

Born in 1976, Fujimura Ryūji is a rarity among a generation that experiments with sense perception, for he is actively engaged in public discourse. In 2007 he published the free paper *Round About Journal* and started a movement. He printed five thousand copies of the first issue and distributed it nationwide through a student network, which immediately gave him influence rivaling that of the commercial architectural journals. He has hosted a symposium of architects of his own generation that featured live editorial coverage from the rear of the audience, and ended with the distribution to attendees of a special edition of *Round About Journal* detailing the events of the symposium. Fujimura has also teamed up with sociologists to proclaim the concept of "critical engineering-ism," searching for a way in which architecture can overcome being assimilated by the logic of capitalism, but in a way that is creative rather than merely critical. This brings to mind Le Corbusier publishing a magazine called *L'Esprit Nouveau*, a kind of forerunner of media strategies on the part of architects.

In Voxel House (2004), which Fujimura designed in collaboration with Vera Jun, the interior walls are covered by a lattice of floor-to-ceiling shelves of varying depths. They are essentially bookshelves, but they undulate topographically, enfold a kitchen and refrigerator, and create a variety of different spaces. At first glance this seems to be a sort of intuitive interior landscape design, but interestingly enough, Fujimura provided a logical explanation of the design process, laying out a series of models used in its development. At each stage they would check various elements and issues with the design that needed to be confirmed before moving on to the next stage, steadily determining the form. A decade earlier, Mikan Gumi had gained attention by advocating an "authorless" architecture— by embracing and fulfilling a diversity of design constraints, they argued, it was possible to eliminate a strong authorial role. However, Mikan Gumi did not reveal their process, so it remained a black box that others could not share. In contrast, Fujimura has developed what he calls "superlinear process theory," an attempt to reach a similar goal by publicly articulating an extremely transparent process.

Fujimura's Building K (2008) fronts a shopping street in the Tokyo neighborhood of Kōenji. Its ground floor is a commercial space; above it rise a cluster of what appear to be narrow towers. Invisible from below is a charming rooftop alleyway located on the fifth floor. And the exterior of the building conceals an intricate megastructural system in which the second through fourth floors are suspended. The complexity of this approach is something you might expect from one of the architects mentored by Sakamoto Kazunari at Tokyo Institute of Technology, such as the members of Atelier Bow-Wow or Mikan Gumi. However, as is indicated by the fact that Fujimura proposed a unique climate control system for Building K, he is aiming at developing a practice that is more like that of a major general

Building K, 2008.
(Photo by Torimura Kōichi, courtesy of
Ryūji Fujimura Architects)

architecture firm than an artsy design studio. And this is what makes him new. Building K won him a place on the cover of *Shin kenchiku* not long after his debut as an architect. It stirred up quite a reaction, with criticism that the architect's intent was difficult to understand, the proportions of the building were unsatisfying, and so on. Some of this was no doubt jealousy, and in any case, Fujimura's media savvy soon had the situation under control. He organized a series of ambitious exhibitions—including *Architect 2.0* (2009) and *City 2.0*, an homage to and further development of Isozaki Arata's *Haishi: The Mirage City* (1995)—and contributed articles to Azuma Hiroki's critical journal *Shisō chizu* (Thought Map), proposing new directions for the architect and the city in the Information Age.

Nakamura Ryūji: The differentiated world of architecture

The exhibition *Phenomenal Resolution: Japanese Architects in Their 30s* at INAX Ginza in 2008 reflected the general tendency to avoid strong architectural statements. The show had a rather feminine feel, expressed in entries such as Ishigami Jun'ya's little picture books and Nakamura Hideyuki's cute drawings. In the midst of all this, Nakamura Ryūji's extraordinarily delicate—one might even say "hyper-differentiated"—works were the most radical development. From a slightly different perspective, they might be viewed as handicraft works. In contrast to large-scale architecture, small-scale craftwork requires refined manual processes. The question even arises, "Is this really architecture?" But by pursuing even more delicate manipulations than is usual in handicrafts, the works approach insubstantiality, and structural issues arise. And because of this, Nakamura's works are able to achieve a transformation from handicraft to full-fledged architectural design. They are architecture of an ultra-differentiated micro realm.

Like Inui Kumiko and Nagayama Yūko, Nakamura is a veteran of Aoki Jun's office, and if his work conveys even more of a feminine atmosphere than that of these two women, it is probably because of the materials he uses: mainly delicate fabrics and paper. Nakamura designed several shops for an eyewear chain, Jin's Global Standard. For the Aoyama shop (2006) he fashioned a display by piercing holes in a large sheet of cloth and hanging eyeglasses from them; the image was one of glasses floating in snow. For the Nagareyama shop (2007), he pinned pieces of stiff paper to the wall and placed the eyeglasses on the upward curve of the sheets. Rather then determining the design on an overall basis, he begins with a concrete image of how the product should be displayed. Then this display design forms the interior landscape of a chain of shops. The Nagareyama shop has a corner location in a shopping mall. Nakamura designed a series of closely set parallel walls slicing across the corner diagonally, with eyeglasses displayed in lines along each wall like stripes on wallpaper, with mirrors inset between the stripes. The repetition of elements and their reflections creates a strange realm in which the scale of the space seems to simultaneously expand and contract.

Insect Cage (2007), a small-scale work using stereolithographic 3D printing technology, is a cage formed by tiny bars of resin (0.3 millimeters in diameter) arrayed in grids with a 7-millimeter pitch. This incredibly fine latticework virtually melts into the air, a fragile structure whose actual boundaries seem ambiguous. As you change your distance and viewing angle, the density of overlapping grid layers changes as well, producing magically shifting effects. The butterflies trapped inside breathe the same air as the viewer but seem to be floating in an entirely different world. *Hechima* (2005) and *Kuma* (2006) produce small, cute volumes by cutting wavy sheets (of plywood in the case of *Hechima,* or paper in the case of *Kuma*) into netlike patterns that are then built up layer by layer. Even then they do not form any continuous solid planes, such that the shapes of these objects are defined by what is essentially a network of holes. As with *Insect Cage,* they are an architecture that demolishes the concept of mass through hyper-differentiation.

Nakamura's *Cornfield* installation, created for the exhibition *Where Is Architecture?* (2010) at the National Museum of Modern Art, Tokyo, is a breathtaking piece. The structural material is paper, and it looks something like an enormous architectural model. The basic units are cubes

Cornfield installation, 2010.
(Courtesy of Ryuji Nakamura & Associates)

14 centimeters on each side, constructed of lattices of paper rods only 1 millimeter thick that are relentlessly replicated to form a triangular prism 1.8 meters high, and sides of 16 meters, 14 meters, and 8 meters in length. Its fabrication employed a fusion of stunningly precise digitally guided laser-cutting technology and mind-bogglingly delicate handiwork, resulting in a structure that seems to be almost made out of air. As you walk around it, your changing field of view produces a variety of moiré1 patterns, almost like video images. This hyper-differentiated structure is design positioned at the cutting edge of Japanese architecture.

Beyond the "wavelet architects"

In 2006, Itō Toyoo wrote a blurb for the jacket of a book by the architectural editor and journalist Nakasaki Takashi on the rising generation that Itō dubbed "a wavelet of architects in a becalmed Japan."[2] The architects covered in the book included Fujimoto Sou, Ishigami Jun'ya, Igarashi Jun, Hirata Akihisa, among many others. While Itō's comment could be read sardonically, he probably had in mind Maki Fumihiko's description of the generation including Hayakawa Kunihiko, Aida Takefumi, Hasegawa Itsuko, Tominaga Yuzuru, and Ishii Kazuhiro as "masterless samurai." Maki was alluding to the masterless samurai following the Warring States period of late medieval Japan to describe the generation of postmodernists born after 1940—the generation to which Itō himself belongs.

Maybe there was a point to seeing the delicate design being done in Japan as mere ripples in comparison to the wave of globalism in contemporary world architecture that was propelling such dynamic, accessible, iconic projects as Frank Gehry's Guggenheim Museum Bilbao and OMA's CCTV headquarters in Beijing.

At the opening of an Atelier Bow-Wow exhibition, Itō touched on the amateur attitude of the younger generation; the old "peacetime warriors" had been called out in similar terms by Maki. History repeats itself. Now,

Itō stands in Maki's shoes. But the "peacetime warriors" advanced to fine careers, and Andō Tadao and Itō in particular to the rank of generalissimos, with portfolios full of projects in every part of the world. Now we've gone from "peacetime" to "becalmed"; from "masterless samurai" to the "wavelet" architects. This phrase is indicative of the younger generation in the early years of the twenty-first century. And we wait, wondering who among the wavelets will be the first to step forward and make a greater wave.

IN CONCLUSION
Architecture after March 2011

The Great East Japan Earthquake struck on March 11, 2011, as I was writing this book. As I know nothing of war, this was the worst disaster that I have directly experienced. It was a personal matter. The building housing the Faculty of Architecture at Tōhoku University, where I work, was badly damaged in the quake and could no longer be used. Having lost access to the building and its large libraries of reference books, I had to suspend my writing activities for a time. An environment I had taken for granted had suddenly disappeared. I did not lose my house to the tsunami, but the disaster radically altered my daily life. I hunted off campus for a place to hold my seminars and managed to borrow classroom space in another building for my undergraduate lectures, which started a month behind schedule. It was not until July that I was able to secure office space on another campus. Eventually I began writing again. Had it not been for the earthquake, I imagine I would have completed this book earlier.

Immediately following March 11, the architectural community was stunned into silence by horrific images of the destruction wrought by the tsunami on the coastal communities of northeastern Japan; before long, a diversity of responses arose almost simultaneously. A number of recovery plans were proposed and workshops held, with plans for improving the temporary housing, including suggestions for room divider systems to pro-vide privacy in the gymnasiums that were being used as shelters for the thousands of people who could not return to their homes. My graduate students and I undertook the design for a community hall for a tempo-rary housing development in the city of Minamisōma and the plan for the restoration and preservation of a collapsed building in the town of Onagawa—activities we would have never imagined before the quake.

In response to the Great East Japan Earthquake, five world-renowned architects—Itō Toyoo, Yamamoto Riken, Naitō Hiroshi, Kuma Kengo, and Sejima Kazuyo—formed the Kishin no Kai as an organization devoted to thinking of "we" rather than "me" and to explore the possibilities of a more socially oriented architecture. These five are members of the gener-ations of architects born in the 1940s and 1950s. Architects of the 1960s–70s generation, like Abe Hitoshi, originally from Sendai, and Tsukamoto Yoshiharu, organized a network for international assistance called Archi-Aid. Compared to the response to the Great Hanshin-Awaji Earthquake of 1995 in Kobe, there was a considerably higher level of activity in the architectural community.

On the other hand, one thing that became clear immediately after the Great East Japan Earthquake was that smaller architectural firms were not being called upon in this emergency. General contractors and engineering consultants had the organizational capacity to be first responders to disas-ter sites; independent architectural practices simply could not match their response time. In addition, while Japan has no shortage of internationally active architects, scarcely any of them were officially invited by local gov-ernments to participate in recovery planning. Even if these architects are widely recognized, urban design is seen as outside their purview. Of course, some of the responsibility for this lies with the architects themselves. In the postwar years Tange Kenzō and the Metabolists conceived grand visions, but after the 1970s, when Isozaki Arata proclaimed his "retreat from the metropolis," with a few exceptions such as Kurokawa Kishō, architects have expressed little interest in urban planning. Since they have not been vocal in this regard, and seem to be beginning to think about it only in the wake of disaster, it is not surprising that no one was particularly quick to call on them for assistance. Because of this, I believe March 2011 will prove to be a catalyst for greater interest by architects in urban planning and projects on the scale of civil engineering. And I believe that in the phase of reconstruction, the spatial literacy of architects—in other words, their ability to read a site and propose outstanding design solutions—will prove to be quite important.

Contemporary Japanese Architects: Profiles in Design begins with the devastation following World War II and ends with what is considered the greatest crisis of the postwar era—the Great East Japan Earthquake—a disaster that plunged Japan into a larger narrative for the first time in many years. Even if it does not immediately change everything about architecture (and personally I do not think it desirable for everyone to act in concert), there is no doubt that when we look back on this time, it will prove to have been a turning point. This book, published at such a historical juncture, can be seen to document the period from the end of World War II to the Great East Japan Earthquake.

NOTES

Chapter 1

1. Sekino Masaru, *Meiji, Taishō, Shōwa no kenchiku*, vol. 25 of *Sekai bijutsu zenshū* (Heibonsha, 1951), 18.
2. Inoue Shōichi, *Senjika Nihon no kenchikuka* (Asahi Shimbunsha, 1995), 36–37.
3. "Kantōgen," *Shin kenchiku* (January 1942).
4. Igarashi Tarō, *Sensō to kenchiku* (Shōbunsha, 2003), 51–54.
5. Adachi Kō, *Nihon kenchikushi* (Chijin Shokan, 1940), 172.
6. Kishida Hideto, *Nihon kenchiku no tokusei* (Naikaku Insatsu Kyoku, 1941), 111.
7. Kishida's position reflects government recognition of Shinto as the national religion and the separation of Shinto and Buddhism, policies that date back to the Meiji period.
8. Fujishima Gaijirō, *Minzoku to kenchiku* (Chikara Shobō, 1944), 18.
9. Igarashi Tarō, *Shinpen: Shin shūkyō to kyodai kenchiku* (Chikuma Shobō, 2007), 219.
10. Kishida Hideto, *Kabe* (Sagami Shobō, 1938).
11. Fujishima Gaijirō, *Ruritō* (Sagami Shobō, 1940), 88.
12. Ibid., 102.
13. Kishida Hideto, "Dai Tōa Kyōeiken kensetsu kinen zōei keikaku no jitsugen o nozomu," *Kenchiku zasshi* (August 1942).
14. Ibid., 583.
15. Kanba Toshio, "Dai Tōa bunka kensetsu no igi," *Kenchiku zasshi* (December 1942), 913–19.
16. "Dai Tōa seichi shukusai toshi keikakuan oboegaki," *Shin kenchiku* (January 1943), 10.
17. Fujimori Terunobu, *Tange Kenzō* (Shin Kenchikusha, 2002), 85.
18. Maekawa Kunio, "Oboegaki," *Kenchiku zasshi* (December 1942), 923.
19. Ikuta Tsutomu, "Kinensei ni tsuite," *Shin kenchiku* (January 1944), 15.
20. Hamaguchi Ryūichi, "Nihon kokumin kenchiku yōshiki no mondai," *Shin kenchiku* (January 1944), 6–12.

Chapter 2

1. Interview with Kurokawa Kishō by Igarashi Tarō and Oda Masanori, *10+1*, no. 36 (2004), 78.

2. Kurokawa Kishō, *Metaborizumu no hassō* (Hakuba Shuppan, 1972), 127.
3. Kurokawa Kishō, "Toshi no shisō," *Shin kenchiku* (October 2004), 51.
4. Kurokawa Kishō, *Kōdō kenchiku ron* (Shōkokusha, 1967), 117.
5. Kurokawa, *Metaborizumu no hassō*, 127.
6. Kurokawa Kishō, *Toshi dezain* (Kinokuniya Shoten, 1965), 123.
7. Kurokawa Kishō, *SD* (April 1978), 12.
8. Kurokawa, *Kōdō kenchiku ron*, 84.
9. Nakamura Hajime, ed., *Bukkyō jiten* (Iwanami Shoten, 1989), 837.
10. Kurokawa, *Kōdō kenchiku ron*, 120–21.
11. Kurokawa Kishō, *Kenchiku ron I: Nihonteki kūkan e* (Kajima Shuppankai, 1982), 86.
12. Interview with Kurokawa Kishō by Igarashi and Oda, 71.
13. Kurokawa Kishō, *Shin kyōsei no shisō* (Tokuma Shoten, 1996), 171.
14. Kurokawa Kishō, *Kenchiku ron II: Imi no seisei e* (Kajima Shuppankai, 1990), 35.
15. Fujimori Terunobu, *Tange Kenzō* (Shin Kenchikusha, 2002), 353.
16. D.T. Suzuki, *Zen and Japanese Culture* (London: Routledge & Kegan Paul, 1959), 24. *Zen to Nihon bunka* (Iwanami Shoten, 1940), 16.
17. Kurokawa Kishō, *Homo movens* (Chūō Kōronsha, 1969), 146.
18. Kurokawa Kishō, *Nomado no jidai* (Tokuma Shoten, 1989), 87.
19. Kurokawa Kishō, *Kurokawa Kishō nōto* (Dōbun Shoin, 1994), 466–67.
20. Umesao Tadao, ed., *Minpaku tanjō* (Chūō Kōronsha, 1978), 145.
21. Interview with Kurokawa Kishō by Igarashi and Oda, 72.

Chapter 5

1. Takiguchi Noriko, *Nihon no kenchikuka: Itō Toyoo kansatsuki* (TOTO Shuppan, 2006), 367.
2. *Detail Japan Talk 2005–2007* (December 2007).
3. Itō Toyoo, "Shōhi no umi ni hitarazu shite atarashii kenchiku wa nai," in *Tōsō suru kenchiku* (Seidosha, 2000), 46.
4. *Toyo Ito 2001*, JA, no. 41 (Spring 2001), 18.
5. Ulrich Schneider et al., *Toyo Ito: Blurring Architecture, 1971–2005* (Milan: Charta, 1999).
6. Sasaki Mutsurō, *Kōzō sekkei no shihō* (Sumai no Toshokan Shuppankyoku, 1997), 177.
7. *Bijutsu techō* (May 2000), 24.
8. Itō Toyoo, "Keitai no yōyū," in *Kaze no henyōtai* (Seidosha, 1989).
9. Itō Toyoo, "Media no mori no Tāzan-tachi," in *Tōsō suru kenchiku* (Seidosha, 2000), 464.
10. Itō Toyoo, "Toshi no tōmei na mori," in *Tōsō suru kenchiku* (Seidosha, 2000), 343.
11. Lecture at the Netherlands Architectural Institute symposium, October 2000.
12. Walter Benjamin, *The Arcades Project*, tr. Howard Eiland and Kevin McLaughlin (Cambridge, MA: Harvard University Press, 2002), 9.
13. *Sendai Mediatēku konseputo bukku* (NTT Shuppan, 2001), 22–23.

14. Itō Toyoo, "Kiriwakeru koto—renzoku saseru koto," GA *Detail 2: Sendai Mediatēku*, A.D.A. EDITA Tokyo, 2001.

15. Lecture at the Netherlands Architectural Institute symposium, October 2000.

16. Itō Toyoo, "Andā konsutorakushon," in Hatakeyama Naoya and Itō Toyoo, *Under Construction* (Kenchiku Shiryō Kenkyūsha, 2001) also expresses the paradox of an eternally incomplete architecture.

17. Artist's talk at the *New Real* exhibition (Sendai Mediatheque, 14 April 2007).

Chapter 6

1. Lecture by Sakamoto Kazunari, "Heisa kara kaihō, soshite kaihō e" (Aichi Shukutoku Daigaku, 27 July 2002).

2. Interview with Sakamoto by Fuchigami Masayuki (http://www.com-et-com/colonne/002/sakamoto/sakusfu.htm).

3. Igarashi Tarō, "Shihonshugi no jidai ni kenchiku no kōsei o tou," *Tosho shimbun* (14 September 1996).

4. Interview with Sakamoto by Fuchigami.

5. Sakamoto Kazunari, "'Tojita hako,' 'kigōteki hyōgen,' soshite 'sokubutsusei,'" in Sakamoto, *Jūtaku: Nichijō no shigaku* (TOTO Shuppan, 2001), 30.

6. Sakamoto, "Heisa kara kaihō, soshite kaihō e," 62.

7. Sakamoto Kazunari and Taki Kōji, *Taiwa: Kenchiku no shikō* (Sumai no Toshokan Shuppankyoku, 1996), 12–13.

8. Sakamoto Kazunari, "Jūtaku ni okeru kenchikusei," in Sakamoto, *Jūtaku: Nichijō no shigaku*, 56.

9. Sakamoto Kazunari, "Shoyū taishō toshite no jūtaku o koete," in Sakamoto, *Jūtaku: Nichijō no shigaku*, 106, 108.

10. Itō Toyoo, *Tōsō suru kenchiku* (Seidosha, 2000), 46.

11. Sakamoto Kazunari, statement in roundtable discussion, "Seiki no kawarime no 'Kenchiku kaigi,'" *Kenchiku gijutsu* (February 1997), 34.

12. Sakamoto Kazunari, statement in roundtable discussion, "Kenchiku to puroguramu," *10+1*, no. 2 (1994), 118.

13. Sakamoto Kazunari, "Kenchiku ni ataeru keishiki," in Sakamoto Kazunari, *Kōsei keishiki toshite no kenchiku* (INAX Shuppan, 1994), 4–5.

14. Sakamoto, *Kōsei keishiki toshite no kenchiku*, 26.

15. Sakamoto Kazunari, "Kōsei no keishiki toshite no kenchiku," in Sakamoto, *Jūtaku: Nichijō no shigaku*, 190.

16. *Kenchiku bunka* (September 1994), 87.

17. Sakamoto, *Jūtaku: Nichijō no shigaku*, 6.

18. Nishizawa Taira, "Gendai jūtaku kenkyū: sunpō, kyōri," *10+1*, no. 23 (2001), 23.

19. Sakamoto Kazunari, as quoted in Sakaushi Taku, "Sozai to kenchiku dezain," *k a*, no. 22 (2002), 3.

20. Fujioka Hiroyasu, "Yori jiritsuteki de, yuruyakana 'kankei' o mezashite," *Kenchiku bunka* (August 1999), 24.

21. Murakami Takashi, "Sūpāfuratto gannen," *Kōkoku* (January–February 2000), 18.

22. Igarashi Tarō, "Sūpāfuratto no kenchiku-toshi o mezashite," in Igarashi Tarō, *Owari no kenchiku / Hajimari no kenchiku* (INAX Shuppan, 2001).

23. Sakamoto Kazunari, "Heisa kara kaihō, soshite kaihō e," 67.

24. Ibid., 66.

25. Sakaushi Taku, "Sozai to kenchiku dezain," *k a*, no. 22 (2002), 4.

Chapter 7

1. Fujimori Terunobu, *Nihon no kindai kenchiku* (Iwanami Shoten, 1993), 257.

2. Fujimori Terunobu, *Shōwa jūtaku monogatari* (Shin Kenchikusha, 1990), 419.

3. Fujimori, *Nihon no kindai kenchiku*.

4. Fujimori Terunobu and Aramata Hiroshi, *Tōkyō rojō hakubutsushi* (Kajima Shuppankai, 1987), 8.

5. Fujimori Terunobu, *Kanpon: Kenchiku tantei nikki* (Ōkokusha, 1999), 24.

6. Fujimori Terunobu, *Meiji no Tōkyō keikaku* (Iwanami Shoten, 1982).

7. Fujimori Terunobu, *Kenchiku tantei no bōken: Tōkyō hen* (Chikuma Shobō, 1986), 137.

8. Fujimori Terunobu and Tange Kenzō, *Tange Kenzō* (Shin Kenchikusha, 2002).

9. Doi Yoshitake, "Kotoba to kenchiku," *Kenchiku gijutsu* (1997), 166.

10. Milan Kundera, *The Art of the Novel*, translated by Linda Asher (New York: Grove Press, 1988).

11. Fujimori Terunobu, *Tenka musō no kenchikugaku nyūmon* (Chikuma Shobō, 2001), 232.

12. Milan Kundera, *The Joke* (New York: Harper & Row, 1967).

13. Milan Kundera, *The Unbearable Lightness of Being* (New York: Harper & Row, 1984).

14. Fujimori Terunobu, *Kenchiku tantei no nazo* (Ōkokusha, 1997), 62.

15. Igarashi Tarō, *Owari no kenchiku / Hajimari no kenchiku* (INAX Shuppan, 2001), 146.

16. Fujimori Terunobu, *Kenchiku tanteijutsu nyūmon* (Bungeishunjū, 1986), 5.

17. Fujimori Terunobu, *Tenka musō no kenchikugaku nyūmon*, 22.

Chapter 8

1. "Tokushū: Interia o kataru," *Kenchiku zasshi* (June 2009), 6.

2. Igarashi Tarō, "Yankī barokku: kaizōsha, interia, kenchiku o megutte," in Igarashi Tarō, *Yankī bunkaron josetsu* (Kawade Shobō Shinsha, 2009).

3. Nishizawa Taira, "Kuramata Shirō no kenchiku ni tsuite," in *Kuramata Shirō to Ettore Sottsass* (ADP, 2010), analyzes Kuramata's residential designs as a tacit critique of architecture.

4. For example, Isozaki Arata, Yokoyama Tadashi, and Andrea Branzi contributed essays to *Kuramata Shirō no sekai* (Hara Bijutsukan, 1996).

5. Iijima Naoki, *Iijima Naoki no dezain / Kazuisuchika / Rinshō kiroku (1985–2010)* (Heibonsha, 2010), 4.

6. *Shōten kenchiku* (September 1999), 112.

7. *Shōten kenchiku* (November 2000), 109.
8. *Shōten kenchiku* (December 2000), 112.
9. *Shōten kenchiku* (January 2005), 86.
10. Nakamura Kimihiko, *Eiga bijutsu ni kaketa otoko* (Sōshisha, 2001).
11. *Shōten kenchiku* (May 2006), 233.
12. *Shōten kenchiku* (September 2007), 83.
13. *Shōten kenchiku* (June 2009), 52.
14. *Shōten kenchiku* (August 2004), 137.

Chapter 11

1. Jonathan Crary, *Techniques of the Observer: On Vision and Modernity in the Nineteenth Century* (Cambridge, MA: MIT Press, 1990).
2. Crary, *Techniques*, 38–39.
3. Kuma Kengo, *Shin · kenchiku nyūmon* (Chikuma Shobō, 1994), 27–28.
4. Beatriz Colomina, *Privacy and Publicity: Modern Architecture as Mass Media* (Cambridge, MA: MIT Press, 1996).
5. Nishizawa Ryūe, "Seikatsu no zentai," *Jūtaku tokushū* (November 1998), 40.
6. Aoki Jun, *Jūtakuron: 12 no daiarōgu* (INAX Shuppan, 2000), 16.
7. "Kūkan jutsu kōza" (Gyararī Ma, 10 November 2000), in *Kūkan kara jōkyō e* (TOTO Shuppan, 2001), 83.
8. Azuma Hiroki, "Nihon-gata posutomodanizumu wa naze ikizumatta ka," *Ronza* (January 2001), 93.
9. Aoki, *Jūtakuron*, 17.
10. Igarashi Tarō, *Owari no kenchiku / Hajimari no kenchiku* (INAX Shuppan, 2001), 405.
11. *Kenchiku bunka* (June 2002), 66.
12. *Shin kenchiku* (January 2003), 46.

Chapter 13

1. Kaijima Momoyo, Kuroda Junzō, and Tsukamoto Yoshiharu, *Mēdo in Tōkyō* (Kajima Shuppankai, 2001).
2. Tsukamoto Yoshiharu, "Shuto kōsoku gaidobukku," *10+1*, no. 16 (1999), 117.
3. Tokyo Institute of Technology Tsukamoto Laboratory and Atelier Bow-Wow, *Petto ākitekuchā gaidobukku* (World Photo Press, 2002).
4. Tsukamoto Yoshiharu, *"Chiisana ie" no kizuki* (Ōkokusha, 2003), 29–30.
5. Alexander Tzonis and Liane Lefaivre, *Architecture in Europe since 1968: Memory and Invention* (London: Thames & Hudson, 1997).
6. Igarashi Tarō, *Owari no kenchiku / Hajimari no kenchiku* (INAX Shuppan, 2001), 287–89.

Chapter 14

1. Andō Kōichi, *Kūkan* (Nyūhausu Shuppan, 2004), 16.
2. Andō Kōichi, *NEW BLOOD* (Rikuyōsha, 2001), 12.
3. Igarashi Tarō, ed., *Sotsugyō sekkei de kangaeta koto, soshite ima* (Shōkokusha, 2005), 36.

Chapter 15

1. Igarashi Tarō, ed., *Sotsugyō sekkei de kangaeta koto, soshite ima 2* (Shōkokusha, 2006), 138.
2. Endō Shūhei, ed., *8-nin wa kōshite kenchikuka ni natta* (Gakugei Shuppansha, 2007), 104–5.
3. Tezuka Takaharu and Tezuka Yui, *Kenchiku katarogu* (TOTO Shuppan, 2006), preface.

Chapter 16

1. Endō Shūhei, ed., *8-nin wa kōshite kenchikuka ni natta* (Gakugei Shuppansha, 2007), 171.
2. Reyner Banham, *Theory and Design in the First Machine Age* (New York: Praeger, 1960).
3. This project was shown in *Fune–>kenchiku: Le Corbusier ga mezashita mono*, an exhibition at the Nippon Yusen Maritime Museum in Yokohama, 4 December 2010–3 April 2011.

Chapter 18

1. See http://www.cybermetric.org/50/50_twisted_column.html.
2. Igarashi Tarō, ed., *Sotsugyō sekkei de kangaeta koto, soshite ima 2* (Shōkokusha, 2006), contains an interview with Ishigami regarding his master's degree project.
3. For further details, see "Venetia Biennale dokyūmento," in Igarashi Tarō, ed., *Kenchiku to shokubutsu* (INAX Shuppan, 2008).
4. Ishigami Jun'ya, *Chiisana zuhan no matomari kara kenchiku ni tsuite kangaeta koto* (INAX Shuppan, 2008).

Chapter 19

1. Gyararī Ma, ed., *Kūkan kara jōkyō e* (TOTO Shuppan, 2001).
2. Nakasaki Takashi, *Yuruyaka ni tsunagaru shakai: kenchikuka 31-nin ni miru atarashii kūkan no yōsō* (Nikkan Kensetsu Tsūshin Shimbunsha, 2006).

REFERENCES

Adachi Kō 足立康. *Nihon kenchikushi* 日本建築史. Chijin Shokan, 1940.

Andō Kōichi 安東孝一. *Kūkan* くうかん. Nyūhausu Shuppan, 2004.

———. *NEW BLOOD*. Rikuyōsha, 2001.

Aoki Jun 青木淳. *Jūtakuron: 12 no daiarōgu* 住宅論：12のダイアローグ. INAX Shuppan, 2000.

Azuma Hiroki 東浩紀. "Nihon-gata posutomodanizumu wa naze ikizumatta ka" 日本型ポストモダニズムはなぜ行き詰まったか. *Ronza* 論座 (January 2001).

Banham, Reyner. *Theory and Design in the First Machine Age*. New York: Praeger, 1960.

Benjamin, Walter. *The Arcades Project*. Translated by Howard Eiland and Kevin McLaughlin. Cambridge, MA: Harvard University Press, 2002.

Bijutsu techō 美術手帖 (May 2000).

Colomina, Beatriz. *Privacy and Publicity: Modern Architecture as Mass Media*. Cambridge, MA: MIT Press, 1996.

Crary, Jonathan. *Techniques of the Observer: On Vision and Modernity in the Nineteenth Century*. Cambridge, MA: MIT Press, 1990.

"Dai Tōa seichi shukusai toshi keikakuan oboegaki" 大東亜聖地祝祭都市計画案覚書. *Shin kenchiku* 新建築 (January 1943).

Detail Japan Talk 2005–2007 ディーテイル・ジャパン・トーク 2005–2007 (December 2007).

Doi Yoshitake 土居義岳. "Kotoba to kenchiku" 言葉と建築. *Kenchiku gijutsu* 建築技術 (1997).

Endō Shūhei, ed. 遠藤秀平編. *8-nin wa kōshite kenchikuka ni natta* 8人はこうして建築家になった. Gakugei Shuppansha, 2007.

Fujimori Terunobu 藤森照信. *Kanpon: Kenchiku tantei nikki* 完本・建築探偵日記. Ōkokusha, 1999.

———. *Kenchiku tantei no bōken: Tōkyō hen* 建築探偵の冒険：東京篇. Chikuma Shobō, 1986.

———. *Kenchiku tantei no nazo* 建築探偵の謎. Ōkokusha, 1997.

———. *Kenchiku tanteijutsu nyūmon* 建築探偵術入門. Bungeishunjū, 1986.

———. *Meiji no Tōkyō keikaku* 明治の東京計画. Iwanami Shoten, 1982.

———. *Nihon no kindai kenchiku* 日本の近代建築. Iwanami Shoten, 1993.

———. *Shōwa jūtaku monogatari* 昭和住宅物語. Shin Kenchikusha, 1990.

———. *Tange Kenzō* 丹下健三. Shin Kenchikusha, 2002.

———. *Tenka musō no kenchikugaku nyūmon* 天下無双の建築学入門. Chikuma Shobō, 2001.

Fujimori Terunobu 藤森照信 and Aramata Hiroshi 荒俣宏. *Tōkyō rojō hakubutsushi* 東京路上博物誌. Kajima Shuppankai, 1987.

Fujimori Terunobu 藤森照信 and Tange Kenzō 丹下健三. *Tange Kenzō* 丹下健三. Shin Kenchikusha, 2002.

Fujioka Hiroyasu 藤岡洋保. "Yori jiritsuteki de, yuruyakana 'kankei' o mezashite" より自立的で、ゆるやかな「関係」をめざして. *Kenchiku bunka* 建築文化 (August 1999).

Fujishima Gaijirō 藤島亥治郎. *Minzoku to kenchiku* 民族と建築. Chikara Shobō, 1944.

———. *Ruritō* 瑠璃塔. Sagami Shobō, 1940.

Gyararī Ma, ed. ギャラリー・間編. "Kūkan jutsu kōza" 空間術講座, 10 November 2000. In *Kūkan kara jōkyō e* 空間から状況へ. TOTO Shuppan, 2001.

Hamaguchi Ryūichi 浜口隆一. "Nihon kokumin kenchiku yōshiki no mondai" 日本国民建築様式の問題. *Shin kenchiku* 新建築 (January 1944).

Igarashi Tarō, ed. 五十嵐太郎編. *Kenchiku to shokubutsu* 建築と植物. INAX Shuppan, 2008.

———. *Owari no kenchiku / Hajimari no kenchiku* 終わりの建築/始まりの建築. INAX Shuppan, 2001.

———. *Sensō to kenchiku* 戦争と建築. Shōbunsha, 2003.

———. "Shihonshugi no jidai ni kenchiku no kōsei o tou." 資本主義の時代に建築の構成を問う. *Tosho shimbun* 図書新聞 (14 September 1996).

———. *Shinpen: Shin shūkyō to kyodai kenchiku* 新編：新宗教と巨大建築. Chikuma Shobō, 2007.

———, ed. *Sotsugyō sekkei de kangaeta koto, soshite ima* 卒業設計で考えたこと、そしていま. Shōkokusha, 2005.

———, ed. *Sotsugyō sekkei de kangaeta koto, soshite ima 2* 卒業設計で考えたこと、そしていま2. Shōkokusha, 2006.

———. "Sūpāfuratto no kenchiku-toshi o mezashite" スーパーフラットの建築・都市をめざして. In Igarashi五十嵐, *Owari no kenchiku / Hajimari no kenchiku* 終わりの建築/始まりの建築.

———. "Venetia Biennale dokyūmento." ヴェネチア・ビエンナーレ・ドキュメント. In *Kenchiku to shokubutsu* 建築と植物.

———. "Yankī barokku: kaizōsha, interia, kenchiku o megutte" ヤンキーバロック：改造車・インテリア・建築をめぐって. In *Yankī bunkaron josetsu* ヤンキー文化論序説. Kawade Shobō Shinsha, 2009.

Iijima Naoki 飯島直樹. *Iijima Naoki no dezain / Kazuisuchika / Rinshō kiroku (1985–2010)* 飯島直樹のデザイン/カズイスチカ/臨床記録 1985–2010. Heibonsha, 2010.

Ikuta Tsutomu 生田勉. "Kinensei ni tsuite" 紀念性について. *Shin kenchiku* 新建築 (January 1944).

Inoue Shōichi 井上章一. *Senjika Nihon no kenchikuka* 戦時下日本の建築家. Asahi Shimbunsha, 1995.

Ishigami Jun'ya 石上純也. *Chiisana zuhan no matomari kara kenchiku ni tsuite kangaeta koto* ちいさな図版のまとまりから建築について考えたこと. INAX Shuppan, 2008.

Itō Toyoo 伊東豊雄. "Andā konsutorakushon" アンダー・コンストラクション. In Hatakeyama Naoya 畠山直哉 and Itō Toyoo 伊東豊雄. *Under Construction*. Kenchiku Shiryō Kenkyū-sha, 2001.

———. "Keitai no yōyū" 形態の溶融. In *Kaze no henyōtai* 風の変様体. Seidosha, 1989.

———. "Kiriwakeru koto—renzoku saseru koto" 切り分けること―連続させること. *GA Detail 2: Sendai Mediatēku*, A.D.A. EDITA Tokyo, 2001.

———. "Media no mori no Tāzan-tachi" メディアの森のターザンたち. In *Tōsō suru kenchiku* 透層する建築.

———. "Shōhi no umi ni hitarazu shite atarashii kenchiku wa nai" 消費の海に浸らずして新しい建築はない. In *Tōsō suru kenchiku* 透層する建築.

———. "Toshi no tōmei na mori." 都市の透明な森. In *Tōsō suru kenchiku* 透層する建築.

———. *Tōsō suru kenchiku* 透層する建築. Seidosha, 2000.

Kaijima Momoyo 貝島桃代, Kuroda Junzō 黒田潤三, and Tsukamoto Yoshiharu 塚本由晴. *Mēdo in Tōkyō* メイド・イン・トーキョー. Kajima Shuppankai, 2001.

Kanba Toshio 樺俊雄. "Dai Tōa bunka kensetsu no igi" 大東亜文化建設の意義. *Kenchiku zasshi* 建築雑誌 (December 1942).

"Kantōgen" 巻頭言. *Shin kenchiku* 新建築 (January 1942).

Kenchiku bunka 建築文化 (September 1994).

Kenchiku bunka 建築文化 (June 2002).

Kishida Hideto 岸田日出刀. "Dai Tōa Kyōeiken kensetsu kinen zōei keikaku no jitsugen o nozomu" 大東亜共栄圏建設記念造営計画の実現を望む. *Kenchiku zasshi* 建築雑誌 (August 1942).

———. *Kabe*壁. Sagami Shobō, 1938.

———. *Nihon kenchiku no tokusei* 日本建築の特性. Naikaku Insatsu Kyoku, 1941.

Kuma Kengo 限研吾. *Shin・kenchiku nyūmon* 新・建築入門. Chikuma Shobō, 1994.

Kundera, Milan. *The Art of the Novel*. Translated by Linda Asher. New York: Grove Press, 1988.

———. *The Joke*. New York: Harper & Row, 1967.

———. *The Unbearable Lightness of Being*. New York: Harper & Row, 1984.

Kurokawa Kishō 黒川紀章. *Homo movens* ホモ・モーベンス. Chūō Kōronsha, 1969.

———. Interview by Igarashi Tarō 五十嵐太郎 and Oda Masanori 小田マサノリ, *10+1*, no. 36 (2004).

———. *Kenchiku ron I: Nihonteki kūkan e* 建築論 I: 日本的空間へ. Kajima Shuppankai, 1982.

———. *Kenchiku ron II: Imi no seisei e* 建築論II:意味の生成へ. Kajima Shuppankai, 1990.

———. *Kōdō kenchiku ron* 行動建築論. Shōkokusha, 1967.

———. *Kurokawa Kishō nōto* 黒川紀章ノート. Dōbun Shoin, 1994.

———. *Metaborizumu no hassō* メタボリズムの発想. Hakuba Shuppan, 1972.

———. *Nomado no jidai* ノマドの時代. Tokuma Shoten, 1989.

———. *SD*スペースデザイン (April 1978).

———. *Shin kyōsei no shisō* 新・共生の思想. Tokuma Shoten, 1996.

———. *Toshi dezain* 都市デザイン. Kinokuniya Shoten, 1965.

———. "Toshi no shisō" 都市の思想. *Shin kenchiku* 新建築 (October 2004).

Maekawa Kunio 前川國男. "Oboegaki" 覚書. *Kenchiku zasshi* 建築雑誌 (December 1942).

Murakami Takashi 村上隆. "Sūpāfuratto gannen" スーパーフラット元年. *Kōkoku* 広告 (January–February 2000).

Nakamura Hajime, ed. 中村元編. *Bukkyō jiten* 仏教辞典. Iwanami Shoten, 1989.

Nakamura Kimihiko 中村公彦. *Eiga bijutsu ni kaketa otoko*. 映画美術に賭けた男, Sōshisha, 2001.

Nakasaki Takashi 中崎隆司. *Yuruyaka ni tsunagaru shakai: kenchikuka 31-nin ni miru atarashii kūkan no yōsō* ゆるやかにつながる社会：建築家31人にみる新しい空間の様相. Nikkan Kensetsu Tsūshin Shimbunsha, 2006.

Nishizawa Ryūe 西沢立衛. "Seikatsu no zentai" 生活の全体. *Jūtaku tokushū* 住宅特集 (November 1998).

Nishizawa Taira 西沢大良. "Gendai jūtaku kenkyū: sunpō, kyori" 現代住宅研究：寸法・距離. *10+1*, no. 23 (2001).

———. "Kuramata Shirō no kenchiku ni tsuite" 倉俣史朗の建築について. In *Kuramata Shirō to Ettore Sottsass* 倉俣史朗とエットレ・ソットサス. ADP, 2010.

Sakamoto Kazunari 坂本一成. "Heisa kara kaihō, soshite kaihō e" 閉鎖から開放、そして解放へ. Aichi Shukutoku Daigaku, 27 July 2002.

———. Interview by Fuchigami Masayuki 淵上正幸. http://www.com-et.com/colonne/002/sakamoto/sakusfu.htm.

———. *Jūtaku: Nichijō no shigaku* 住宅: 日常の詩学. TOTO Shuppan, 2001.

———. "Jūtaku ni okeru kenchikusei" 住宅における建築性. In *Jūtaku: Nichijō no shigaku* 住宅: 日常の詩学.

———. "Kenchiku ni ataeru keishiki" 住宅に与える形式. In *Kōsei keishiki toshite no kenchiku* 構成形式としての建築.

———. "Kenchiku to puroguramu" 建築とプログラム. *10+1*, no. 2 (1994).

———. *Kōsei keishiki toshite no kenchiku* 構成形式としての建築. INAX Shuppan, 1994.

———. "Kōsei no keishiki toshite no kenchiku" 構成の形式としての建築. In Sakamoto, *Jūtaku: Nichijō no shigaku* 住宅: 日常の詩学.

———. "Seiki no kawarime no 'Kenchiku kaigi'" 世紀の変わり目の「建築会議」. *Kenchiku gijutsu* 建築技術 (1997).

———. "Shoyū taishō toshite no jūtaku o koete" 所有対象としての住宅を超えて. In *Jūtaku: Nichijō no shigaku* 住宅:日常の詩学.

———. "Sozai to kenchiku dezain" 素材と建築デザイン. *k a*華, no. 22 (2002).

———. "'Tojita hako,' 'kigōteki hyōgen,' soshite 'sokubutsusei'" 「閉じた箱」、「記号的表現」、そして「即物性」. In *Jūtaku: Nichijō no shigaku* 住宅: 日常の詩学.

Sakamoto Kazunari 坂本一成 and Taki Kōji 多木浩二. *Taiwa: Kenchiku no shikō* 対話・建築の思考. Sumai no Toshokan Shuppankyoku, 1996.

Sakaushi Taku 坂牛卓. "Sozai to kenchiku dezain" 素材と建築デザイン. *k a*華, no. 22 (2002).

Sasaki Mutsurō 佐々木睦朗. *Kōzō sekkei no shihō* 構造設計の詩法. Sumai no Toshokan Shuppankyoku, 1997.

Schneider, Ulrich, et al. *Toyo Ito: Blurring Architecture, 1971–2005*. Milan: Charta, 1999.

Sekino Masaru 関野克. *Meiji, Taishō, Shōwa no kenchiku* 明治、大正、昭和の建築. Vol. 25 of *Sekai bijutsu zenshū* 世界美術全集. Heibonsha, 1951.

Sendai Mediatēku konseputo bukku せんだいメディアテークコンセプトブック. NTT Shuppan, 2001.

Shin kenchiku 新建築 (January 2003).

Shōten kenchiku 商店建築 (September 1999, November 2000, December 2000, August 2004, January 2005, May 2006, September 2007, June 2009).

Suzuki, D.T. *Zen and Japanese Culture*. London: Routledge & Kegan Paul, 1959.

———. *Zen to Nihon bunka* 禅と日本文化. Iwanami Shoten, 1940.

Takiguchi Noriko 瀧口範子. *Nihon no kenchikuka: Itō Toyoo kansatsuki* にほんの建築家伊東豊雄・観察記. TOTO Shuppan, 2006.

Tezuka Takaharu 手塚貴晴 and Tezuka Yui 手塚由比. *Kenchiku katarogu* 建築カタログ. TOTO Shuppan, 2006.

"Tokushū: Interia o kataru" 特集：インテリアを語る. *Kenchiku zasshi* (June 2009).

Tokyo Institute of Technology Tsukamoto Laboratory and Atelier Bow-Wow 東京工業大学塚本研究室; アトリエ・ワン. *Petto ākitekuchā gaidobukku* ペット・アーキテクチャー・ガイドブック. World Photo Press, 2002.

Toyo Ito 2001 伊東豊雄 2001. *JA: The Japan Architect*, no. 41 (Spring 2001).

Tsukamoto Yoshiharu 塚本由晴. *"Chiisana ie" no kizuki* 「小さな家」の気づき. Ōkokusha, 2003.

———. "Shuto kōsoku gaidobukku" 首都高速ガイドブック. *10+1*, no. 16 (1999).

Tzonis, Alexander, and Liane Lefaivre. *Architecture in Europe since 1968: Memory and Invention*. London: Thames & Hudson, 1997.

Umesao Tadao, ed. 梅棹忠夫編. *Minpaku tanjō* 民博誕生. Chūōkōronsha, 1978.

About the Author

Igarashi Taro, architectural historian and critic, was born in 1967 in Paris. After graduating from the Department of Architecture in the Faculty of Engineering at the University of Tokyo, he received a master's degree and a doctorate (in engineering) from the same institution. He is now a professor in the Graduate School of Engineering at Tōhoku University. He served as commissioner for the Japan Pavilion at the Venice Biennale of Architecture in 2008 and artistic director of the Aichi Triennale in 2013. Publications include *Kenchiku wa ika ni shakai to kairo o tsunagu no ka* [How Does Architecture Connect with Society?] (Sairyūsha, 2010); *Shinpen: Shin shūkyō to kyodai kenchiku* [New Edition: The New Religions and Monumental Architecture] (Chikuma Shobō, 2007); *Gendai kenchiku ni kansuru 16-shō* [Sixteen Chapters on Contemporary Architecture] (Kōdansha, 2006); *Gendai kenchiku no pāsupekutibu* [Perspectives on Contemporary Architecture] (Kōbunsha, 2005); *Kabōbi toshi* [The Overprotected City] (Chūōkōron-Shinsha, 2004); and *Sensō to kenchiku* [War and Architecture] (Shōbunsha, 2003). He has also been a contributing editor for a number of books, including *Yankī bunkaron josetsu* [An Introduction to Yankee Culture] (Kawade Shobō Shinsha, 2009) and *Mienai shinsai* [Invisible Earthquakes] (Misuzu Shobō, 2006).

About the Translator

David Noble grew up in Nashville, Tennessee. After graduating from Vanderbilt University with a degree in East Asian studies, he did graduate work in Japanese language, history, and literature at the University of Chicago and Princeton University. He then worked for three years as the executive editor of *Japan: An Illustrated Encyclopedia* (Kodansha, 1993) and five years at Weatherhill, Inc., before establishing an independent practice as a translator, editor, and book designer. He has translated more than a dozen books, focusing on history, political science, and the humanities. He lives on the Olympic Peninsula in Washington State.

（英文版）**現代建築家列伝**—社会といかに関わってきたか
Contemporary Japanese Architects: Profiles in Design

2018年3月27日　第1刷発行

著　　者　　五十嵐　太郎

訳　　者　　ディビッド・ノーブル

発 行 所　　一般財団法人出版文化産業振興財団
　　　　　　〒101-0051 東京都千代田区神田神保町3-12-3
　　　　　　電話　03-5211-7282（代）

ホームページ　http://www.jpic.or.jp/

印刷・製本所　　大日本印刷株式会社

定価はカバーに表示してあります。
本書の無断複写（コピー）、転載は著作権法の例外を除き、禁じられています。

© 2011 by Igarashi Taro
Printed in Japan
ISBN 978-4-86658-021-0